FROM RIGHTS
TO LIVES

BLACK LIVES & LIBERATION

SERIES EDITORS

Brandon Byrd, *Vanderbilt University*
Zandria F. Robinson, *Georgetown University*
Christopher Cameron, *University of North Carolina, Charlotte*

BLACK LIVES MATTER. What began as a Twitter hashtag after the 2013 acquittal of George Zimmerman for the murder of Trayvon Martin has since become a widely recognized rallying cry for black being and resistance. The series aims are twofold: 1) to explore social justice and activism by black individuals and communities throughout history to the present, including the Black Lives Matter movement and the evolving ways it is being articulated and practiced across the African Diaspora; and 2) to examine everyday life and culture, rectifying well-worn "histories" that have excluded or denied the contributions of black individuals and communities or recast them as entirely white endeavors. Projects draw from a range of disciplines in the humanities and social sciences and will first and foremost be informed by "peopled" analyses, focusing on everyday actors and community folks.

FROM RIGHTS TO LIVES

The Evolution of the Black Freedom Struggle

EDITED BY

FRANÇOISE N. HAMLIN
AND
CHARLES W. MCKINNEY JR.

VANDERBILT UNIVERSITY PRESS
Nashville, Tennesee

Copyright 2024 Vanderbilt University Press
Introduction and Postscript ©2024 by Françoise N. Hamlin and Charles W. McKinney Jr.
All rights reserved
First printing 2024

Library of Congress Cataloging-in-Publication Data

Names: Hamlin, Françoise N., editor. | McKinney, Charles Wesley, 1967- editor.
Title: From rights to lives : the evolution of the Black Freedom Struggle / edited by Françoise N. Hamlin & Charles W. McKinney, Jr.
Other titles: Evolution of the Black Freedom Struggle
Description: Nashville, Tennessee : Vanderbilt University Press, [2024] | Series: Black lives and liberation
Identifiers: LCCN 2023051883 | ISBN 9780826506658 (paperback) | ISBN 9780826506665 (hardcover) | ISBN 9780826506672 (epub) | ISBN 9780826506689 (pdf)
Subjects: LCSH: Black lives matter movement. | Civil rights movements—United States. | African Americans—Civil rights. | African Americans—Violence against. | Racial profiling in law enforcement—United States. | Police brutality—United States.
Classification: LCC E185.615 .F77 2024 | DDC 323.0973—dc23/eng/20231204
LC record available at https://lccn.loc.gov/2023051883

Front cover images: (top) "I Am a Man, copyright by Richard L. Copley, used with permission; (bottom) Justice for George Floyd Protest, Washington, DC, May 31, 2020, photograph by Johnny Silvercloud

We thank the generations of activists—the folks on the front lines of the Black Freedom Struggle—who have shaped the contours of this volume in immeasurable ways with their vision, work, and determination to drag the world toward its stated principles. We hope that this small offering helps illuminate that mighty work and chart a path forward. We dedicate this book to you.

Contents

Acknowledgments ix

    Introduction. From Rights to Lives: History Matters   1

1. "Sincerely, Your Grandparents' Hands": Elucidating Similarities between the Trayvon Martin Generation of #BlackLivesMatter and the Emmett Till Generation of the Civil Rights Movement   17
   Charity Clay

2. Continuity and Change: The Spirituality of Liberation in the Black Lives Matter Movement   44
   Christophe D. Ringer

3. Good Cops?   71
   Peter Pihos

4. "We May Have to Defend Ourselves": Black Women and Campaigns against Police Sexual Violence during the Civil Rights and Black Lives Matter Eras   99
   Althea Legal-Miller

5. Revolts of the Black Athletes: Race, Sport, and Activism from the Civil Rights Movement to Black Lives Matter   130
   Scott N. Brooks and Aram Goudsouzian

6. The Search for Truth and Justice: A Diasporic Black
   Freedom Struggle   157
   Kishauna Soljour

7. The Ambivalence of Activist Photography: July 10, 2016   184
   David V. Mason

8. When the Cultural Revolution Comes: Anthem Making
   in the Era of BLM   215
   Mickell Carter

Postscript. "Miraculous, Magnificent, and Messy":
Rights, Lives, and the Movement in Real Time   239
Françoise N. Hamlin and Charles W. McKinney Jr.

Contributors   257

Acknowledgments

All books are collaborative endeavors, but none are more so than edited collections. We would like to thank our contributors for both their writing and their willingness to build a community in the process. As we all navigated the pandemic, they hung in and did the work with grace, accommodating our long lapses and our quick requests!

We hold immense gratitude for Vanderbilt University Press in their encouragement to create this book, albeit long before the global pandemic. We thank the editors of the series where this book resides and give a special shout out to series editor Zandria Robinson, who championed this project early. We are truly grateful for Gianna Mosser, our fearless press director and editor, who shepherded the book through and graciously accommodated all the starts and stops that incurred along the way.

We thank the Department of History at Brown University, for the publication funds that offset costs, and the Royce Family Fellowship through Brown University, which enabled us to hold workshops in Providence and execute the strategy of collaboration that we had envisioned. We had the privilege to workshop face-to-face, but with modern technology, where there is a will, there is a way.

Furthermore, we would like to thank Frank Rivera-Marin for lending his artistic talents in the initial cover design and Claire Nelson, who brought clear, unjaded, knowledgeable, and constructive eyes to the work as we turned the penultimate corner. We are truly blessed that Richard Copley's iconic image graces the front cover. Thank you!

• • •

First, I thank my family and friends (near and far) for the support they gave along the journey. While this is not the project they thought I was working on, this is the project I *needed* to work on. More often than not they asked no questions and let me do my thing. For that I am grateful. Elijah Malik, all I do is for you—and this one especially. I pray for a better world where you are safe and I do not have to worry about you not coming home. Right now that world seems like science fiction, but I wish that for you and for all our children.

This project is among a few, and amid lots of other research, teaching, and work, so here I thank those who engaged with me directly on this book by providing a sounding board and/or tangible support. This is in no particular order. Among my colleagues at Brown, I thank: Caroline Castiglione, Rebecca Nedostup, Vazira Zamindar, Naoko Shibusawa, Noliwe Rooks, Lisa Biggs, Keisha Blain, and Paget Henry. To my students (past and present) who make me a better scholar and teacher: our discussions in the classroom helped us see the repeating questions and comparisons about the past and our present and motivated us to create this book. Thank you to the Department of History, who gave me the funds to aid the publication process, and to the Royce Family for the endowed chair, which funded the workshop. Beyond Brown, there is the Spain Train (IYKYK): Katherine Charron, Robin Morris, George Trumbull IV, Tammy Ingram, Aaron Wong, Adriane Lentz-Smith, and Claire Nelson. Then there is Frank Rivera, Marjolein Sopjes, Madison Burke, John Hickey, Charlotte Stutz, Emily Franchetti, and Karen Cox. Thank you for your friendship, and/or counsel on this project specifically, during this process.

Lastly, I want everyone to know that Chuck is the best co-conspirator. We both juggled multiple projects, our families, and, oh yes, a pandemic and our paying jobs, yet we found time to focus and get tasks done efficiently and effectively. We stayed on the same page throughout, and I wish everyone were so lucky to have such a perfect co-editing experience. Thank you for suggesting this way back when.

FH

• • •

Mom, Dad, and Teresa: it all starts with you. Thank you for your love and support across every stage of my life, up to and including this one.

A wide swath of my community was a great help to me as we slowly made our way to this point. My colleagues in the Africana Studies Program at Rhodes College—Evie Perry, Samson Ndanyi, Charles Hughes, Earl Wright II, Duane Loynes Sr., and Shatavia Wynn—continually challenged me to think in capacious ways about race, power, and social change. My thanks to Charles Hughes, Robert Widell, and Simon Balto (the Clown Society), fellow historians and friends who were thoughtful interlocutors from the beginning days of the project to its completion. I thank my colleagues in the Rhodes College Department of History for their insistence that good history can, in fact, change hearts and minds. We thank Kathy Bassard and Rashna Richards in the Office of Academic Affairs at Rhodes College for institutional support and words of encouragement. Special thanks to the T. Hardy Debonairs Book Club (Paul Taylor, Eddie Glaude, Mark Jefferson, Charles Peterson, Ron Sullivan, and Cornel West) for creating one of the most rewarding intellectual spaces I've ever had the privilege of joining. Our regularly scheduled musings on Black life, the blues, freedom dreams, and the prospects of our democratic tradition always renew my faith in what King called "the beautiful struggle to make a new world."

I thank my children Vanessa, Ayo, and Chioke for being sources of light throughout this process. My wife, Natalie, lived with this project through the pandemic and while providing hospice care for her mother. (Rest well, Beverly Davis: we miss you mightily.) Thank you, Nat, for reminding me what matters.

Françoise, thank you for taking this journey with me. Your insight, instincts, and intellect set us on our path. Thank you in particular for convening us all at Brown to workshop the book. That process enabled us to forge something special, I think. It was an absolute joy to work with you.

CM

INTRODUCTION
From Rights to Lives
History Matters

In 2019, we issued a call for essays to critically engage the dynamic relationship between two moments of liberatory possibility on the Black Freedom Struggle (BFS) timeline: the Civil Rights/Black Power moment and the #BlackLivesMatter (#BLM) era. We shaped our query with a few guiding questions: What can we learn when we place these moments of struggle in dialogue with each other? How can/should our understanding of the mass movements after World War II shape our analysis of #BLM? What are the (dis)continuities we should keep in mind? Conversely, how can our understanding of #BLM shape/reshape our analysis of the larger BFS as a whole? What analytical tools have we developed in the effort to understand #BLM that can be applied to better explicate the BFS? In what ways does #BLM challenge our understanding of the BFS? What are the lessons to be gleaned for future moments of insurgency?

We come to this work as two students of the era commonly known as the Civil Rights Movement (CRM). To that end, we are deeply committed to making sense and meaning of the myriad movements built—slowly and intentionally—all across the nation in the middle of the previous century. Trained by scholars who have chronicled the movement, as well as the activists who forged it, we know that the BFS that occurred in the middle of the twentieth century was a local, national, and international mass of movements that profoundly shaped a wide array of institutions and the cultural, political, and legal terrain of the nation. The CRM was also a moment of culmination, with local efforts to gain greater freedom connecting with national (and international) strategies to advance the work of justice. However, while the Movement fundamentally altered many aspects of Black/American life, the enduring nature of racial inequality continues to delimit the possibilities and potentials surrounding the full expression of Black humanity. Activists and scholars attest to the perils and prospects of this momentous epoch and understand the tenuous nature of the advancements won—and subsequently eroded.

Fourteen-year-old Emmett Till's brutal killing in 1955 both traumatized and galvanized a generation of Black youth who identified with, and recognized themselves in, the murdered Black boy: the Emmett Till Generation.[1] Similarly, seventeen-year-old Trayvon Martin's murder in 2012 culminated in collective fury and spurred a new generation of young activists to action. After the acquittal of Martin's killer, activists organized around a hashtag: #BlackLives Matter.[2] Short and clear, the hashtag powerfully encapsulated the spirit of the moment by declaring simply and loudly: *Our lives matter. Stop killing us.* Initially crafted and promoted by three queer Black feminists (Patrisse Cullors, Alicia Garza, and Opal Tometi), the hashtag evolved into a critical tool to mobilize Black folks (and their allies) across the country (and then internationally) in an effort to confront unmitigated murder and police brutality.

Almost immediately, the aims and goals of #BLM expanded, in recognition of the deeply interconnected and complex nature of racial oppression in American (and, ultimately, Western) society. Just as the previous high point of Black activism contained multitudes, so too does the contemporary moment. Protests about police brutality and murder expanded outward to encompass and confront other facets of racial domination. As in years past, protests about policing promoted larger conversations (and confrontations) related to housing, employment, segregation, gentrification, poverty, and the multiplicity of challenges faced by Black folks across the nation. #BLM highlighted the growth and development of a new era of movement building and struggle, one that continues to grow and evolve as we write. The current moment also finds #BLM activists and their allies engaged in vigorous debate and dialogue about the best way forward for Black self-determination and safety—all the while contending with the protean nature of white supremacy, white rage, and the coordinated pushback from governmental entities at all levels.[3]

We realize the challenge associated with making critiques and observations about #BLM in real time as we make comparisons between the CRM and the #BLM moment. Looking back on the Civil Rights period, we can view how the analysis of contemporaneous events spanned a range: from the insightful to the spurious. For example, when Black students began sitting in at lunch counters in 1960, white college officials across the South characterized the phenomenon as the Black-student version of the "panty raid," a popular pastime on white college campuses at the time. Others saw something much more substantive: the groundwork of a social revolution that, if nurtured, could have the potential to reshape American society. The space between prank and social revolution can be complicated. Explication of the sit-ins—and the burgeoning mass movement they portended in the early 1960s—grew in sophistication and complexity along with the movement itself.[4]

Scholars and others who have critically engaged the aims, tactics, and ideologies of #BLM have constructed a capacious entryway into dialogues that span the range from crucial illumination to unproductive dissembling. Much like during the Civil Rights era, this engagement shares the burden of constructing an analysis of the moment as it unfolds. In the initial months of the mass movement catalyzed by #BLM, pundits, scholars, activists, and others chastised the movement as "leaderless."[5] This critique reflected (and continues to reflect) an adherence to a traditional leadership model, one that centers the role of one (usually male) leader, dispensing directions and charting the course of the movement. For civil rights activity in the United States, this represents the default mode of leadership, exemplified by Martin King Jr.'s relationship with the Southern Christian Leadership Conference and by his (assumed) leadership over the totality of the struggle.[6] For many, the absence of this particular type of leadership could only be read as a lack of leadership structure. Garza, Cullors, Tometi, and others have clearly articulated their intention to create and cultivate a style of leadership shaped largely by a Black feminist orientation, one that understood the perils of elite, top-down leadership. Yet this orientation also reflects Miss Ella Baker's vision of leadership, which she articulated as the Student Nonviolent Coordinating Committee formed in 1960.[7] However, the current critique did open up the space to engage in an ongoing analysis of the merits and challenges of the structural choices made by key personnel. What *does* group-centered leadership look like? How does a national/international entity accomplish successful activism for real change? How can it function effectively in the heat of social protest, when unforeseen developments demand a tactical course correction on short notice? These and other questions are both crucially relevant in this moment and also have their moorings in the previous moment of social upheaval.

Questions related to the efficacy of #BLM also reveal expansive and productive venues for critical assessments. Black Studies scholar Keeanga-Yamahtta Taylor's 2019 review of the movement thus far concluded that, "confronted by an array of internal and external obstacles," the movement had "stalled," even as an unrepentant white supremacist ascended to the highest political office in the land. Essayist and scholar Jesse McCarthy wrote that #BLM has "done more to explode the Overton window in American politics than any movement since the 1960s" and "has to be fully and duly appreciated for the extraordinary achievement that it is." Both Taylor and McCarthy frame #BLM as a significant, substantive moment in movement history, one that—despite hefty internal and external challenges—has fundamentally reshaped the conversation around policing and has shifted the terrain of the politically possible. Conversely, political scientist Adolph Reed Jr. has characterized the #BLM Movement as a "branding exercise" replete with a "liturgy of empty slogans," a moment and movement that, ultimately, detracts from more serious efforts to explicate the root causes of racial inequality and police brutality. Political scientist Cedric Johnson echoes Reed's sentiment, claiming that #BLM has inhibited a more nuanced assessment of the role class—across racial lines—plays in shaping the contours of police brutality. All of these assertions bear consideration. We contend that comparative historical analysis can bring this moment of protest, deliberation, and reaction into clearer view. The work of the historian is, at its core, to examine change over time. By extending and expanding the window of analysis with regard to #BLM's impact, we hope to provide a perspective that is mindful of the long view necessary to exploring the gains and setbacks accrued over the past decade.[8]

There have been countless books and articles produced on the CRM, and the two of us have contributed to that vast historiography.[9] Participants and scholars have examined the movement in interesting and multifaceted ways. Scholarly work on #BLM has only just begun to emerge in the past few years.[10] While historians and others have created work that places #BLM on the longer timeline of the Black liberatory movement, very few volumes seek to put these two similar yet distinct moments in conversation with each other. We attempt to do this work in *From Rights To Lives*. Broadly speaking, the traditionally conceptualized mid-twentieth century CRM and the newer Black Lives Matter Movement (BLMM) possess some similar qualities. They both represent dynamic, complex moments of possibility and progress. They also share mass-based movement activities, policy/legislative advocacy, grassroots organizing, and targeted media campaigns. Innovation, growth, and dissension—core aspects of movement work—mark them both. Crucially, these moments also engender aggressive, repressive, multi-level responses to these assertions of Black humanity. The systems and structures that constitute the infrastructure of our society—forged in the fire of white supremacy—work as they are designed and seek to blunt, if not extinguish, these tentative efforts to create a new world that actualizes democracy.

We began this work before the global health pandemic hit; then the process slowed considerably as we all encountered varying degrees of instability, illness, and loss. In addition to exacerbating deficiencies in health care access and employment, the pandemic further highlighted the structural challenges within policing and the justice system. On May 25, 2020, in Minneapolis, Minnesota, Derek Chauvin slowly choked the life from George Floyd for the whole world to witness, and pushed #BLM onto the streets again.[11] Millions marched across the country (and the world) to protest the insidious *racial* pandemic that ravaged the nation. Those who took to the streets in 2020 did so in numbers never before seen in American history, and they did so in lockstep with a virulent, deadly virus that would claim the lives of millions around the world. The summer of 2020 became another summer of discontent (akin to those in the 1960s), heightened by the risks of protesting during the spread of a deadly, unseen, and highly contagious virus.[12]

However, in the midst of chaos and uncertainty, we found a sliver of a silver lining. We used the forced delays to create space to pause and congregate. We wanted to use this project to also build the intellectual community in which we wanted to dwell and thrive—to replace the impersonal (and often isolating) production of knowledge with a process that sought to embody the spirit of the movements in which we belong as well as study. In August 2022 we held a one-day workshop in Providence, Rhode Island, where everyone met (in person and virtually for some) and read one another's revised essays in advance. Contributors got the benefit of general, thoughtful interventions and suggestions, courtesy of their fellow authors. Part editing, part community building, part support group, this was a powerful experience that invested in and bonded scholars from around the country (and across the pond) and from diverse academic ranks and institutions all around a common project. We modeled the beloved intellectual community and highly recommend it as a best practice.

As editors we are primarily teachers, always pushing the importance of historical knowledge, bringing these ideas, and the tools with which to analyze them, to students and beyond the academy. As scholars we acknowledge our responsibility to communicate in a way that makes this book legible to multiple audiences. That means writing for a broad audience and then avoiding or clarifying and defining oft-used/misused/overused terms. Let us begin with a few terms we have already used. We define the CRM as the mass of movements that occurred in the decades of the 1950s and 1960s. Given the porous nature of local movements, assigning rigid dates makes little sense to how people navigate their realities, so we generally begin in the early fifties after World War II ended and the United States settled into a measure of post-war prosperity while Black veterans, union members, activists, and others crafted new understandings of life's possibilities beyond Jim Crow. The CRM sits on the timeline of the BFS, which we can date from the moment of contact (on the original continent leading to enslavement) to the present. The Black Power Movement's (BPM) porous boundaries on the BFS timeline begin in the mid-1960s to the mid-1970s, depending on the place, organization, or individual. Scholars disagree about the definitions of both the CRM and BPM: some pitch them as oppositional, whereas others see the BPM as an evolution of the CRM. Regardless, there are ideological, rhetorical, organizational, and often generational and geographical connections between the two. The BLMM sits on the BFS timeline from 2012 and, as of publication, has not ended.

Once we understand how we use our basic temporal terms, we can move forward with our comparisons. History matters because it tells us where we once stood and compels us to understand, appreciate, and acknowledge space and change over time. History forces us to think about what folks in the past did given the information *they* had. It means knowing and caring about the specificities, rather than leaning into blanket generalizations that only distort and distract. For example, as teachers we routinely have to burst the bubble about the CRM as a wholesome love fest with altruistic Black folk prepared to martyr themselves for "the cause." Joyce Ladner, a Mississippian (and later Howard University interim president) who actively participated in the Mississippi CRM in the early sixties, dissuades us of this unified mirage when she explained her thought process during those years. She stated that she and those around her "did it for ourselves. We weren't aware of history at that time, or that one day it would go down in history, because these events were in the moment. We didn't have time to focus on long-term strategies."[13] In no way does Ladner's assertion negate those who modeled their activism using different perspectives. In fact, her experience challenges us to expand our notions related to how and why people joined the movement. Additionally, Ladner's actions brought her in contact with people shaped by Mahatma Gandhi's perspective, one that demanded deep faith and love for one's enemies to break down systemic hatred, individual by individual. The various theologies of James Lawson in Nashville, Tennessee, or Martin Luther King Jr. all drew strength from these moral arguments, which dictated their nonviolence as more than a strategy. Ladner and her peers helped forge the movement in real time, along with the people whose names we all recognize.[14]

Rather than erasing this legacy, we put these powerful motivations and dynamics in conversation with each other, all the while remembering that both the young people on the ground doing the thoughtful, intentional work of justice "for themselves" and the well-known actors crafting theories of engagement and transformation have always been in dynamic tension with one another as they often toiled shoulder-to-shoulder in the streets. Conflicts of strategy, pace, and leadership endemic among organizations, individuals, and generations have always existed, even with shared goals—from dismantling Jim Crow to ending apartheid to transforming policing. These fissures were national, regional, and local and constitute the mass of movements that most accurately describe what we call the Civil Rights and Black Lives Matter Movements.

History matters when we consider the advances in technology and how the dissemination of information has changed the nature of organizing and protest. Without the filters and the requisite delays of print media or even television, personal digital devices and the Internet present opportunities for instantaneous, unfiltered broadcast worldwide and easy global access. For those of us who remember life before Internet, we recognize the double-edged sword. Instant access also means most viewers do not receive enough context or critical analysis (at best), which can lead to swift reactions that tend to be emotive rather than strategic. Yet, instant access provides more visual proof of what most Black folk knew (and still know) as their truth: that Black lives do not matter in a society structured by racism, and that Black death happens too often and with impunity.

Our challenge is in having to talk about an active movement in progress. Essays drafted in 2019 have needed updating for 2024, and the factual details may have further shifted or been resolved by the end of this book's production. The comparative themes, however, persist, and the flashpoints in these essays highlight the politics of respectability, generational strife, gendered conflicts in leadership, perception versus reality, the broad impact of #BLM in American culture, the religious dimension of protest, and the limits of integration. Let this serve as a snapshot of now: how scholars situated and contextualized *this* moment while also taking part in building the alternative, the freedom dream.

In the opening essay, sociologist Charity Clay grapples with what is perhaps the largest (mis)conception of the relationship between the Civil Rights and #BLM moments: that the contemporary moment represents clear-cut tactical and methodological distinctions that make it a "clean break" from the Civil Rights era of the 1960s. Utilizing Julian Bond's "master narrative" of the CRM as an interpretive lens, Clay considers how the perception some BLMM activists have forged of themselves (fueled by images on social media) is distinct from the *perceived* embodiment of traditional, "respectable" CRM leaders and foot soldiers. Public education in the nation has boiled the Black Freedom Struggle down to digestible chunks of non-confrontational historical knowledge. Students understand that there was, at some point, something called a "movement" and that this "movement" fixed any and all problems Black folks faced. The depth and complexities of the movement remain largely hidden from current generations raised on myths, misunderstandings, and simplistic renderings in popular culture. The politics of respectability shaped and defined the visual and cultural cues of the movement. Images of young people clothed in their Sunday best and engaged in nonviolent struggle, while accurate, obscured the deep intellectual, tactical, spiritual, and epistemological work those occasionally well-dressed people performed. It is that work that connects movement folks in the past and present. Ultimately, Clay shows how the present is not that different from the past and that the wildly popular yet problematic notion that this is "not your grandma's movement" may obscure more than it reveals about the nature of social change in this moment.

In that same vein, religious ethicist Christophe Ringer argues against a powerful oversimplification of the BLMM: that, unlike the CRM, it is devoid of an enervating spirituality. Ringer insists that spirituality should be the vehicle through which we understand the BFS. Utilizing the work of the late activist, historian, and writer Vincent Harding, Ringer focuses on the spiritual experience of protest, the presence of faith and love that is not necessarily religious but, like Black religion itself, transgresses the boundaries between religious institutions and spirituality. For Ringer, a thorough examination of a Black spirituality of liberation in BLMM reveals both a distancing and a reclamation of Black religious meaning, a meaning that—like the best of Black religion—merges the secular and sacred in an effort to lay claim to greater freedom.

Peter Pihos offers a compelling reminder about the prospects and perils of police reform that originates within police departments themselves. Using Chicago as a case study, his essay explains how, over the past half century, the police department met reform efforts with coordinated, consolidated repression. As gains won through the CRM forced open a space for more Black men in blue, some of those Black officers tried to reform the institution from within. It was a brief moment of possibility for change—a door that opened but quickly closed as the system restructured to insulate itself and make sure that moment would never occur again. An understanding of internal police department dynamics remains a crucial area of inquiry in both the past and present.

Remaining in the realm of policing, Althea Legal-Miller writes about two campaigns fifty years apart that both focused on Black women's vulnerabilities and police sexual crimes against them. Her essay begins with Dorothy Height, the long-time president of the National Council of Negro Women and a national leader, who tried to force (without much success) the federal government to take seriously the crimes against women arrested for their civil rights activities. Legal-Miller considers the limits of national politics in local issues while also showcasing the extraordinary work that Height could do with her rare national access. Then in 2014, two artists in Oklahoma, Candace Liger and Grace Franklin, drew attention to the multiple sexual attacks police officer Daniel Holtzclaw committed against women in his custody by creating the advocacy group OKC Artists for Justice. Their grassroots efforts in Oklahoma, centered on survivor support, highlighted a stunning lack of regard by the justice system for Holtzclaw's victims and generated national attention to the case. The essay, like many in this volume, highlights the limitations and possibilities of case studies but ultimately lays out several crucial factors: the pernicious determination of the state to protect itself, often at the expense of Black women's bodies, and the enduring, transformative power of Black women's organizing in defense of themselves and their safety.

Scott Brooks and Aram Goudsouzian's contribution provides a comparative exploration of Black athletic activism during the CRM and BLMM. Their work reminds us of how the actions (or inactions) of Black athletes frequently mirror the range of responses to racial inequality in the larger society. To this end, their essay reveals and reminds us of the broad, dynamic range this action can take: while some athletes contemplated boycotting the 1968 Olympics, others did not. While some athletes expressed vigorous support for the BLMM, others did not. Nevertheless, in both moments, the actions of Black athletes—whether individual or collective—played a key role in shifting the political terrain of sports in ways that made social dissent possible, and always behind a backdrop of intense racial animosity and resentment, both within the sports world and in the larger society. In both eras, there is a price to pay for activism; in both eras, athletes make choices and weigh their options with regard to speaking out about the injustices they witness. Finally, the essay also shows us how racial activism can be co-opted and marketed for corporate profit, a move that always threatens to complicate—and dilute—the message and intent of social protests.

In contrast, Kishauna Soljour offers a perspective beyond the US border by teasing out some of the historical connections between blackness and activism in the United States and France. Excavating a historical dynamic she refers to as "transnational collaboration," Soljour extends the transatlantic racial dialogue between Black folks in France and the United States back in time, with moorings in Black abolitionist efforts that began in the Revolutionary era. With her primary focus on the transnational work done in 1947 and 1968, she dissects two critical moments in Black French/US history, moments catalyzed by a rich tradition of literary activism that gave powerful language to the work of liberation in both nations. Rejecting a US-centric analysis that might credit the BLMM as a singular catalyst in France, Soljour documents how Black France, also energized in the wake of a police killing, utilized the momentum created by the BLMM to organize an expansive mass movement that challenged French racial discrimination and police brutality. Soljour's essay chronicles how in response to this uprising the metropole sought to maintain the status quo and whiteness by literally erasing the category of race, a move designed to subvert racial identity and subsequent racial disruptions by invoking the nation's entrance into a new, "post-racial" era.

The last two chapters turn more fully to cultural production. In an era of instantaneous photographic reproduction and social media, performance theorist David Mason considers *who* makes the images that have shaped mainstream perceptions of the action unfurling on America's streets. In an era of #BLM, to what extent does the identity of the person behind the camera matter? In what ways are photographers' choices affected by the worldview they bring to the endeavor of chronicling Black protest? Mason provides a thoughtful meditation on photography and the photographer in the documentation of social movements, using his own personal experiences photographing a BLMM protest in Memphis, Tennessee, in 2016. Through his case study, Mason discusses how photographs have contributed to the master narrative told and retold about the mass movement for civil rights. His essay also explores the implications of Black protest captured in photographs by white photographers for white editors in real time and expands the discussion on the medium itself as a tool for both activists and the media.

Settling into the moments' media, Mickell Carter's essay considers how the role and impact of the BLMM necessitates a re-examination and remix of the Black Arts tradition timeline. For her, the work produced by Black artists articulating Black freedom dreams in the Black Power moment of the 1960s and 1970s served as the anchor for the rich musical contours produced by Black artists making similar articulations in later decades. BLMM provides an explicit through line by which to excavate this larger tradition. Black culture producers in recent years, in direct response to the BLMM, have crafted sonic landscapes that have shaped, and will continue to shape, our understanding and interpretation of the social, cultural, and political terrain created by Black activism over the past decade. To do this work, Carter explores the role of anthems—sonic monuments/memorials—and how they help illuminate the boundaries of resistance through Black expressive culture. Comparing the Black Arts Movement to contemporary artistic expressions that elide with the BLMM, Carter explores whether art shapes movements or vice versa.

If nothing else, these essays demonstrate the messiness of movements, activism, politics, and history in the midst of relentless global structural racism and white supremacy. None of these writers provide neat, hopeful conclusions to persistent, centuries-old, complicated and multi-layered struggles. Our selections purposefully represent a broad spectrum. There is no one answer, no one explanation, no magical elixir. Unfortunately, so much of this nation's history, particularly its racial history, is saturated with violence, death, and brutality. Yet we rise and find ways to thrive. We would be remiss, however, if we did not warn readers that these pages document trauma of many kinds. This is the history we must confront so that the next generations might have more guidance and not have to resurrect these themes when the next mass movement occurs. History matters.

History allows us to better understand processes, trends, collisions, and collusions. This volume encourages a multi-pronged interrogation of our contemporary moment in the BFS in light of an era from the most recent past on that timeline. With an intention to tease out continuities or ruptures, these essays offer hope—a hope that knowledge brings strength, power, and action that propel the struggle forward despite the obstacles.

NOTES

1. Many from the Till generation wrote or spoke poignantly about how the murder awoke their racial consciousness and galvanized their drive to end such terror. His slaughter was a defining moment—regardless of the range of upbringing circumstances. For scholarship on the Emmett Till generation, consider Jordana Y. Skakoor, *Civil Rights Childhood* (Jackson: University Press of Mississippi, 1999); Christopher Metress, *The Lynching of Emmett Till: A Documentary Narrative* (Charlottesville: University of Virginia Press, 2002); Devery Anderson, *Emmett Till: The Murder That Shocked the World and Propelled the Civil Rights Movement* (Jackson: University Press of Mississippi, 2015); Timothy Tyson, *The Blood of Emmett Till* (New York: Simon and Schuster, 2017); Elliott Gorn, *Let the People See: The Story of Emmett Till* (Oxford: Oxford University Press, 2018); Richard Mayer, *In the Name of Emmett Till: How the Children of the Mississippi Freedom Struggle Showed Us Tomorrow* (Montgomery, AL: NewSouth Books, 2021); and memoirs by movement veterans like the late John Lewis in *Walking with the Wind: A Memoir of the Movement* (Durham, NC: Duke University Press, 1998), and Anne Moody, *Coming of Age in Mississippi: The Classic Autobiography of Growing up Poor and Black in the Rural South* (New York: Dell, 1992).
2. For a quick history of the hashtag with sources for further reading consider: "Black Lives Matter: Herstory," Black Lives Matter, accessed January 23, 2024, https://blacklivesmatter.com/herstory; "This Day in History: July 13, 2013," HISTORY, July 12, 2021, https://www.history.com/this-day-in-history/blacklivesmatter-hashtag-first-appears-facebook-sparking-a-movement; and "A Brief History of Civil Rights in the United States: The Black Lives Matter Movement," Vernon E. Jordan Law Library, January 6, 2023, https://library.law.howard.edu/civilrightshistory/BLM.
3. For early examples, see Keeanga-Yamahtta Taylor, *From #BlackLivesMatter to Black Liberation* (Chicago: Haymarket Books, 2016) and Barbara Ransby, *Making All Black Lives Matter: Reimagining Freedom in the Twenty-First Century* (Berkeley: University of California Press, 2018).
4. On southern officials thinking the sit-ins were the Black version of panty raids, see Taylor Branch, *Parting The Waters: America in the King Years, 1954–1963* (New York: Simon and Schuster, 1988). Activist and organizer Ella Baker always stressed the importance of activist autonomy and the power of the young to affect change. See https://snccdigital.org/people/ella-baker for an overview and more sources on Ella Baker.
5. For instance, see Sandhya Somashekhar, "Oprah Says Protesters Lack Clear Demands. Here's What They Do Want," *Washington Post*, January 6, 2015, https://www.washingtonpost.com/news/post-nation/wp/2015/01/06/oprah-says-protesters-lack-clear-demands-heres-what-they-do-want.

6. Many scholars have noted how the placement of King on the leadership pedestal never reflected the reality of the movement for most activists beyond his immediate circles and SCLC. For examples, see Charles Payne, *I've Got the Light of Freedom: The Organizing Tradition and the Mississippi Freedom Struggle* (Los Angeles: University of California Press, 1995); Françoise N. Hamlin, "Collision and Collusion: Local Activism, Local Agency and Flexible Alliances," in *The Civil Rights Movement in Mississippi*, ed. Ted Ownby (Jackson: University Press of Mississippi, 2013), 35–58; Jeanne Theoharis, *A More Beautiful and Terrible History: The Uses and Misuses of Civil Rights History* (Boston: Beacon Press, 2018); Charles McKinney, "Complicating Martin Luther King, Jr.: Teaching the Life and Legacy of the Movement's Most Iconic Figure," in *Understanding and Teaching the Civil Rights Movement*, ed. Hasan Jeffries (Madison: University of Wisconsin Press, 2019), 113–30.
7. See Barbara Ransby, *Ella Baker and the Black Freedom Movement: A Radical Democratic Vision* (Chapel Hill: University of North Carolina Press, 2003), 239–47. Both she and Septima Clark, two vital activists and organizers in the mass movement for civil rights, had much to say about Dr. King and the very masculinist structure of SCLC's top-down leadership. For examples, also see Vicki L. Crawford et. al., eds., *Women in the Civil Rights Movement: Trailblazers and Torchbearers, 1941–1965* (Bloomington: University of Indiana Press, 1993); Katherine Mellon Charron, *Freedom's Teacher: The Life of Septima Clark* (Chapel Hill: University of North Carolina Press, 2009); Emilye Crosby, ed., *Civil Rights History From the Ground Up: Local Struggles, A National Movement* (Athens: University of Georgia Press, 2011); and Theoharis, *A More Beautiful and Terrible History*.
8. Keeanga-Yamahtta Taylor, "Five Years Later, Do Black Lives Still Matter?," *Jacobin Magazine*, September 30, 2019, https://jacobin.com/2019/09/black-lives-matter-laquan-mcdonald-mike-brown-eric-garner; Jesse McCarthy, "On Afropessimism," *Los Angeles Review of Books*, July 20, 2020, https://lareviewofbooks.org/article/on-afropessimism; Adolph Reed Jr., "How Racial Disparity Does Not Make Sense of Patterns of Police Violence," Nonsite.org, June 9, 2020, https://nonsite.org/how-racial-disparity-does-not-help-make-sense-of-patterns-of-police-violence-2; Cedric Johnson, *After Black Lives Matter* (New York: Verso Books, 2023).
9. Our works include Charles W. McKinney Jr., *Greater Freedom: The Evolution of the Civil Rights Struggle in Wilson, North Carolina* (Lanham, MD: University Press of America, 2010); Françoise N. Hamlin, *Crossroads at Clarksdale: The Black Freedom Struggle in the Mississippi Delta after World War II* (Chapel Hill: University of North Carolina Press, 2012).
10. For examples, see Ransby and Taylor, as well as Christopher Lebron, *The Color of Our Shame: Race and Justice in Our Time* (Oxford: Oxford Univer-

sity Press, 2013), and *The Making of Black Lives Matter: A Brief History of an Idea* (New York: Oxford University Press, 2017); Patrisse Khan-Cullors, *When They Call You a Terrorist: A Black Lives Matter Memoir* (New York: St. Martin's Press, 2018); Veronica Chambers, *Call and Response: The Story of Black Lives Matter* (New York: Versify, 2021); Deva Woodly, *Reckoning: Black Lives Matter and the Democratic Necessity of Social Movements* (Oxford: Oxford University Press, 2021); Brandon Hogan, Michael Cholby, Alex Madva, Benjamin Yost, eds., *The Movement for Black Lives: Philosophical Perspectives* (New York: Oxford University Press, 2023); On the convergence of #BLM protests and the global pandemic, see Barnor Hesse and Debra Thompson, eds., "2020: One Pandemic, Two Pandemics, Black Lives Matter," special issue, *South Atlantic Quarterly* 121, no. 3 (July 2022).

11. For a synopsis of the murder of George Floyd and the protests that followed, consider Helier Cheung, "George Floyd Death: Why US Protests Are So Powerful This Time," BBC, June 8, 2020, https://www.bbc.com/news/world-us-canada-52969905; Derrick Bryson Taylor, "George Floyd Protests: A Timeline," *New York Times*, Nov. 5, 2021, https://www.nytimes.com/article/george-floyd-protests-timeline.html.

12. See Benjamin Press and Thomas Carothers, "Worldwide Protests in 2020: A Year in Review," Carnegie Endowment for International Peace, December 21, 2020, https://carnegieendowment.org/2020/12/21/worldwide-protests-in-2020-year-in-review-pub-83445; Michael Powell, "Are Protests Dangerous? What Experts Say May Depend on Who's Protesting What," *New York Times*, July 6, 2020, https://www.nytimes.com/2020/07/06/us/Epidemiologists-coronavirus-protests-quarantine.html.

13. Elahe Izadi, "Black Lives Matter and America's Long History of Resisting Civil Rights Protesters," *Washington Post*, April 19, 2016.

14. For examples with deep descriptions of these positions, see David Halberstam, *The Children* (New York: Random House, 1998); C.T. Vivian, *It's in the Action: Memories of a Nonviolent Warrior* (Montgomery, AL: NewSouth Books, 2021); James Lawson Jr., *Revolutionary Nonviolence: Organizing for Freedom* (Oakland: University of California Press, 2022).

CHAPTER 1

"Sincerely, Your Grandparents' Hands"

Elucidating Similarities between the Trayvon Martin Generation of #BlackLivesMatter and the Emmett Till Generation of the Civil Rights Movement

Charity Clay

We Are Not Our Grandparents! The Collective Consciousness for Black Youth of #BlackLivesMatter

At a Ferguson protest on October 13, 2014, activist and HipHop artist Kareem Jackson, known as Tef Poe, announced to the public: "This ain't your grandparents' Civil Rights Movement!" He continued in his address, specifically recognizing the "young men with their shirts off and bandanas on, [and] the girl who should be in school but isn't" as the people who had been the most involved during the street protests and local organizing efforts in response to the police killing of eighteen-year-old Mike Brown two months earlier. His comments praised Black youth for their commitment to justice and consistent presence and simultaneously called out those Black elders who were quick to critique Black youth for their personal style and protest tactics while remaining largely absent from the local organizing efforts themselves.[1]

Tef Poe's statement articulated a rejection of the politics of respectability tactic used by previous generations of Black people to achieve racial equality. It also marked an early assertion of a developing collective consciousness for Black youth protestors of the emerging movement later referred to as #BlackLivesMatter (#BLM).[2] Two subsequent exchanges in late 2014 between Black youth aligned with #BLM and Black elder public figures aligned with the Civil Rights Movement (CRM) further contributed to the development of Black youth's collective consciousness: one was the presence of Ferguson protestors at Rev. Al Sharpton's "Justice for All" March; the other was Black youth's social media responses to Oprah Winfrey's critiques of their protests.[3]

Sharpton held the "Justice For All" March in Washington, DC, on December 13, 2014, in response to the failures to indict the police officers who had killed Eric Garner and Mike Brown earlier in the summer and the recent police killing of twelve-year-old Tamir Rice in November. Black youth who had been protesting in the streets, organizing meetings with local officials, establishing community outreach centers, and participating in hashtag social media campaigns since the summer felt that Sharpton organized the march in an attempt to insert himself as the leader of the emerging movement without having any prior involvement. Ferguson protestor Johnetta Elzie spoke to this sentiment at the march, informing the crowd: "This movement was started by the young people, and I don't see no young people talking," referring to the march as "a publicity stunt" and claiming that Sharpton and his organization "are not doing anything but standing around." She contrasted the march with her experiences in Ferguson, where law enforcement constantly attacked and even hit her with rubber bullets while on the front lines with other protestors.[4]

While mainstream media portrayed the presence of Ferguson protestors at Sharpton's march as a disruption, Elzie's efforts to acknowledge the importance and necessity of young Black people in the movement spoke directly to a collective consciousness that insisted on recognizing the current generation of Black youth as creating a movement separate from their "grandparents." Ferguson protestors and other Black youth expressed this consciousness by showing up to Sharpton's march confrontational and demanding, a stark contrast to the passive and accommodating ways they perceived as characterizing their CRM elders.

A week after the "Justice For All" March, another incident served as an early assertion of Black youth's collective consciousness, this time on Twitter, the outlet that would become #BLM's signature social media platform. This second incident occurred when Oprah Winfrey's comments about the protests, made while promoting her film *Selma*, went viral.[5] When asked on *Good Morning America* what viewers could learn from the movie, Winfrey stated: "All people who are protesting now could benefit from seeing the strategic intention that had to happen in order for real progress to be made."[6] Then she added the following comments, seemingly directed at Black youth: "You can't just be marching without an intention. . . . You got to have a clear strategic intention of what it is you want to accomplish, and you cannot be heard unless you come in peace."[7] In an exclusive *People Magazine* article released the same week, Winfrey stated that she was looking for "some kind of leadership to come out of [the protests] to say 'this is what we want. This is what has to change, and these are the steps that we need to take to make these changes, and this is what we're willing to do to get it.'"[8]

Black youth received Winfrey's comments as an uninformed and inaccurate assessment of their movement and responded immediately by directing tweets @Oprah. One tweeter typed, "If @Oprah doesn't see 'leadership' in Ferguson, it's cuz she's not really looking. It's grass-roots – she has to do work to see the teams." Another tweeter questioned Winfrey's criteria for determining leadership, typing, "So does @Oprah expect someone to raise their hand at a Protest when they ask 'who is your leader'? That messiah style leadership is not us." One Ferguson organizer tweeted, "Once again a Black 'celebrity' shows just how out of touch they are. So, while @Oprah searches for an outdated leadership model, #weworkin."[9] @TefPoe even extended an invitation, tweeting, "@Oprah there are youth orgs set up and ready to roll. How about some of the black elite sit at the table w/us and discuss our demands?"[10] While direct responses to Winfrey's comments ranged from complete dismissal of her words' validity to invitations for her to support Black youth in their efforts, a common sentiment among them was that Black youth did not wish to follow the traditions of a CRM whose leadership style and tactics they believed to be obsolete and, furthermore, that they did not seek the approval of Black elders whom they viewed as elitist and out of touch.

Similar to the media coverage of the Black youth presence at Sharpton's march, mainstream outlets framed Black youths' direct Twitter responses to Winfrey as disrespectful and added the exchange to the growing narrative that included stories linking property destruction and violence to Black youth protestors. This narrative overshadowed the positive impact Black youth were having in their communities and invited such criticism from Winfrey and other Civil Rights–aligned Black elders. In addition to their direct responses to Winfrey, Black youth also used Twitter to counter the narratives that portrayed them as unintentional, disorganized, and violent by creating and sharing social media posts highlighting the roles that they had played and were currently playing in the movement on the ground nationwide. For many Black youth, engagement with #BLM via social media introduced them to the Black Freedom Struggle (BFS). In this way, this use of social media also showcased Twitter as an effective platform of communication and organization for the developing movement, presenting social media technology as a nuanced tool for youth of this generation that separated them from their CRM elders who never had the option to individually broadcast directly to local and global audiences.

In both highlighted exchanges, Black youth asserted a collective consciousness marked by their unflinching commitment to grassroots direct action, their rejection of respectability, and their use of social media as a new tool of activism. My analysis of their approach views it as an evolution of the BFS: an era-specific response to the unique manifestations of systemic racial oppression these youth were experiencing. This era is marked by the failure of a proposed "post racial" United States that the presidential election of Barack Obama supposedly ushered in, bringing improved conditions for Black people. The broken promises of Obama's "Change" for Black

Americans coupled with the rise of social media, which increased the visibility of racial incidents ranging from workplace and public-space micro aggressions to fatal encounters with law enforcement. Thus, Black youth entering the BFS during this era questioned the effectiveness of their elders' tactics and began to develop their own, in attempts to carry on the tradition they associated more with Black Power than the CRM. As a result, the efforts of the Black youth of #BLM to accept the challenge of the BFS was framed by negative media portrayals associating them with violence, destruction, and chaos in the same way Black youth of the Black Panther Party were half a century ago. In 2017, the FBI used portrayals of #BLM youth to create a new domestic terrorism program category called the "Black Identity Extremism Movement."[11] In 1969, FBI Director J. Edgar Hoover stated in an annual report that the organization had increased its investigations of "violence-prone Black Extremists groups" and that, amongst them, "The Black Panther Party, without question, represents the greatest threat to the internal security of the country."[12] Ironically, these negative public portrayals of Black youth during both time periods contributed to Civil Rights-aligned Black elders viewing both their Black Power Movement peers and the Black youth of #BLM as misaligned with the CRM, dividing people on the same side of the fight.

Defending themselves against the criticisms and negative media portrayals, Black youth of #BLM expressed their collective consciousness by echoing Tef Poe's early statement. They asserted that they are "not their grandparents" and added the closing, "sincerely, these hands," indicating their willingness to "throw hands," or physically fight, for their freedom in opposition to their nonviolent "grandparents" of the CRM. Though the initial statement from Tef Poe was intended as a rejection of respectability, Black youth began asserting it as a rejection of not only the Civil Rights-aligned Black elders who critiqued them but also the entire CRM as an extension.

So, while the 2014 police killings of unarmed Black males ranging in age from twelve years old to forty-three should have catalyzed intergenerational solidarity within the BFS, media framing of both the CRM and the Movement responding to those killings widened the gap between Black youth and their elders. I offer that the media-created master-narrative myths of the CRM drove both the Black elders' critiques of Black youth and the Black youths' defensiveness in response to those critiques, and they deserve interrogation. This chapter elucidates how both generations have adopted CRM master narratives and how this has created conflict between them detrimental to the BFS. As an attempt to foster intergenerational solidarity within the BFS, I also provide counter narratives of the CRM to reveal the similarities between the Black youth of #BLM and their CRM elders.

Master Narrative Myths of the Civil Rights Movement

Author Toni Morrison characterizes a master narrative as "whatever ideological script is being imposed by the people in authority on everybody else."[13] With respect to race, master narratives describe dominant social mythologies that mute, erase, and neutralize features of racial struggle in ways that normalize and perpetuate whiteness.[14] These mythologies become so ingrained in our psyche and normalized in our culture that, when effective, even members of racially marginalized groups will accept, adopt, and perpetuate them. For the CRM, scholar Ashley W. Woodson identifies four master narrative themes: first, they essentialize Black people and Black struggle; second, they portray racism as an accident; third, they center stories of myths, martyrs, and messiahs; and fourth, they suggest that the CRM ended racism.[15] Myths along these themes were constructed in real time, largely through television media content, spun and presented as accurate, unbiased accounts of historical events. Activist and educator Julian Bond masterfully presents the following CRM master narrative script in his book designed to teach CRM history:

> Traditionally, relationships between the races in the South were oppressive. In 1954, the Supreme Court decided this was wrong. Inspired by the court, courageous Americans, Black and white, took protest to the

street, in the forms of sit-ins, bus boycotts and freedom rides. The protest movement, led by the eloquent Dr. Martin Luther King Jr., aided by a sympathetic federal government, most notably the Kennedy brothers and a born-again Lyndon Johnson, was able to make America understand racial discrimination as a moral issue. Once Americans understood that discrimination was wrong, they quickly moved to remove racial prejudice and discrimination from American life, as evidenced by the Civil Rights Acts of 1964 and 1965. Inexplicably, just as the civil rights victories were piling up, many African Americans, under the banner of Black power, turned their backs on American Society.[16]

As such, these myths mute the CRM's myriad of voices, positioning the Rev. Dr. Martin Luther King Jr. as the sole representative of the sentiments of Black people. They erase the generations of Black resistance to racial injustice, discrimination, and violence by crediting the Supreme Court for sparking the CRM with the 1954 *Brown* decision. They neutralize the systemic racial oppression of Jim Crow segregation by presenting it as simply an interpersonal issue of race relations between Black and white people in the American South.

For Black elders, adopting these CRM myths leads them to use two criteria to measure the legitimacy of Black youth and #BLM: first, the presence of charismatic leadership like Dr. King and, second, whether their responses to white violence are peaceful. By those criteria then, #BLM, with its decentralization via localized organizing and globalized social media engagement and its protestors' combative responses to law enforcement, is fundamentally misaligned with the CRM. Ironically, although Black youth may recognize that Black elder critiques of their #BLM protest activities come from absorbing CRM master narrative myths, Black youth adopt them as well. Their adoption leads them to consider the CRM as based solely in respectability, characterized by conservative messiah leadership and passive nonviolence. In turn, Black youth view this version of respectability as ineffective and irrelevant for #BLM and dismiss their elders altogether. Thus, comparisons made between #BLM and the mythologized CRM only increase intergenerational conflict and sabotage opportunities for Black youth to learn from movement elders whose protest experiences align more with theirs than CRM master narrative myths show.

This chapter presents Black youth of #BLM as the Trayvon Martin Generation and reintroduces them to their "grandparents," presented here as the Emmett Till Generation: the radical youth of the CRM. I elucidate three major similarities between the Black youth of #BLM and their CRM elders. The first similarity is that both generations' entry into the BFS responded to the tragic killing of one of their peers by white vigilantism not punished by the criminal justice system. The second similarity is how both generations of youth organized in radically different ways than their elders, specifically in ways that introduced nuanced movement ideologies, tactics, and tools. The third similarity is that master narratives have operated to mute, erase, and neutralize the impacts of both generations' movements within the BFS. The similarities between these generations also provide counter narratives to the two major master narrative myths: that Dr. King was the sole leader of the CRM, and that Civil Rights nonviolence was passive and synonymous with not fighting back against white violence. The chapter concludes by offering some common ground for building intergenerational solidarity between the Trayvon Martin and Emmett Till generations, which I consider useful as the BFS moves into what I present as the Post #BLM era.

The Trayvon Martin Generation: Black Youth of #BlackLivesMatter

In 2012, Black youth nationwide witnessed one of their peers, seventeen-year-old Trayvon Martin, posthumously criminalized after a white vigilante in Sanford, Florida, killed him. They watched as media, police, and his killer's defense attorneys labeled Martin as a thug for wearing a hoodie and posting social media content showing him with gold teeth, giving the middle finger, and smoking cannabis. Black youth saw how these portrayals led to narratives that held his Blackness as more responsible for his death than George Zimmerman, the twenty-eight-year-old who shot the teenager, claiming that he looked suspicious. Through this incident, many Black youth who looked, dressed, and expressed themselves like Martin increasingly understood their vulnerability to fatal white violence. Already heavily engaged in social media for entertainment and even education, Black youth began to respond to in-person racial injustices through social media as well. They posted pictures in hoodies, holding Skittles brand candies and Arizona brand iced tea (the items Martin carried when he was killed), and hashtagged #IAmTrayvon in solidarity on social media.

Responding in the moment, using an emerging tool literally at their fingertips, Black youths' early social media engagement around Trayvon Martin's killing pioneered the use of social media as a tool of the BFS and became their entry into activism. Eight years later, in May 2020, seventeen-year-old Darnella Frazier captured cellphone footage of George Floyd, a forty-six-year-old Black man, dying of asphyxia as a Minneapolis Police Department training officer held his knee on Floyd's neck for over eight minutes. Frazier shared the footage via social media, and it immediately went viral, sparking global #BLM protests in the middle of the COVID-19 pandemic. Frazier herself and other Black youth on the front lines represent the Trayvon Martin Generation.

Poet Elizabeth Alexander refers to the Trayvon Martin Generation as young Black people who have grown up in the past twenty-five years and had their adolescence shaped by social media engagement that has increased visibility of fatal violence perpetuated upon unarmed Black people by law enforcement. In her exquisite definition, quoted below at length, she asserts that the widespread broadcasting of Black victimization resulting from fatal police violence

> formed [the Trayvon Martin Generation's] world view. These stories helped instruct young African Americans about their embodiment and their vulnerability. These stories were primers in fear and futility. These stories were the ground soil of their rage. These stories instructed them that anti-Black hatred and violence were never far. They watched these violations up and close and on their cell phones, so many times over. They watched them in near-real time. They watched them crisscrossed

and concentrated. They watched them on a school bus. They watched them under the covers at night. They watched them often outside of the presence of adults who loved them and were charged with keeping them safe in body and soul.[17]

The collective consciousness of the Trayvon Martin Generation can be characterized in three ways: first, their ability to reflect on and articulate their responses to this violence through social media via written word, visual art, dance, music, and other forms of expression; second, their willingness to engage in conversations among their peers and with members of their parents' and grandparents' generations who care to engage; and third, their commitment to resistance, via hashtag campaigns, organizing within their communities, and as participants of larger protests movements.

In addition, activist and journalist Rahiel Tesfamariam, whose "This ain't yo mama's Civil Rights Movement" t-shirt worn at a Mike Brown protest is displayed in the National African American Museum of History and Culture (NAAMHC), articulated the following observation of the Trayvon Martin Generation: "For this generation, there's no need to hide behind a veil of purity or wear a suit to have an authoritative seat at the table. This is a movement that encourages all to come as you are. Natural, Bohemian, Rebellious, Tatted up. Provocative. Ratchet. It seems like everything is acceptable – except the constraining rules of our elders' day."[18] In this context, the Trayvon Martin Generation showed up to protests, city council meetings, and other activities fully understanding that they may be negatively stereotyped because of their appearance. They showed up in these ways as an intentional statement that Black respectability does not, nor has it ever, guaranteed safety for Black people interacting with the state. This rejection of this particular brand of respectability is essential to the Trayvon Martin Generation; as such, the slogan on Tesfamariam's t-shirt and others with the same sentiment were popularized via apparel, protest signs, and various social media platforms during the #BLM protest activities between 2014 and 2016.

Indeed, it was in this span of two years that the Trayvon Martin Generation carried out historic disruptions with their protest events in response to police killings of more unarmed Black people across the nation. For examples, on Black Friday in 2014, the Blackout Collective successfully shut down the San Francisco Bay Area Rapid Transit (BART) trains at the West Oakland station.[19] The following year, in 2015, the Trayvon Martin Generation shut down Chicago's Michigan Avenue "Magnificent Mile" shopping district after footage was released of police fatally shooting unarmed seventeen-year-old Laquan McDonald sixteen times.[20] They also marched from Baltimore's city hall to the Inner Harbor after twenty-five-year-old Freddie Gray was killed in police custody.[21] In 2016, after the Facebook live broadcast of the police slaughtering of thirty-two-year-old Philando Castile in the Minnesota Twin Cities area, the Trayvon Martin Generation shut down Interstate 94 in protest.[22] The success of these disruptive protests are evidence of the commitment and organization of the Trayvon Martin Generation, amid the Black elder critiques and loved ones' concerns for their safety.[23] The Trayvon Martin Generation, through these actions, sent the message that they viewed themselves as more courageous and more confrontational than their CRM elders. They viewed themselves as the generation that would accomplish the goals that their elders could not and proclaimed again that they are "not their grandparents. Sincerely, these hands." While misguided in their proclamation regarding their CRM elders, the Trayvon Martin Generation was seriously engaged with the BFS.

In addition to these major disruptive protests, the Trayvon Martin Generation led local organizing: with efforts to physically repair communities affected by property destruction committed in response to police killings and the subsequent failures to indict; with healing initiatives to assist residents suffering from systemic racial oppression caused by major institutions like housing, education, social welfare, and of course law enforcement; and with programs to provide intervention and de-escalation as an alternative to engaging law enforcement in efforts to reduce intracommunal violence. They were also involved in global social media mobilizing efforts with organizations in solidarity throughout the African diaspora and on the continent. Yet, while the Trayvon Martin Generation constantly combatted master narrative myths created about

#BLM in real time, they simultaneously adopted the master narrative myths of the CRM, causing them to distance themselves from their elders rather than recognize the significant similarities. Thus, it is necessary to reintroduce the Trayvon Martin Generation to their "grandparents," the Emmett Till Generation.

The Emmett Till Generation: Radical Black Youth of the Civil Rights Movement

White vigilantes in Mississippi kidnapped, tortured, and lynched fourteen-year-old Emmett Till, visiting from Chicago in 1955, for allegedly whistling at a white woman. When his mother returned his body to Chicago for his funeral, she requested that his casket be opened for public viewing to show the world the extent of white violence against Black people in the South. Photos of Till's mutilated body were printed in *Jet* magazine and circulated across the world, analogous to how videos of police killings of Black people "go viral" on social media today.

Mississippi-born Student Nonviolent Coordinating Committee (SNCC) activist and sociologist Joyce Ladner was twelve years old when Emmett Till was lynched. She refers to herself and her peers, Black people who were born predominately in the 1940s and galvanized to become involved in the BFS because of Till's case, as the Emmett Till Generation. She states, "I can name you ten SNCC workers who saw that picture [of Till's body] in *Jet* magazine, who remembered it as the key thing about their youth and that was emblazoned in their minds. . . . [One] of them told me how they saw it and thought that one day they would avenge his death."[24] Fellow SNCC member Cleveland Sellers, who was eleven years old when Till died, recalls that he and his peers had discussions in their class after bringing copies of the *Jet* magazine issue to their South Carolina elementary school.[25] The former chairman of SNCC (and later US Congressman) John Lewis was a fifteen-year-old in Alabama, and he wrote that he would never forget that moment.[26]

Though often overlooked by the master narrative of the CRM, members of the Emmett Till Generation were significantly involved with every major televised BFS event from 1955 to 1963. Fifteen-year-old Claudette Colvin, who refused to give up her bus seat to a white woman in March 1955, has more recently been recognized as a catalyst for the Montgomery Bus Boycott.[27] In 1957, members of the Emmett Till Generation famously known as the "Little Rock Nine" were thrust onto the frontlines of the movement and into the spotlight of the national media when the governor of Arkansas prohibited them from entering Little Rock Central High School. On February 1, 1960, four students from North Carolina A&T State University engaged in a sit-in at a local Greensboro Woolworth's dining counter. I suggest that the sit-ins were a turning point in the CRM, because they increased the scope, presence, and leadership of Black youth and led to the development of SNCC after 126 student delegates gathered in April 1960 for a conference at Shaw University in Raleigh, North Carolina.[28] Black Freedom Struggle veteran Ella Baker organized the conference in her role as executive director of the Southern Christian Leadership Council (SCLC). Her goal was to gather youth leaders from college campuses and Black communities to meet and mobilize into a radical, democratic, youth-led organization.[29] Less than three years after its founding, SNCC, alongside long-time labor organizer Asa Philip Randolph and other entities, organized the 1963 March on Washington for Jobs and Freedom.

The master narrative myth of the CRM attends to SNCC and its legacy in the following three ways: it either ignores the organization completely; it reduces it to a youth subsidiary of Dr. King's SCLC or Roy Wilkins's NAACP; or it presents SNCC's efforts as antithetical to the CRM, citing its later proclamation of Black Power in 1966.[30] In these ways, the myths of the CRM erase the significant contributions of the Emmett Till Generation, who created a movement alongside their respective elders, whom they also viewed as too accommodating and passive in their pursuits of gradual Civil Rights gains via legislative amendments. On the one hand, adopting master narrative myths has lead to Black elder critiques of the Trayvon Martin Generation; on the other hand, it has lead to the Trayvon Martin Generation assessing their elders' CRM protests by modern-day standards of social engagement. Unknowingly, Black youth assessments fail to consider the ever-present threat and reality of violence their

CRM elders faced under the Jim Crow system of racial oppression that regularly attacked Black people with impunity for attempting to assert their humanity. The result is a conclusion that their "grandparents" were passive and cowardly. In addition to master narrative treatments of SNCC making it difficult for Black youth to see similarities between them and their "grandparents," the ahistorical comparisons between #BLM and the CRM also sabotage intergenerational solidarity within the BFS. Thus, introducing counter narratives operates here as an attempt to reconnect Black youth to their elders.

Finding Common Ground for Intergenerational Solidarity

Both the Emmett Till and Trayvon Martin Generations were inspired by the killing of one of their peers to step boldly onto the front lines of a major movement and do things differently than their elders. Both elders and community leaders received their tactics and attitudes as dangerous and reckless. While their legacies have been distorted by master narratives of both the CRM and #BLM, members of both generations provide first-person counter narratives to highlight contributions erased by mainstream media.[31]

These similarities provide fertile common ground to build intergenerational solidarity. To further conversations between the two generations, this chapter proceeds by unpacking counter narratives to the major CRM myths both generations have adopted. It counters the myth of Dr. King's messiah leadership by showcasing examples of SNCC's decentralized leadership and counters the myth of Civil Rights nonviolence as passive and cowardly by reframing passive nonviolence as aggressive confrontations and highlighting the role armed self-defense played in supporting the CRM nonviolent activities. Overall, the following sections aim to show the Trayvon Martin Generation that their elders possessed the very qualities they believe set them apart while also illustrating to Black elder critics of #BLM the important roles these youth play within the BFS.

SNCC Counter Narratives to the Myth of Dr. King's Messiah Leadership

Despite master narrative myths of Martin Luther King Jr. as the national spokesman of the CRM, King himself recognized the increasing participation and leadership of the Emmett Till Generation. At a speech delivered in Durham, North Carolina, on February 16, 1960, after stores across the state had closed due to the growing youth-led sit-in movement, he stated to the crowd:

> You students of North Carolina have captured this dynamic idea in a marvelous manner. You have taken the undying and passionate yearning for freedom and filtered it in your own soul and fashioned it into a creative protest that is destined to be one of the glowing epics of our time. For the past few days, you have moved in a uniquely, meaningful orbit imparting heat and light to distant satellites.... What is fresh, what is new in your fight is the fact that it was initiated, fed and sustained by students. What is new is that American students have come of age. You now take your honored places in the world-wide struggle for freedom.[32]

While King's statement may be taken as an official welcome into the CRM to members of the Emmett Till Generation, SNCC co-founder and longtime Tennessee activist Avon Rollins, Sr. insisted that SNCC was the vanguard of the BFS, responsible for bringing King's SCLC and other organizations into *their* movement of the 1960s.[33]

SNCC historian Clayborne Carson designates the 1963 March on Washington as the shift from the CRM under King's leadership to the "Freedom Struggle" under the leadership of SNCC. He marks the march as his first SNCC demonstration and adds that when he met SNCC organizers Kwame Ture, then known as Stokely Carmichael, and Bob Moses, he realized that "Martin Luther King was following *them.*"[34] While King's "I Have a Dream" speech immortalized him as the perceived leader of the CRM, movement veteran Avon Rollins explained SNCC's initial intentions for the march:

> The actual march was very different from that which some had suggested and recommended take place. For example, some had sought to form

a "human petition" on the National Mall in Washington, D.C. The purpose of this "human petition" would be to demand an end to the disenfranchisement of African Americans from exercising the voting rights guaranteed to them under the Constitution of the United States. For some of the more radical among us, the March on Washington was to be a rally through which individuals would engage in activities to disrupt the Federal government, by swamping the telephone switchboards of the various departments of government, by chaining themselves to the White House and other government buildings, and by stopping traffic in the District. Government would cease to function. As history has reported, these actions did not take place.[35]

While SNCC ultimately made concessions in their initial plans to include conservative elders like King, Roy Wilkins, and Whitney Young, deferring to them as featured speakers, SNCC members and march organizers elected twenty-year-old John Lewis to speak on the organization's behalf. As the youngest speaker at the march, Lewis proclaimed:

To those who have said, "be patient and wait," we have long said that we cannot be patient. We do not want our freedom gradually; we want to be free now! We are tired. We are tired of getting beaten by policemen. We are tired of seeing our people locked up in jail over and over. And then you holler, "be patient." How long can we be patient? We want our freedom, and we want it now. We do not want to go to jail, but we will go to jail if this is the price we must pay for love, brotherhood and true peace. I appeal to all of you to get into this great revolution that is sweeping this nation.[36]

Lewis's speech represented the Emmett Till Generation: those on the front lines of voter registration drives, sit-ins to desegregate public establishments, and other activities where they were routinely brutalized by police and white civilians. His words reflect their sense of urgency and indicate how their actions moved past the conservative gradualism of their elders' actions, even though they may have presented themselves "respectfully" with their clothing.[37] Through

Lewis's words, the Emmett Till Generation bravely embraced being criminalized in their pursuit of justice and rejected gradual legislative efforts that resulted in little to no changes to the economic and political conditions for Black people.

In fact, the original version of Lewis's speech was even more radical. It stated explicitly that SNCC did not support the existing Civil Rights Act created by the Kennedy administration because it did not protect Black people from police brutality, especially those who were attacked while peacefully protesting for their constitutional rights.[38] While Dr. King's "Dream" has become, arguably, the grandest symbol of the CRM master narrative myths, SNCC's organization, participation, and speech at the March on Washington not only counter the myth of Dr. King's messiah leadership but also showcase the success of SNCC's decentralized leadership, which led to the March's success. The SNCC model operated along three lines: intergenerational solidarity, support of local leadership, and the pursuit of economic and political autonomy for southern Black communities.

While most SNCC members were part of the Emmett Till Generation, they were trained and mentored by veterans of the BFS like Ella Baker and Gloria Richardson. They were also guided through communities by local leaders like C. C. Bryant in Mississippi and John Hulett in Alabama.[39] Ranging from radical to conservative, these SNCC mentors were members of Dr. King's generation, and, while they respected King, some departed from his nonviolent tactics and encouraged the young SNCC members to balance their radical approaches with thoughtful tactics that could be successful within the context of extremely violent white opposition to any attempts to pursue Black equality.

The myth of Dr. King as a messiah leader implies that he was viewed as the savior of Black southerners. SNCC's leadership was the opposite. When SNCC organizers entered rural Black communities in Georgia, Louisiana, Alabama, and Mississippi, they aided local leaders and existing initiatives instead of positioning themselves as saviors. In fact, before SNCC workers began their campaigns, they shadowed residents, stayed in their homes, and listened to their stories to become acclimated to each unique environment.

After building rapport with residents, SNCC workers focused on supporting voter registration campaigns. This allowed local leaders to focus on running political campaigns to draft legislation and supporting candidates who would serve the interests of rural Black southerners striving to obtain political and economic autonomy instead of integration.

While SNCC chairman Stokely Carmichael's (later Kwame Ture) call for Black Power in 1966 aligned him with the militancy of later organizations like the Black Panther Party, it was actually a slogan taken from the Lowndes County Freedom Organization (LCFO) in Alabama. As a member of SNCC, Carmichael worked with the LCFO in 1965 to establish the first independent political party of the era after witnessing the refusal to recognize the Mississippi Freedom Democratic Party (MFDP) at the 1964 Democratic National Convention and the passing of the Voting Rights Act earlier in 1965. When Carmichael entered Lowndes County, 80 percent of the population was Black, but only one Black person was registered to vote due to the extreme political and economic disenfranchisement and white violence of Jim Crow. He and other SNCC workers launched a massive campaign to support the LCFO, not only helping Black residents register to vote but also campaigning for Black nominees for sheriff, tax collector, tax assessor, coroner, and the school board to be included on the 1966 ballot. Meanwhile, LCFO members provided economic support and set up tent cities to house Black residents either evicted from their homes or fired from their jobs for trying to register to vote. They also provided armed self-defense for community members and SNCC organizers. Though their efforts were successful in producing candidates for the ballot, white voter fraud and intimidation prevented the nominees from winning.[40] Still, the LCFO model of political autonomy and their efforts to provide economic support and public safety for Black residents inspired Carmichael's public announcement of "Black Power" as a framework for liberation. Thus Black Power emerged from the Emmett Till Generation's participation in the BFS through SNCC.

The Importance of Armed Self-Defense for Successful SNCC Nonviolence

In his book *We Will Shoot Back*, scholar Akinyele Omowale Umoja insists that armed southerners provided a "blanket of protection" for SNCC organizers that included night patrols and trained snipers.[41] His work suggests that while SNCC adopted practical nonviolent tactics, they embraced the support of communities trained in armed self-defense and that this support increased the likelihood that their nonviolent campaigns could be carried out successfully against white southerners' threats of extremely violent opposition. Stories of armed southerners protecting nonviolent protestors counter master narrative myths that manufacture a false dichotomy between nonviolence and physical resistance by disconnecting Black southerners' organized armed self-defense from the activities of major organizations affiliated with the CRM. This dichotomy is played out by media coverage that portrays Black people as passive victims of white violence to garner empathy and to assuage concerns of any Black uprising.

In doing so, such portrayals construct a myth that mutes the ways that civil rights organizations intentionally engaged in nonviolent demonstrations, erasing the tradition of Black people and organizations that did defend themselves and their communities against white violence and neutralizing the courage required to withstand white violence without public retaliation. The myth also results in the Trayvon Martin Generation viewing their nonviolent elders as passive and cowardly. However, the absence of Black self-defense in nationally televised CRM events does not equate to its absence from the struggle. Black armed self-defense during the CRM was a localized tactic largely carried out by Black veterans who had served in World War II and the Korean War. An early example is Robert F. Williams' Black Armed Guard that provided defense for Freedom Riders in North Carolina in 1961. Another example is the Deacons of Defense, founded in 1964 in Louisiana to protect Black residents and nonviolent activists from violence and intimidation of the local Ku Klux Klan and law enforcement.

Additionally, accounts of Black physical resistance to white violence often feature individual incidents that were not part of any organized events.⁴² Sadly, many of these stories, like one shared by Lyman Johnson for the Southern Oral History Program, indicated that these individual acts of resistance often forced Black people to flee their homes and resulted in greater white violence against Black residents to instill fear and deter further resistance.⁴³ Thus, counter narratives that celebrate how Black people risked their lives fighting back against the everyday assaults under Jim Crow aid in removing the false dichotomy that led the Trayvon Martin Generation to view their CRM elders as passive and cowardly. Within this context, collective nonviolent action is a tactic used by specific organizations, separate from but occurring alongside the daily practices of self-defense by Black southerners. Moreover, nonviolence is not passive or cowardly but active and courageous because of the resolve it required.

From Cowardice to Courageousness: SNCC Counter Narratives of Passive Civil Rights Nonviolence

In reframing nonviolence in *This Nonviolent Stuff'll Get You Killed*, CRM veteran and author Charles Cobb explains that SNCC nonviolent protests, like sit-ins, "were not acts of hate or brutality toward white people, who were themselves ignorant of their imprisonment by a system that led them to believe in white supremacy. They were, instead, aggressive confrontations that challenged the *system*, and recognizing this refutes the notion that nonviolence was a passive tactic."⁴⁴ Cobb's term "aggressive confrontations" provides alternative language to describe nonviolent protests like boycotts, sit-ins, marches, and voter registration efforts. In fact, participation in nonviolent protests was very tactically orchestrated and required training to prepare participants for the onslaught of violent attacks from whites.⁴⁵ Nonviolent efforts were anything but passive, because they required Black people to intentionally place themselves in harm's way during demonstrations; to have their families and communities targeted for violence; and possibly to be imprisoned and/or retaliated against by the loss of housing and jobs. For these reasons, Cobb presents "aggressive confrontations" as the ultimate show of courage, as death-defying actions that diminished the fear weaponized to keep many Black people in the South from standing up for their rights and mobilizing communities to fight back against systemic racial oppression and individual and organized white violence.

Counter narratives of SNCC nonviolence as aggressive confrontations also reframes the approach behind tactics like boycotts, sit-ins, and marches in ways that clearly articulate their alignment with specific goals of the struggle. Boycotts were intended for economic impact; sit-ins were aimed at bringing public attention to segregation of public accommodations; and marches were intended to communicate solidarity and express statements of protest to various types of injustice and inequality. Understanding the intentionality of SNCC initiatives that are often oversimplified as nonviolence can inform the Trayvon Martin Generation that not only were such initiatives localized, but tactics were also selected in response to various types of inequality and injustice.

Conclusion

The intent of this chapter is not to romanticize SNCC. As with all organizations, their legacy is complicated. Despite support from locally organized armed resistance in the rural South, SNCC organizers experienced extreme and sometimes fatally violent white opposition. The recruitment of white college students for Freedom Summer in 1964 to increase visibility of the Movement is critiqued for going against the focus on localized organizing. Some consider the shift from "nonviolence" to Black Power in 1966 as the organization's downfall. Members of the Trayvon Martin Generation who enter the BFS could learn valuable lessons for their own participation. The SNCC counter narratives presented here elucidate some similarities between the youth of #BLM and the youth of the CRM. The aim is to show that the Trayvon Martin Generation has not abandoned or rejected the ideologies and tactics of their elders but rather developed era-specific adaptations of them to address evolved methods of systemic racial oppression in the era of failed post raciality and increased social media.

The Trayvon Martin Generation has evolved sit-ins to die-ins and "Black brunch" protests. Both use small, dedicated groups of people in large public spaces intent on disrupting comfort and bringing awareness to existing racial oppression. Hashtag campaigns transition boycotts from the physical to the digital marketplace, where Black social media users leverage the social influence of Black buying power to decrease the profit of corporations operating in the interest of whiteness through their discriminatory treatment of Black consumers and employees. Organizing large-scale marches to encourage solidarity and provide international visibility is a tactic adopted directly from the CRM. In fact, while the Trayvon Martin Generation perceives themselves as more confrontational, their ability to have nonviolent standoffs with riot police and other types of law enforcement is made possible by the brutality suffered by the Emmett Till Generation during the aggressive confrontations of the CRM. Thus, nonviolence and "respectability" aside, the Trayvon Martin Generation owes a debt of gratitude to these elders.

To be clear, I offer that #BLM is a nonviolent, direct-action movement led by Black youth of the Trayvon Martin Generation primarily between 2014 and 2016. The shift away from grassroots organizing to political lobbying, which occurred during the 2016 election cycle, was the beginning of the end for the movement sparked by the vigilante killing of Trayvon Martin and which exploded after the police killing of Mike Brown.[46] By 2020, much of what we witnessed, though it may have looked similar on the surface to the protest activities of 2014, was much more celebritized, corporatized, and politicized. As of this writing in 2024, we are witnessing attempts to construct a master narrative of #BLM that mutes the efforts of grassroots, youth-led organizations by conflating property damages caused by nihilists, anarchists, and saboteurs with Black protesters. This master narrative also erases the voices of local communities by designating outsiders like DeRay Mckesson, Alicia Garza, and others as the movement's national spokespeople. Finally, it neutralizes the intensity dedicated to Black liberation by presenting the movement as "intersectional" and highlighting the involvement of whites and nonblack People of Color (POC). The script of #BLM has converted the movement into a brand to be monetized by showcasing involvement from celebrity entertainers and professional athletes, performances from politicians, and monetary investment from corporations as evidence of progress, all as part of what I term the Black Protest Industrial Complex (BPIC).[47]

Countering these myths will be the task of the Trayvon Martin Generation as the BFS moves into what I offer as the Post #BLM era. This era began with the January 6, 2021, attack on the United States Capitol by Donald Trump supporters refusing to accept his defeat in the 2020 presidential election. In this Post #BLM era, those participating in the freedom struggle will have to find alternatives to social media networks that law enforcement now use to surveil and criminalize protestors under suspicion of being "Black Identity Extremists," akin to the FBI wiretapping during the CRM and the Black Power Movement. They will have to reconcile the reality that scores of opportunists used #BLM to access funds to build personal brands and networks to achieve their professional aspirations without any commitment to Black liberation. Thus, understanding how master narratives of the CRM have caused unnecessary intergenerational conflict within the BFS and learning from the experiences of their "grandparents" is indeed necessary to prevent history from wholly repeating itself. Finally, SNCC counter narratives expand beyond what is provided here and contain the Emmett Till Generation's insight into leadership models, engagement with media and white outsiders, variability of tactics, and much more about the dynamics of Black youth organizing vital for us all, but offered specifically to the Trayvon Martin Generation:

In Struggle,
Sincerely,
Your Grandparents' Hands.

NOTES

1. Matt Pearce, "Ferguson October Rally Shows Divide over Civil Rights," *Detroit Free Press*, October 14, 2014, https://www.freep.com/story/news/nation/2014/10/13/ferguson-october-rally-shows-divide-civil-rights/17196139.
2. Throughout this chapter #BlackLivesMatter (#BLM) with the stylized hashtag will be used to refer to Black youth involved in grassroots organizing, large-scale street protests, and hashtag campaigns in response to the law enforcement and vigilante killing of unarmed Black people beginning with the Ferguson protests in 2014. It is intended to be viewed distinctly from the national "Black Lives Matter" organizations supported largely by political and corporate funding that have increasingly been scrutinized since 2020 as being opportunistic at best and fraudulent at worst. For more about collective consciousness, see Emile Durkheim, *The Division of Labour in Society* (New York: Free Press, 1893).
3. I use the term "aligned with the Civil Rights Movement" as a reference to Black elders, like the Rev. Al Sharpton and Oprah Winfrey, who were born in the movement era of the 1950s and 1960s but did not participate until later, if at all. Most of those who would become involved engaged in activities aligned with the nonviolence of Dr. King.
4. Geneva Sands and Jordan Fabian, "Young Voices from the 'Justice For All' March in D.C.," *Splinter News*, December 13, 2014, https://splinternews.com/young-voices-from-the-justice-for-all-march-in-d-c-1793844491.
5. *Selma* is a 2014 biopic that focuses on Martin Luther King Jr.'s involvement in the events leading up to Bloody Sunday. The film was released just four months after the movement that would later be known as #BlackLivesMatter began in Ferguson, Missouri, after the police killing of eighteen-year-old Michael Brown on August 9, 2014.
6. "Oprah Winfrey on the powerful biopic of Martin Luther King Jr." *Good Morning America*, December 17, 2014, https://www.goodmorningamerica.com/amp/news/video/oprah-winfrey-powerful-biopic-martin-luther-king-jr-27660556.
7. Jennifer Pereira, "The Lesson Oprah Winfrey Hopes Protestors Learn from 'Selma,'" *ABC News*, December 17, 2014, https://abcnews.go.com/Entertainment/lesson-oprah-winfrey-hopes-protesters-learn-selma/story?id=27641601.
8. "Oprah Winfrey's Comments about Recent Protests and Ferguson Spark Controversy," *People Magazine*, January 1, 2015, https://people.com/celebrity/oprah-on-recent-protests-and-ferguson.
9. "Oprah Winfrey's Comments."
10. Sandhya Somashekhar, "Protestors Slam Oprah over Comments That They Lack 'Leadership,'" *Washington Post*, January 2, 2015, https://www.washington

post.com/news/post-nation/wp/2015/01/02/protesters-slam-oprah-over-comments-that-they-lack-leadership.
11. Jana Winter and Sharon Weinberger, "The FBI's New US Terrorist Threat: 'Black Identity Extremists,'" *Foreignpolicy.com*, October 6, 2017, https://foreignpolicy.com/2017/10/06/the-fbi-has-identified-a-new-domestic-terrorist-threat-and-its-black-identity-extremists.
12. "J. Edgar Hoover Calls BPP Greatest Threat," Newspapers.com, *Chicago Tribune*, July 16, 1969, https://www.newspapers.com/article/chicago-tribune-j-edgar-hoover-cals-bpp/30004654.
13. *Toni Morrison: The Pieces I Am*, directed by Timothy Greenfield-Sanders (New York: Magnolia Pictures, 2019), DVD.
14. I use the term "whiteness" to represent the system of racial oppression that provides structural power and individual privilege for upholding the idea that whiteness is superior to other racialized categories. I distinguish it from "white supremacy," presenting whiteness as an indication of the normalized system, whereas white supremacy often evokes notions of extremism.
15. Ashley N. Woodson, "'There Ain't No White People Here': Master Narratives of the Civil Rights Movement in the Stories of Urban Youth," *Urban Education* 52, no. 3 (March 2017): 316–42, doi:10.1177/0042085915602543.
16. Julian Bond, *Julian Bond's Time to Teach: A History of the Southern Civil Rights Movement* (Boston: Beacon Press, 2021), xiv–xv.
17. Elizabeth Alexander, "The Trayvon Martin Generation: For Solo, Simon, Robel, Maurice, Cameron, and Sekou," *New Yorker*, June 15, 2020, https://www.newyorker.com/magazine/2020/06/22/the-trayvon-generation.
18. Rahiel Tesfamariam, "Why the Modern Civil Rights Movement Keeps Religious Leaders at Arm's Length," *Washington Post*, September 18, 2015, https://www.washingtonpost.com/opinions/how-black-activism-lost-its-religion/2015/09/18/2f56fc00-5d6b-11e5-8e9e-dce8a2a2a679_story.html.
19. The People's Minister JR, "Blackout Collective Obstructs BART trains on Black Friday in Protest of Police Killings," *San Francisco Bay View*, December 1, 2014, https://sfbayview.com/2014/12/blackout-collective-obstructs-bart-trains-on-black-friday-in-protest-of-police-killings.
20. Juan Perez Jr., Grace Wong, Kate Thayer, Lolly Bowean, and Jeff Coen, "Crowds Close Stores, March on Mag Mile to Protest Laquan McDonald Killing," *Chicago Tribune*, November 28, 2015, https://www.chicagotribune.com/news/breaking/ct-laquan-mcdonald-black-friday-protest-met-20151127-story.html.
21. Brandon Soderberg "Baltimore Protestors March through the Inner Harbor the First Day of Police Trial in Death of Freddie Gray," *Baltimore City Paper*, December 8, 2015, https://www.baltimoresun.com/citypaper/bcp-120915-mobs-protest-test-run-20151208-story.html.

22. Randy Furst, "Protestors Shut Down I-94 in St. Paul for Hours," *Star Tribune*, July 11, 2016, https://www.startribune.com/marchers-block-i-94-to-westbound-traffic/386158771.
23. I am not suggesting that the Trayvon Martin Generation is solely responsible for these large-scale demonstrations. I am recognizing that their participation is evidence that they could engage in disciplined, organized, intergenerational efforts.
24. Dorie Ann Ladner and Joyce Ladner, "Oral History Interview," Library of Congress, September 20, 2011, https://www.loc.gov/item/2015669153.
25. Cleveland Sellers, "Oral History Interview," Library of Congress, March 21, 2013, https://www.loc.gov/item/2015669180.
26. John Lewis, "Together, You Can Redeem the Soul of Our Nation," *New York Times*, July 30, 2020, https://www.nytimes.com/2020/07/30/opinion/john-lewis-op-ed.html.
27. Although Colvin was one of five plaintiffs in the first federal case challenging segregation in Alabama, she was pregnant and unmarried at the time of the case, and Civil Rights organizers believed that white media and prosecutors would successfully frame Colvin as criminal, potentially sabotaging their efforts.
28. Charles M. Payne, "Ella Baker and Models of Social Change," *Signs: Common Grounds and Crossroads. Race, Ethnicity and Class in Women's Lives* 14, no. 4, (1989): 885–99. SNCC is an acronym for the Student Nonviolent Coordinating Committee.
29. Payne, "Ella Baker." Here I focus on SNCC, but there were other organizations with members of the Emmett Till Generation, like the Congress of Racial Equality (CORE) and the NAACP Youth Councils.
30. NAACP is an acronym for the National Association for the Advancement of Colored People.
31. While the Trayvon Generation has used social media, the Emmett Till Generation has contributed their experiences to various oral history projects and various memoirs and autobiographies. The first I was introduced to was Anne Moody's *Coming of Age in Mississippi*, published in 1968.
32. Martin Luther King Jr., "A Creative Protest," in *The Papers of Martin Luther King Jr., Volume V: Threshold of a New Decade*, ed. Clayborne Carson, Tenisha Armstrong, Susan Carson, Adrienne Clay, and Kieran Taylor (Berkeley: University of California Press, 1992). Available online at https://kinginstitute.stanford.edu/king-papers/documents/creative-protest.
33. Avon Rollins Sr., "The March on Washington as Remembered by Avon Rollins Sr.," interview by D. C. Everest Oral History Project, August 28, 1963, available online at *Veterans of the Civil Rights Movement—March on Washington*, rev. June 14, 2008, https://www.crmvet.org/info/mowrolin.htm.
34. Allison Miller, "The Politics of the Past in the Black Freedom Struggle" (blog), *The Future of the African American Past*, Conference, May 19–21, 2016,

Washington, DC, https://futureafampast.si.edu/blog/politics-past-black-freedom-struggle.
35. Rollins, "The March on Washington."
36. Lauren Feeney, "Two Versions of John Lewis' Speech," *Bill Moyers*, July 24, 2014, https://billmoyers.com/content/two-versions-of-john-lewis-speech/#original.
37. Civil Rights Movement protestors are thought to be playing into respectability politics by being well dressed, but this ignores that their protest clothing was also their everyday wear. Black youth during Jim Crow tended toward more professional dress than current youth standards. However, for the Emmett Till Generation, their clothing was not considered an assertion of their political views.
38. Feeney, "Two Versions."
39. Clayborne Carson, *In Struggle: SNCC and the Black Awakening of the 1960s, with a New Introduction and Epilogue by the Author* (Cambridge: Harvard University Press, 1995).
40. Hasan Kwame Jeffries, *Bloody Lowndes: Civil Rights and Black Power in Alabama's Black Belt* (New York: New York University Press, 2009).
41. Akinyele Omowale Umoja, *We Will Shoot Back: Armed Resistance in the Mississippi Freedom Movement* (New York: New York University Press, 2013), 54.
42. These accounts are often shared through informal oral histories maintained by family members of those who participated in and witnessed these brave acts of resistance. Historically, they have not been widely shared for fear of retaliation by whites. However, over the last thirty years, these stories have begun being documented via collections in the Library of Congress and other outlets like Duke University's "Behind the Veil" Oral History Project.
43. Interview with Lyman Johnson by John Egerton, *Southern Oral History Program Collection*, July 12, 1990, https://docsouth.unc.edu/sohp/playback.html?base_file=A-0351.
44. Charles E. Cobb Jr., *This Nonviolent Stuff'll Get You Killed: How Guns Made the Civil Rights Movement Possible* (Durham, NC: Duke University Press, 2014), 3.
45. Carson, *In Struggle*.
46. Keeanga-Yamahtta Taylor, *From #BlackLivesMatter to Black Liberation* (Chicago: Haymarket Books, 2016).
47. Charity Clay, "S1 - Episode Three: The Aftermath," September 28, 2020, in *The CatalystCast*, podcast, MP3 audio, 23:39, https://podcasters.spotify.com/pod/show/urfavcharity/episodes/S1-Episode-Three---The-Aftermath-efe4lr/a-a2fej0s.

CHAPTER 2

Continuity and Change

The Spirituality of Liberation in the Black Lives Matter Movement

Christophe D. Ringer

In the National Museum of African American History and Culture on the Mall in Washington, DC, hangs a black shirt with the phrase "This Ain't Yo Mama's Civil Rights Movement" emblazoned across the front. Theologian and activist Rahiel Tesfamariam donated the shirt she wore when she was arrested on July 13, 2015, with sixty other faith leaders in an act of civil disobedience after the killing of Michael Brown in Ferguson, Missouri, the year before. Kareem Jackson, known as Tef Poe, musician, rapper, activist, and co-founder of the Hands Up United movement, had authored the phrase, but it was the photo of Tesfamariam wearing the shirt when she was arrested that went viral. Tesfamariam donated the shirt to the museum in order to document the emergence of a "non-violent but militant resistance."[1] More specifically, she argues that the image went viral because it articulates a rejection of social movements whose leadership is dominated by "well dressed, respectable clergymen" steeped in hierarchal leadership, respectability politics, and the principles of reconciliation and nonviolence, and that this message has resonated with young activists today. In addition, she notes that many activists keep religious leaders at a distance precisely because of churches that bar women from ordination, use scriptural references to marginalize the LGBTQ community, and value the lives and leadership of charismatic straight men more than other lives.[2] However, I argue this phrase, "This Ain't Yo Mama's Civil Rights Movement," conceals a far more complex reality than mere repudiation. More specifically, the Black Lives Matter Movement (BLMM) represents a moment of distancing as well as reclamation, a rupture and reproduction, simultaneously drawing and departing from previous movements in the Black Freedom Struggle.[3] This essay analyzes the religious dimensions of the BLMM. I argue that scholar and activist Vincent Harding's classic 1968 essay "The Religion of Black Power" contributes to the practice of critical memory.[4] Specifically, Harding's work provides an example of how we might discern the ways that the Movement for Black Lives is deeply engaged in questions and issues often associated with religious traditions.

I argue that a Black spirituality of liberation describes the personal and collective efforts dedicated toward building a world beyond white supremacy and anti-Blackness that satisfies the material and subjective needs of human life.[5] This spirituality of liberation wrestles with the spiritual, moral, and political ambiguities often associated with established religious traditions in the struggle for freedom. In many ways, Harding's life and work reflect this spirituality of liberation, which in turn represents the religious significance of Black Power and the Movement for Black Lives.

The Inspiration of Vincent Harding

Vincent Harding's spirituality of liberation draws from his experiences as a social activist, writer, educator, minister, and historian. He served for twenty-three years as a professor of religion and social transformation at the Iliff School of Theology, after having first served as the director of the King Center and as a founding member of the Institute for the Black World.[6] Harding was born in 1931 and raised by his mother in Harlem, New York. In his youth, he was introduced to the peace activism of Mohandas K. Gandhi through Victory Tabernacle Church, but it was his experience in the Army at Fort Dix in New Jersey from 1953 to 1955 that impressed upon him the "dehumanizing power of the military."[7] After leaving the military, he earned a PhD in History from the University of Chicago, where he became enamored with the legacy and writings of sixteenth-century Anabaptists. In particular, he was struck by their commitment to self-sacrificing love and their willingness to accept death rather than inflict suffering. Inspired by this legacy, Harding joined the Woodlawn Mennonite Church on the South Side of Chicago, where he met his wife Rosmarie and was eventually called to serve as its associate pastor in 1958. Harding and Rosmarie shared their life with the Movement.

In 1961, the couple relocated to Atlanta to start a Mennonite Voluntary Service unit that would serve as a residence and refuge for local Movement workers, social service volunteers, and interracial reconciliation. Over the next decade, Harding and his wife became thoroughly integrated in the world of civil rights activism and Mennonite life, and Harding's stature in the Civil Rights Movement in Atlanta grew as their friendships with Martin Luther and Coretta Scott King deepened.[8] Harding became a trusted ally and advisor to King, eventually penning his historic 1967 Riverside Speech that condemned the escalating war in Vietnam. However, Harding's unflinching commitment to the Movement would test the commitment of the Mennonite community to live up to its own legacy of self-sacrifice as it relates to racial justice.

Mennonite traditions rooted in gradualism and quietism made them reluctant to participate in nonviolent direct action, and this profoundly influenced Harding's activism and scholarship. His seminal "The Religion of Black Power" (1968) is the culmination of a series of probing essays: "What Answer to Black Power" (1966), "Where Have All the Lovers Gone?" (1966), and "Black Power and the American Christ" (1967).[9] These essays show how Harding's relationship with the Black Power Movement evolved and matured in two primary respects. First, as a historian, he interprets the emerging movement as part of the long "harrowing and terrifying beauty" of the Black experience in America that includes the ebbs and flows of movements for justice.[10] Second, they reveal his evolution as a person of faith. The rise of the Black Power Movement raised existential questions for Harding regarding his relationship with the Mennonite tradition. In "What Answer to Black Power?" the urgent challenges posed to him by his own colleagues in the Movement are worth quoting at length:

> How can you stay with them when they have participated by their silence and complacency in the exploitation of your people? Yes, your people, Vincent. You go to the Mennonites, and they say, "brothers," and they say, "we're all one in Christ," but they still say, "your people," Vincent because they know that you are not really brothers. They still say, "your people, how do your people feel, Brother Harding? What do your people think, Brother Harding?" Do they really consider you "brother" if they are still talking about "your people"? You need to break Vincent. You need to break with them because they are not for real.[11]

Eventually, Harding would answer these questions by leaving the Mennonite world. The world of social activism became both an expression of his spirituality and the focus of his scholarship. Harding's essays and subsequent scholarship during this pivotal period provide a unique perspective on the emergence of Black Power and connect it to broader historical movements for social justice. As a scholar activist, Harding participated in social movements with a critical eye that refused romantic nostalgia for the past in order to keep alive possibilities in the present for a different future.[12] It is for this reason that Harding provides an interesting lens for thinking about the ruptures and retrievals in our contemporary understanding of the BLMM.

In the essay "The Religion of Black Power," Harding examines the religious aspects and implications of Black Power. He defined Black Power as a necessary stage in the development of the Black struggle for freedom, emphasizing Black self-definition and a radical critique of American society.[13] First, he engages Black Power's call for creating a new humanity through self-love that both cultivates a new sense of community and commands social respect.[14] This vision of a new Black humanity encourages African Americans to identify with the oppressed of the world rather than solely with America, bringing "Black Power into the orbit of a universality more authentic than the largely parochial sentiments of a 'Judeo-Christian' Western commitment."[15] Harding discerns the presence of messianism, prophetic leadership, and historical judgment within Black Power, tracing it through movements associated with Marcus Garvey and Malcolm X. A salient point for Harding is that Black Power expresses a recurring religious quality of Black radicalism—the tension between redemption and atonement or a day of destruction and judgment.[16] This includes a reflection on what possibilities may emerge for the institutionalization of these religious intuitions present in Black Power.[17] Harding also issues a challenge to those familiar with "comforting religious symbols" to attend to the issues of "anthropology, incarnation, the nature of the universe and of God . . . hope and faith, questions of eschatology and the nature of the kingdom, problems of love and its functions."[18] Harding closes the essay by recognizing the religious contributions of Black Power in acknowledging the depth of evil in America and in placing their ultimate concern in something beyond that reality.

To appreciate the historical intervention of "The Religion of Black Power," it is important to contrast it with another seminal essay, "Black Power: A Statement from the National Committee of Negro Churchmen (NCNC)." This essay, a statement of sorts, was published simultaneously in the *New York Times* and *Los Angeles Times* on July 31, 1966. Historian Gayraud Wilmore argues that the NCNC, an ad hoc group of clergymen, were concerned about the "hysterical reaction of some white clergymen to Black Power, the way many whites were distorting the slogan and many blacks thoughtlessly bandying it about."[19] The statement is a philosophical and theological treatment of Black Power aimed at both ecclesiastical and political leaders who felt betrayed, horrified, or confused by its emergence. More specifically, it argues that political and economic power is the prerequisite to genuine interracial fellowship. And, while deploring the "overt violence" of riots, the statement critiques the silent and covert types of violence that tie "a white noose of suburbia around the necks and which pin the backs of the masses of Negroes against the steaming ghetto walls" with inequitable jobs, housing, and education.[20] The eruptions in the cities were God's judgment upon the nation for its failure to establish the well-being of its people, they argue. Harding, however, rightly discerns that the NCNC's statement was not merely an affirmation of "Black Power"; it was also a particular rendering of Black Power that curtailed the more radical aspects of the Movement to focus squarely on the inclusion of Black people in all areas of American life.[21] Harding's "The Religion of Black Power" does not argue for the compatibility of Black Power with the Christian tradition or American ideals; rather, through the language of the Christian tradition, Harding perceives the possibility of Black Power as a religion itself through which Black people might express their spirituality in the face of anti-Blackness.[22] One example of a spirituality of liberation's enduring presence, both in previous iterations of the freedom struggle and in the BLMM, is the necessity and ambiguity of love.

The Politics of Love in the Struggle for Liberation

Martin Luther King Jr.'s early philosophy of nonviolence reveals the conceptual and practical challenges around love in the Freedom Struggle. Nonviolence for King was the ability of non-retaliation and unearned suffering to affect white people's conscience.[23] This is rooted in the theological and philosophical convictions that all persons are made in the image of God, objective moral laws exist, and the universe is imbued with value.[24] The practical consequence is the belief that, regardless of psychological and cultural conditioning, all persons—and white people, in particular—possess a conscience that can be awakened. Those most committed to the practice of nonviolence are those whose actions might best awaken that conscience. Although nonviolence for King was rooted in resistance to oppression and not simply in passive suffering, activists such as Stokely Carmichael worried about tying Black self-determination to this awakening of white conscience.[25] The strategic challenges inherent in King's philosophy, which rely on a strong relationship between Black nonviolent resistance and the stimulation of white conscience, became clear in the face of white intransigence. Ultimately, King does not offer a strategic, theological, or philosophical alternative to the Black Power appraisal that America needed judgment rather than redemption.[26] Rather, King reaffirms that "Our most fruitful course is to stand firm, move forward nonviolently, accept disappointments and cling to hope. Our determined refusal not to be stopped will eventually open the door to fulfillment."[27] This hope is also present in the work of his contemporary activist Ruby Sales. For Sales, religion prepares the foundation for standing against the "winds of segregation, the winds of society that by its very nature conspired to render us very, very small."[28] Moreover, religion serves as an equalizer by transforming oppressed people into full human beings as well as recognizing the oppressors as humans.[29] This spirituality, informed by Black Christian communities, was not accepted by all expressions of the Freedom Struggle.

The Black Power Movement posed challenging questions to more established religious traditions regarding the role of love in the pursuit of freedom, and to those Christian traditions that counsel believers to love their enemies, in particular. Harding recounts a 1966 forum on Black Power where someone remarked, "Martin King was trying to get us to love white folks before we learned to love ourselves, and that ain't no good."[30] Harding rightly argues that self-esteem in many religious traditions is a "prerequisite to the establishment of community" and is the "bedrock of love."[31] More importantly, he recognizes that the call to self-love acknowledges the psychological challenges of establishing self-respect in a society constituted by anti-Blackness. However, this call to self-love is not without its ambiguities. Harding did question whether some Black Power advocates had sufficiently examined their expectations that self-love would produce mutual respect with whites.[32] Harding quotes writer and activist John Oliver Killens, who argues that Black love is "so powerful that it will settle for nothing short of love in return. Therefore, it does not advocate unrequited love, which is sick under any guise or circumstance. Most black folk have no need to love those who would spit on them or practice genocide against them.... Profound love can only exist between equals."[33] To this, Harding registers a key concern that while Black love may powerfully anchor self-esteem, it cannot demand a predetermined outcome. Specifically, it cannot guarantee reciprocity from white people or ensure that Black folk will only devote their love solely toward their own communities. The Black Power Movement thus challenged the strategic value of love in the context of King's philosophy of nonviolence.[34] The dilemmas around the spiritual, moral, and strategic value of love remain present for today's activists in the BLMM.

The most visible similarity and difference between earlier freedom struggles and the BLMM is the reconfigured theme of self-love with all of its complexities. In 2013, Alicia Garza penned a "Love Letter to Black Folks" on Facebook, stating emphatically, "We don't deserve to be killed with impunity. We need to love ourselves and fight for a world where Black lives matter. Black people I love you. I love us. We matter. Our lives matter."[35] Patrisse Cullors created the social media hashtag #BlackLivesMatter, and Opal Tometi created the website and social media platforms that circulated the message far and wide. Two of these activists identify as queer. Their queer identity disrupts the *iconography/hagiography/mythology* of a heterosexual cisgendered Black man as the default image of leadership within Black social movements (even when the community knew Black women did the lion's share of the work). This open centering of their queerness similarly challenges the religious and cultural politics within the African American community in general and social justice movements in particular. Historian Jeffrey Ogbar notes that the Black Power Movement, by contrast, "lionized black men as macho leaders, fighters and defenders of black people," reflecting the times and the historical legacies up to that point.[36] Moreover, these BLMM activists also reclaim a legacy of women's labor within freedom struggles that is too often rendered invisible by historical accounts focusing primarily on men (the "Great Man Theory" of history). As activist scholar Barbara Ransby argues, the BLMM is deeply rooted in Black feminist politics.[37]

The influence of Black feminism is felt within the BLMM through the recognition of how racism and violence affect LGBTQIA communities. What the Combahee River Collective defines in the 1970s as "interlocking" systems of oppression, such as racism, sexism, heterosexism, and exploitation, similarly informs the political organizing of BLMM.[38] More specifically, Black feminism articulates why the oppression of Black women cannot be reduced to a single category. Rather, multiple forms of oppression simultaneously mark Black women's experience. In addition, Ransby notes that the BLMM introduces recent articulations of this theme, through ideas such as intersectionality, to a new generation of activists via the political struggle itself rather than solely through textbooks.[39] The religious significance of this self-affirmation of Black life by Black and queer-identified women enlarges the range of humanity we consider sacred and thus who is worthy of self-love.

The BLMM evidences a spirituality of liberation that continues to place an emphasis on love. In a 2016 episode of the radio program *On Being*, host Krista Tippett engages in a conversation with Patrisse Cullors and Dr. Robert Ross (a physician and psychiatrist), in which Tippett asks Cullors why rage and not love is at the forefront of the movement.[40] Cullors is quick to point out that the phrase "Black lives matter" originated as a love letter to Black people. She poignantly argues that blocking traffic on freeways, being chained together in protest, and other acts of resistance are acts of love for the Black community and the nation. In addition, Cullors notes the other spiritual practices that accompany protests, such as prayer, acts of remembrance, the use of altars, and Indigenous practices such as burning sage. In their conversation, Tippett recalls hearing Ruby Sales, speaking in 2016 at the American Academy of Religion, reflect upon the role of religion in the Black Freedom Struggle:

> None of us considered ourselves to be religious in the way our parents or grandparents were and there was a lot of religion, but we were rejecting so much of what we'd grown up with. We didn't think that defined us. And

we only realized later that even though that was true, we were steeped in that tradition, in the hope, in the sense of love, in the songs, in the community. We had our armor on. . . . And then we became involved in policy, and we sent our children out into the empire without their armor on.[41]

Sales describes a moment of similarity and difference in the Civil Rights Movement, in which she had rejected aspects of a religious tradition while carrying forth a deep commitment to hope, love, culture, and community. Hearing Sales's words, Cullors responds, "Many of us in the Black Lives Matter movement have either been pushed out of the church because many of us are queer and out . . . the church has become very patriarchal for us as women, and so that's not necessarily where we have found our solace. And I think we have had to contend with that during this movement."[42] Cullors is forthright about the ambiguities relating to organized religion in general, and to Black churches in particular. Churches with long histories of involvement with social justice have been ambivalent about embracing those who unapologetically identify as queer. Although this is an important point of difference, there is an important point of retrieval, too: Sales and Cullors evidence the presence of what I have termed a Black Spirituality of Liberation, which continues to creatively engage and expand on themes such as love, justice, hope, community, and culture. They both have rejected aspects they associate with established religious traditions while carrying forward those aspects they find liberating.

There is another important point of continuity between Cullors and Sales in their respective focus on becoming fully human. Recall Sales's emphasis on religion's transforming the oppressed into full human beings. Cullors, in a similar fashion, states:

> Black Lives Matter is a rehumanizing project. We've lived in a place that has literally allowed for us to believe and center only Black death. We've forgotten how to imagine Black life. Literally whole human beings have been rendered to die prematurely, rendered to be sick, and we've allowed for that. Our imagination has only allowed for us to understand Black people as a dying people. We have to change that. That's our collective imagination. Someone imagined handcuffs; someone imagined guns;

someone imagined a jail cell. Well, how do we imagine something different that actually centers Black people, that sees them in the future? Let's imagine something different.[43]

Beyond the historical differences in the experiences of Cullors and Sales is a spirituality of liberation that reclaims and transforms the humanity of Black people in the face of enduring anti-Blackness. BLMM stands in a long tradition of resisting racism, inscribing collective memory, cultivating hope, and nurturing self-love.

Patrisse Cullors sees the concept of "healing justice," as first articulated by Cara Page, as critical to the rehumanizing project of #BlackLivesMatter. Page, a Black queer feminist organizer, curator, and cultural memory worker, developed the concept in direct response to an increase in fascist, anti-Black racism in the US South in the early 2000s. Page and others witnessed severe burnout among organizers, resulting in their having to leave social movement work, which, in turn, raised serious questions about how to heal their relationship with land, work, body, and spirit while in the context of white supremacy. Through conversations with southern-based spiritual and healing practitioners as well as with organizers, "healing justice" emerged to address the connections between collective wellness, economic justice, environmental justice, and disability justice. As a cultural worker, Page was also interested in reclaiming lineages of healing practices within Black culture that did not separate the work of healing from liberation.[44] This reclaiming of a history of healing also addresses they ways collective trauma can result in collective dissociation, in which Black people lose knowledge of traditions created for survival and resilience.

This retrieval is a key reason why, for Cullors, the work is not only about policy. She states, "I think some people get so confused by us. They're like, 'Where's the policy?' I'm like, 'You can't policy your racism away.' We no longer have Jim Crow laws, but we still have Jim Crow hate."[45] There is a profound commonality between Cullors' remarks and those of past freedom struggles that refuse to separate social transformation and self-transformation. Whether it is the self-purification required for the practice of nonviolent direct action or the transformation of consciousness for Black Power, the personal and the social are deeply intertwined.[46] The BLMM expresses this by focusing on how oppression lives in the body and psyche; this emphasis reclaims self-care from its popular contemporary focus on individual wellness by embracing its origins as a political act.[47]

Cullors articulates a profound public faith that is prophetic, actively creating community through rituals that include prayer and various spiritual practices through which people can find meaning. American popular culture is often accused of sampling various religious practices as merely another mode of consumption.[48] However, Cullors' account of the BLMM evidences a plurality of religious practices that serve to provide spiritual sustenance in the work of social justice. Such practices may include acupuncture, reiki, herbal remedies, art therapy, and divination. Raised as a Jehovah's Witness, Cullors found that the all-male leadership structure did not allow her to feel peace, so she began to explore other forms of spiritual practice and traditions, eventually settling on Ifa, which she describes as her spiritual home. However, she also faced discrimination in Ifa, as her first babalawo, an initiating priest, refused to initiate her because of her sexuality. Although Ifa is her spiritual home, she notes, "I've done ten-day Vipassana retreats. I've done all types of spiritual quests. I have a deep practice of generative somatics. I have a mediation practice. I go to therapy."[49] For Cullors, a signature aspect of such practices is that they restore and reclaim the health and well-being of activists from interpersonal, social, and state trauma and violence. This focus on restoration and reclaiming within community distinguishes the spiritual pluralism of BLMM from the individualism of American religious consumption.

The Politics of Violence in the Struggle for Liberation

There is a long history of using urban unrest to discredit the Black Freedom Struggle. Black activists have always had to remove the veil of deception that obscures their critiques of the status quo. The rebellions in Watts (1965), Miami (1980), Los Angeles (1992), Ferguson

(2015), and Minneapolis (2020) all responded to police violence, and all were widely condemned in the popular media as the disparities Black people experience in education, housing, health, unemployment, incarceration, and myriad other racial injustices have been ignored or tolerated.

In 1967, Martin Luther King Jr. argued that "riots are socially destructive and self-defeating" but that he needed to vigorously condemn the social conditions that sparked the unrest in the first place. With his trademark eloquence, he responded to critiques of the urban uprisings that had transpired, noting that as long as "America postpones justice, we stand in the position of having these recurrences of violence."[50] Understanding systemic racism as the root of the uprisings, King remained resolute that social justice was the best means of preventing social unrest even as he decried the use of violence. The question of violence represents another moment of continuity and change as the BLMM finds itself at the crossroads of having to respond to social uprisings labeled as violent and the use of violence as a political tactic.

During the summer of 2020, the murder of George Floyd sparked widespread social turmoil, exacerbated by the global pandemic whose lockdown orders increased the amount of time people spent viewing news on television and social media. This allowed more people to witness these ritual crimes against Black people. Less than 10 percent of the 2,400 demonstrations associated with the BLMM in the wake of George Floyd's killing featured violence or property destruction of any kind; however, the media's framing of the protests has shaped their image in the popular imagination so that 42 percent of Americans believe protesters associated with the BLMM are inherently violent.[51] In the June 2020 issue of the *New Yorker*, Opal Tometi responds to these myths to reiterate the BLMM's focus on the systemic nature of anti-Blackness, state-sanctioned violence, and killing of Black people, rather than on individual instances of moral transgression. She argues:

> I just don't equate the loss of life and the loss of property. I can't even hold those two in the same regard, and I think for far too long we have seen that happen. We have had these conversations where we are conflating

very different realities and operating from different value systems.... We are really focused on how to get our demands out and stay focused on the main thing, which is people, and we want to value our love of people over property.[52]

Likewise, after the "Unite the Right" rally in Charlottesville on August 12, 2017, Alicia Garza argued that the rhetoric of violence and nonviolence often "obscures the relationships of power."[53] The myths act like smoke and mirrors to detract from the BLMM's critique of racial capitalism that values property more than people. The BLMM, like King, uses non-violence as a strategic and moral imperative. However, they do not explicitly condemn or condone the use of violence during unrest, effectively delegitimizing the concern as a barrier to moving toward genuine solutions. However, this creates an interesting contrast with the Black Power rhetoric from half a century ago.

In October 2016, Elaine Brown, former Chairwoman of the Black Panther Party (BPP), caused a stir when asked her thoughts about the BLMM in *Ebony* magazine. In the interview, she states that she is not sure what Black Lives Matter does and sees no comparison with the BPP: "We [BPP] advocated community self-defense organizations to be formed, so that we would not be assaulted by the police, so that we would bear arms and assume our human rights.... [Black Lives Matter] to me is a plantation mentality. It smacks of 'master, if you would just treat me right.' And it has nothing to do with self-determination, empowerment and a sense of justice, or anything else."[54] I argue that Brown's viewpoint is a consequence of the BLMM's attempt to hold a nuanced position. More specifically, it is a position that reclaims nonviolent direct action as the primary strategy of social change while not advocating for armed overthrow of the state yet still recognizes a long tradition of armed community self-defense against white vigilante and police violence, much like the Deacons for Defense.[55]

The Politics of Respectability and Charisma

The question of self-love and self-esteem that arises from living in an anti-Black society occasions another concern: self-fashioning and self-representation in the "politics of respectability." Respectability politics first received its major academic articulation by Evelyn Brooks Higginbotham in her classic *Righteous Discontent: The Women's Movement in the Black Baptist Church, 1890–1920*, published in 1994. The terms have traveled beyond the academy, and within public discourse they have come to signify one aspect of the cultural and political tensions within our current freedom struggles.[56] Although space does not allow for a full treatment of Higginbotham's rich explanation, I want to highlight key themes relevant for the analysis here. She situates her study of the politics of respectability in the maturing of the women's movement known as the Women's Convention, an auxiliary organization within the National Baptist Convention in the early twentieth century, when Black women increasingly expressed and crafted their public voices across a range of issues such as migration, urbanization, employment, consumer culture, the suffragist movement, and world war.[57] However, Black women's voices emerged in a society whose anti-Blackness received legitimation from science in the form of social Darwinism during the Jim Crow era.[58] Higginbotham argues persuasively that at that time, "Black manhood was represented as male sexuality run rampant," whereas, "Black womanhood and white womanhood were represented with diametrically opposed sexualities" with images such as the immoral Black female teacher and mother degrading Black families receiving legitimation from historians and sociologists.[59] The politics of respectability in the Progressive Era represented a counter-discourse designed to challenge and refute mainstream racist bias used to justify Jim Crow.

At the heart of the politics of respectability of the Women's Convention was the process of "self-construction and self-presentation," undertaken so that poor and working-class Black women could establish "self-esteem and self-determination" independent of the social markers of race and income. More specifically, Higginbotham persuasively argues that this program of "manners and morals" represented a self-conscious effort to refute the rationalizations that were used to justify their oppression, even including an interpretive reversal that positioned themselves as morally superior to whites.⁶⁰ However, Higginbotham notes this frequently occasioned biting criticism of other Black folks who did not conform to these women's vision of how the race should comport themselves in order to be worthy of respect. Such critiques were leveled through a wide array of public strategies such as leaflets, newspaper articles, and personal visits that discouraged "gum chewing, loud talking, gaudy colors, the nickelodeon, jazz, littered yards, and a host of other perceived improprieties."⁶¹ Imbued with evangelical fervor, the gospel of the Women's Convention tied the collective fate of Black people to the ability of individuals to regulate their behavior in accordance to the values of the dominant culture—to *prove* the legitimacy of the race as equals. Higginbotham notes that one of the unfortunate moral consequences of this project was that the "focus on individual behavior served inevitably to blame blacks for their victimization and, worse yet, to place an inordinate amount of blame on black women."⁶² It is precisely this ambiguity that reverberates today. The politics of respectability ultimately lodges itself between proving false the rationalizations for oppression and exclusion—by African Americans fashioning themselves to fit dominant cultural norms—while not expressly critiquing the dominant racist culture for the systemic biases in the first place.

The BLMM challenges the influence of respectability politics within the cultural politics of the Black Public Sphere. However, the meaning of respectability politics has shifted after one hundred years and the end of the Jim Crow era. In an insightful 2014 essay, "The Rise of Respectability Politics," political scientist Fredrick C. Harris argues that now respectability politics among Black elected officials primarily works to accommodate neoliberalism by recommending self-care and self-correction as strategies to lift the conditions of the Black poor by preparing them to compete in a market economy." Moreover, he argues that the idea of "racial uplift" in contemporary respectability politics sees individual deviance or non-conformity to dominant cultural norms as an explanation for individuals—and not the entire race—being left behind instead of advancing in American life.⁶³ Rather than underscoring the linked fate of all Black people, contemporary respectability politics purports to explain the fates of *some*. The BLMM critiques this shift by highlighting that systemic racism affects even those Black people deemed "respectable." More importantly, the BLMM challenges the persistent character assassination and moral judgment used to justify police killings, such as the media's posthumous focus on Freddie Gray's possible drug use, rumors of Michael Brown's stealing cigarettes, Eric Garner's selling loose cigarettes, Renisha McBride's possible intoxication, and Trayvon Martin's hoodie.[64] Such politics, the BLMM recognizes, limit a more transformational vision of social justice.[65]

Organizer and co-founder of #BlackLivesMatter, Alicia Garza, provides a poignant account of this sensibility in *The Purpose of Power: How We Come Together When We Fall Apart*, her account of her experience as an organizer and the emergence of #BlackLivesMatter. In the wake of Michael Brown's murder by Darren Wilson, Garza traveled to Ferguson, Missouri, at the request of a colleague to support two local grassroots organizations, Organization for Black Struggle (OBS) and Missourians Organizing for Reform and Empowerment (MORE). In addition, a Black Lives Matter Freedom Ride, modeled after the Freedom Rides in the 1960s, and a Weekend Resistance effectively leveraged support from Black people across the country to sustain local organizing efforts. Garza recognized that resistance in Ferguson focused on predatory policing *and* the rejection of traditional religiously influenced forms of Black leadership as exemplified by Rev. Dr. Martin Luther King Jr., Rev. Jesse Jackson, and Rev. Al Sharpton.[66] This rejection was exemplified in the tension between local activists and protesters and Rev. Jackson and Rev. Sharpton.

Alicia Garza attributes the public rejection of Rev. Jackson's leadership to an insensitive and inopportune appeal for donations to a local church when he visited, which was met with boos from the crowd. Although Brown's family welcomed Rev. Sharpton, many activists criticized his appeal for calm, his emphasis on voting, and his denouncing only the "bad apples" in the Ferguson Police Department rather than systemic predatory policing.[67] Garza interprets this as a rejection of respectability politics as articulated by Higginbotham. Garza is worth quoting at length:

Higginbotham would argue that the politics of respectability gives you the moral high ground, a notion that mistakenly assumes that the dehumanizing structures of racism have any moral nature to which to appeal.... In rejecting Jackson and Sharpton's approach and Higginbotham's respectability politics, the Ferguson rebellion marked a major shift, a moment when Black protesters stopped giving a fuck about what white people or "respectable" Black people thought about their uprising. This turning point did not hurt the growing movement, as figures like Higginbotham would claim—if anything it helped open up new political space through which we could explore the pervasive nature of anti-Blackness and internalized white supremacy among Black communities. The Ferguson rebellion helped create a new common sense among Black people.... Had Black Lives Matter or the Ferguson rebellion or the subsequent Baltimore uprising heeded Higginbotham's advice about respectability, had folk listed to Al Sharpton asking them to go home and instead turn out to the polls or not to tear up their own community, there would have been no reckoning, no calling to account—we would have simply continued in the same pattern as always.[68]

Garza mistakenly interprets Higginbotham as evaluating and recommending respectability politics as an effective strategy (Higginbotham herself has noted some of the unfortunate consequences that Garza has named). However, Garza's reflections reveal how the BLMM in Ferguson challenges our current iteration of respectability politics that tolerate any justification for police killings of Black people. The BLMM also challenges a hierarchy of valuing Black lives based upon their conformity to socially dominant cultural norms. Together, these cultivate a piety and politics that refocus concerns on the anti-Black violence of America's systems beyond the individual culpability of victims or "bad apples" within police departments. The BLMM's challenge to respectability politics represents a change in our understanding of the value of linked fate in the spirituality of liberation.

Intergenerational collaboration and conflict are expected in social movements. The challenge posed to respectability politics by the BLMM represents a retrieval and rupture in the concept of linked fate.

Political scientist Michael C. Dawson articulates that linked fate predicts the ways African Americans perceive their own individual self-interest and life chances as intertwined with the interests of other members of their racial group.[69] A recent empirical study by political scientists shows that respectability politics leads African Americans who place a high value on linked fate to withdraw solidarity from those who experience multiple forms of marginalization.[70] In particular, this study shows that African Americans who see heterosexual two-parent households as normative and accept racial profiling as a consequence of maintaining social order are 20 percent more willing to marginalize Black LGBTQ+ people.[71] As such, the BLMM has identified a critical barrier to retrieving a deep sense of linked fate among Black folk, creating a rupture in the current iteration of respectability politics. This leverages Vincent Harding's insight about the religion of Black Power as far more attuned to a genuinely universal morality. In the religion of Black Lives, that universal sense is reconfigured within the understanding of Blackness itself to counter the devaluing of those experiencing multiple forms of marginalization.

Another enduring question in the spirituality of the Black Freedom Struggle is the relationship of leadership to charisma. The spirituality of liberation in the BLMM represents a significant shift beyond the models of leadership that depend on a single person. More specifically, there is a critique of clergy-centered male leadership that fails to recognize the full contributions and talents of women while also preferring top-down decision-making rather than organizing power through democratic grassroots processes.[72] Organizer Charlene Carruthers, Founding National Director of Black Youth Project 100, argues that the problem with relying on charismatic leadership in movement building is twofold: first, if a leader becomes inactive (or becomes a martyr), the movement work may not continue. Moreover, organizing efforts around personalities carries the risk that the movement will become sidetracked from meeting the concrete needs of the people. Second, Carruthers suggests, charismatic leadership can provide an inaccurate picture of the nature of social movements. She argues: "King was an exceptional leader, but still it took countless leaders and countless people on the ground to create what we reflect back on as one of the greatest social movements ever."[73] I argue that BLMM seeks to model an alternative version of charisma and leadership that avoids these pitfalls.

Charisma as it relates to social and political movements has often been interpreted as offering something transrational or sacred to a secular world oriented around a bureaucracy that legitimates political authority, and those recognized as wielding such authority are normatively men, even as examples of women's charismatic authority abound.[74] Conversely, the BLMM introduces a new formation of charismatic leadership centered on women. In addition, the BLMM's challenge to respectability politics opens the door for new iterations of charisma to emerge; specifically, the BLMM enlarges the range of Black life considered sacred, thus creating more diverse possibilities for legitimating political authority. There is also the undeniable way in which figures such as Alicia Garza, Opel Tometi, and Patrisse Cullors are engaging new movement constituencies by reaching across a number of new media platforms. In doing so, they claim a form of charismatic authority that is not constitutively male, clerical, or dependent upon the "individual hero" narrative. Nevertheless, there are some similarities between BLMM leadership and other celebrated leaders in the Black Freedom Struggle. The concept of the charismatic scenario articulated by literary scholar Erica R. Edwards is helpful here: she defines the charismatic scenario as a cosmology or mythology that is simultaneously a performative technology for Black mass mobilization that shapes desires for political leadership.[75] The story of how the hashtag #BlackLivesMatter came to be a love letter to Black people operates as an origin story: in it, the activist or organizer is one moved to love by the sufferings of their people. And the charismatic scenario is the sight of a person—or in the case of BLMM, persons—wrestling meaning as well as a social movement from death. It is a rewriting of the charismatic scenario beyond the lone heterosexual man with clerical authority: leaders in the Black Freedom Struggle are no longer ordained, but they are no less sacred.

The Spirituality of Liberation in the Black Lives Matter Movement

There is no doubt that the BLMM represents a new political formation in American life. It is also the case, as I have argued here, that the BLMM evidences a spirituality that migrates across social movements and established religious traditions. Moreover, this spirituality takes as its starting point past Black freedom struggles. The BLMM has continued the practice of affirming the sacredness of Black life in the midst of its devaluation, while challenging the gender politics that have left LGBTQ+ populations on the margins of the sacred within many established religious traditions. Through the development of a new social movement, members of the BLMM are practicing a spirituality that situates them beyond both armed self-defense and non-violent direct action. Rather, theirs is a healing justice that embraces a radical love of Black people while eschewing narratives of sacrifice for self-care and rewriting the ways charisma can expand our definitions of leadership. The religion of the BLMM is not one of traditional revolution or redemption but of a possible rebirth of the nation through the power of social movements. Vincent Harding would be pleased to know that a vibrant Black Spirituality of Liberation continues to evolve to meet the demands of our time.

NOTES

1. Peggy McGlone, "'This Ain't Yo Mama's Civil Rights Movement' T-shirt from Ferguson Donated to Smithsonian Museum," *Washington Post*, March 1, 2016, https://www.washingtonpost.com/news/arts-and-entertainment/wp/2016/03/01/this-aint-yo-mamas-civil-rights-movement-t-shirt-from-ferguson-donated-to-smithsonian.
2. Rahiel Tesfamariam, "Why the Modern Civil Rights Movement Keeps Religious Leaders at Arm's Length," *Washington Post*, September 2015, https://www.washingtonpost.com/opinions/how-black-activism-lost-its-religion/2015/09/18/2f56fc00-5d6b-11e5-8e9e-dce8a2a2a679_story.html.
3. I use BLMM to refer to two distinct but related movements: 1) the Black Lives Matter Global Network started by Alicia Garza, Opal Tometi, and

Patrisse Cullors; and 2) the Movement for Black Lives, a coalition of over fifty Black organizations (https://m4bl.org).

4. Vincent Harding, "The Religion of Black Power," in *The Religious Situation*, ed. Donald R. Cutler (Boston: Beacon Press, 1968), 3–38. In "Critical Memory and the Black Public Sphere," Houston Baker argues that within modernity, critical memory is co-present with nostalgia. The latter is often the function of Black conservative interpretations of Black life that marginalize the role of the Black masses while centering the roles of middle-class Blacks and whites. Critical memory, however, recovers the complexities of the suppressed past and draws them into the present. See *The Black Public Sphere Collective* (Chicago: University of Chicago Press, 1995), 5.

5. I use this definition to capture: 1) Harding's emphasis on liberating spirituality and the role of the Black Freedom Struggle in human transformation; 2) to discern issues of religious meaning and significance beyond formal religious institutions as well as within social movements; and 3) to describe matters of ultimate concern as well as matters considered sacred without assuming belief in God or deities. See Dwight Hopkins, *Black Theology, USA and Africa: Politics, Culture and Liberation* (Eugene: Wipf and Stock Press, 1989), 81–83 for Harding's use of the phrase "liberating spirituality."

6. "Harding, Vincent Gordon," Stanford University, The Martin Luther King, Jr. Research and Education Institute. https://kinginstitute.stanford.edu/encyclopedia/harding-vincent-gordon.

7. Tobin Miller Shearer, *Daily Demonstrators: The Civil Rights Movement in Mennonite Homes and Sanctuaries* (Baltimore: John Hopkins Press, 2010), 102.

8. Shearer, 106.

9. See Vincent Harding, "Where Have All the Lovers Gone?," *Mennonite Life* 23, no. 1; "Black Power and the American Christ," *Christian Century*, January 4, 1967, 10; "What Answer to Black Power?," *Gospel Herald*, December 26, 1966; and "The Religion of Black Power."

10. Vincent Harding, *There is a River: The Black Struggle for Freedom in America* (New York: Harcourt Brace, 1981), xii.

11. Vincent Harding, "What Answer to Black Power?," 1115.

12. Harding's involvement in the Movement included being arrested during the Albany Movement as well as other campaigns throughout the South. See "Harding, Vincent Gordon," Stanford University, The Martin Luther King Jr. Research and Education Institute, https://kinginstitute.stanford.edu/encyclopedia/harding-vincent-gordon.

13. Vincent Harding, "Out of the Cauldron of Struggle: Black Religion and the Search for a New America," *Soundings: An Interdisciplinary Journal* 61, no. 3 (Fall 1978): 349. Although Harding does not offer a precise conceptual definition of the Black Power Movement, his interpretation of the movement as an evolution of the Black Freedom Struggle is similar to Peniel E.

Joseph's critique of narratives that see BPM as hastening the decline of the Civil Rights Movement. See Peniel E. Joseph, ed., *The Black Power Movement: Rethinking the Civil Rights-Black Power Era* (New York: Routledge, 2006), 3.

14. Vincent Harding, "The Religion of Black Power," in *Black Theology: A Documentary History Volume One: 1966–1979*, ed. James H. Cone and Gayraud Wilmore (Maryknoll: Orbis Books, 2003), 40.
15. Harding, "Religion," 46.
16. Harding, "Religion," 54.
17. Harding, "Religion," 58. It is also important to note that Harding's essay complicates the historical narrative that the Black Power Movement solely represents a repudiation of the religious, and in particular Christian, traditions among those activists associated with Martin Luther King Jr. As such, Harding allows us to see the BPM as more complex that the term "secular" might imply. For recent scholarship on this point, see Kerry Pimblott, "Beyond De-Christianization: Rethinking the Religious Landscapes and Legacies of Black Power in the Age of #BlackLivesMatter," in *Race, Religion, and Black Lives Matter: Essays on a Moment and a Movement*, ed. Christopher Cameron and Phillip Luke Sinitiere (Nashville: Vanderbilt University Press, 2021), 39–66.
18. Harding, "Religion," 58.
19. Gayraud S. Wilmore, *Pragmatic Spirituality: The Christian Faith through an Africentric Lens* (New York: New York University Press, 2004), 188.
20. National Committee of Negro Churchmen, "Black Power," *New York Times*, July 31, 1966.
21. Wilmore, 190.
22. In the development of Black religious thought, there are ongoing methodological conflicts and debates about what constitutes "Black Religion" as a field. In particular, there are historical concerns about the field being overdetermined by theological discourse in general and the influence of Black Protestantism in particular. James H. Cone and Charles H. Long are often seen as seminal figures in the study of Black theology and Black religion, respectively. Long was particularly influential in critiquing the use of methods drawn from theology to interpret Black religion. Harding's account of the religion of Black power is drawn from Christian traditions. However, I argue that his usage is not purely confessional and is compatible with Long's concept of religion as ultimate orientation.
23. See Martin Luther King Jr., "Pilgrimage to Nonviolence," in *A Testament of Hope: The Essential Writings and Speeches of Martin Luther King, Jr.*, ed. James M. Washington (New York: Harper San Francisco, 1986), 39.
24. Space does not allow for a full treatment of the relationship between these concepts. See Rufus Burrow Jr., *Martin Luther King, Jr. and the The-*

ology of Resistance (Jefferson: McFarland, 2015); Burrow Jr., *God and Human Dignity: The Personalism, Theology and Ethics of Martin Luther King, Jr.* (Notre Dame, IN: University of Notre Dame Press, 2006); John J. Ansbro, *Martin Luther King, Jr.: The Making of a Mind* (Maryknoll: Orbis Books, 1982).
25. Aram Goudsouzian, *Down to the Crossroads: Civil Rights, Black Power and the Meredith March against Fear* (New York: Farrar, Straus, and Giroux, 2014), 254.
26. Harding, "Religion," 63.
27. Martin Luther King Jr., *Where Do We Go From Here: Chaos or Community?* (Boston: Beacon Press, 1968), 48.
28. Ruby Sales, interview by Vincent Harding, Veterans of Hope Project, 2016, https://www.veteransofhope.org/veterans/ruby-sales.
29. Ruby Sales, interview by Vincent Harding.
30. Harding, "Religion," 41.
31. Harding, "Religion," 42.
32. Harding, "Religion," 43.
33. Harding, "Religion," 42.
34. I use King's philosophy of nonviolence as a representative example of a particular practical social challenge while recognizing there were many other influential figures central to this aspect of the movement.
35. Daniel Taylor, "Morning Start: 'BlackLivesMatter' Started with a Love Letter," *Vernon Morning Star*, June 20, 2020, https://www.vernonmorningstar.com/trending-now/morning-start-blacklivesmatter-started-with-a-love-letter-3314983.
36. He also notes that the Black Panther Party was the first major Black organization to align itself with the women's liberation movement as well as the gay liberation movement. See Jeffrey Ogbar, "Rainbow Radicalism: The Rise of the Radical Ethnic Nationalism," in *The Black Power Movement: Rethinking the Civil Rights-Black Power Era*, ed. Peniel Joseph (New York: Routledge, 2006), 222.
37. Barbara Ransby, *Making All Black Lives Matter: Reimagining Freedom in the Twenty-first Century* (Oakland: University of California Press, 2018), 2.
38. Keeanga-Yamahtta Taylor, ed, *How We Get Free: Black Feminism and the Combahee River Collective* (Chicago: Haymarket Books, 2017), 181.
39. Ransby, 3.
40. Krista Tippett, "The Spiritual Work of Black Lives Matter," *On Being*, February 18, 2016, https://onbeing.org/programs/patrisse-cullors-and-robert-ross-the-spiritual-work-of-black-lives-matter-may2017.
41. Tippett, "The Spiritual Work."
42. Tippett, "The Spiritual Work."
43. Tippett, "The Spiritual Work."

44. See Cara Page, "A Conversation about Healing Justice with Cara Page," Center for Law and Social Policy, Facebook Live, September 16, 2020, www.clasp.org/events/conversation-about-healing-justice-cara-page/; Evelyn Lynn, Noemi Y. Molitor, Cara Page, and Lamont Sims, "A Conversation about Southerners on New Ground: Transformation, Legacy, and Movement Building in the US South," *Scholar and Feminist Online* (Barnard Center for Research on Women) 8, no. 3 (summer 2010), https://sfonline.barnard.edu/polyphonic/print_song.htm.
45. Tippett, "The Spiritual Work."
46. The use of the term "self-purification" here is a reference to one of the four steps in nonviolent direct action campaigns. See Martin Luther King Jr., "Letter from a Birmingham Jail," in *A Testament of Hope: The Essential Writings and Speeches of Martin Luther King, Jr.*, ed. James M. Washington (New York: Harper San Francisco, 1986), 291.
47. See Janan P. Wyatt and Gifty G. Ampadu, "Reclaiming Self-Care: Self-Care as a Social Justice Tool for Black Wellness," *Community Mental Health Journal* 58, no. 2 (2022): 214; and Aisha Harris, "A History of Self-Care: From Its Radical Roots to Its Yuppie Driven Middle Age to Its Election Inspired Resurgence," *Slate*, April 5, 2017, https://www.slate.com/articles/arts/culture box/2017/04/the_history_of_self_care.html.
48. See Jeremy Carrette, *Selling Spirituality: The Silent Takeover of Religion* (New York: Routledge, 2005) for a representative critique of how "spirituality" emerges through the commercialization of religion, which promotes personal development and spiritual meaning by shifting from "traditional religion" to "private spirituality." Also see Karyn Lofton's *Consuming Religion* (Chicago: University of Chicago Press, 2017) and *Oprah: The Gospel of an Icon* (Berkeley: University of California Press, 2011) for accounts of cultural consumption and religion. For accounts thematizing religion in society as a religious/spiritual marketplace, see Wade Clark Roof, *Spiritual Marketplace: Baby Boomers and the Remaking of American Religion* (New Jersey: Princeton University Press, 1999); Shayne Lee and Phillip Sinitiere, *Holy Mavericks: Evangelical Innovators and the Spiritual Marketplace* (New York: New York University Press, 2009); and Omar M. McRoberts, *Streets of Glory: Church and Community in a Black Urban Neighborhood* (Chicago: University of Chicago Press, 2003).
49. Habah Farrag, "The Spirit in Black Lives Matter: New Spiritual Community in Black Radical Organizing," *Transition* 125 (2018): 81.
50. Martin Luther King Jr. "The Other America," (speech, Stanford University, Stanford, CA, April 14, 1967).
51. See Roudabeh Kishi and Sam Jones, "Demonstrations and Political Violence in America: New Data for Summer 2020," Armed Conflict Location and Event Data (ACLED), September 3, 2020, https://acleddata.com/2020/09/03/demonstrations-political-violence-in-america-new-data-for-summer-2020.

52. Isaac Chotiner, "A Black Lives Matter Co-Founder Explains Why This Time Is Different," *New Yorker*, June 3, 2020, https://www.newyorker.com/news/q-and-a/a-black-lives-matter-co-founder-explains-why-this-time-is-different.
53. Brandon Patterson, "There's No Middle Ground," *Mother Jones*, September 8, 2017, https://www.motherjones.com/politics/2017/09/theres-no-middle-ground.
54. Tom Slater, "Black Lives Matter has a 'Plantation Mentality,'" *Spiked*, October 19, 2016, https://www.spiked-online.com/2016/10/19/black-lives-matter-has-a-plantation-mentality.
55. See Dr. Akinyele Umoja at 16:57 in "We Keep Us Safe," Black Lives Matter, January 19, 2021, https://blacklivesmatter.com/we-keep-us-safe-community-call-video. Umoja details the history of arms within the Black community, such as vigilance committees that protected fugitive slaves from being captured. In addition, he notes examples of nonviolent actors being protected by those with arms. A primary example is the Deacons for Defense, formed in 1964 in Jonesboro, Louisiana. The Deacons were a self-defense organization that protected Movement workers from vigilante and police violence. See Lance Hill's *The Deacons for Defense: Armed Resistance and the Civil Rights* (Chapel Hill: University of North Carolina Press, 2004).
56. It should be noted that organizers and activists such as Ella Baker and Stokely Carmichael were engaged in similar tensions in their work. See Barbara Ransby, *Ella Baker and the Black Freedom Movement* (Chapel Hill: University of North Carolina Press, 2003), 188–92, and Stokely Carmichael, "What We Want," *New York Review of Books* 7, September 22, 1966, 5–6.
57. Evelyn Brooks Higginbotham, *Righteous Discontent: The Women's Movement in the Black Baptist Church, 1890–1920* (Cambridge: Harvard University Press, 1994), 185.
58. Higginbotham, 115.
59. Higginbotham, 190.
60. Higginbotham, 191–93.
61. Higginbotham, 195.
62. Higginbotham, 202.
63. Frederick C. Harris, "The Rise of Respectability Politics," *Dissent* (Winter 2014), https://www.dissentmagazine.org/article/the-rise-of-respectability-politics.
64. "Geraldo Rivera: Trayvon Martin's Hoodie Sweatshirt as Guilty as George Zimmerman," *Slate*, March 23, 2012, https://slate.com/news-and-politics/2012/03/geraldo-rivera-trayvon-martins-hoodie-sweatshirt-as-guilty-as-george-zimmerman-video.html.
65. In a very insightful debate titled "Respectability and Politics" at the Schomburg Center, Khalil Gibran Muhammad raises the interesting point that the ethos of respectability might be better understood as internal to Black

culture as a matter of sustaining institutions rather than solely as a strategy for social change. See "Stage for Debate: Respectability and Politics," February 2, 2016, Schomburg Center for Research in Black Culture, https://livestream.com/accounts/7326672/events/4710955/videos/111296873.
66. Alicia Garza, *The Purpose of Power: How We Come Together when We Fall Apart* (New York: Random House, 2020), 124.
67. Garza, 132.
68. Garza, 133.
69. See *Behind the Mule: Race and Class in African American Politics* (New Jersey: Princeton University Press, 1994), 76.
70. See Tehama Lopez Bunyasi and Candis Watts Smith, "Do All Black Lives Matter Equally to Black People? Respectability Politics and the Limitations of Linked Fate," *Journal of Race, Ethnicity, and Politics* 4 (2019), 180–215.
71. Bunyasi and Smith, 204.
72. Barbara Ransby's chapter "The Preacher and the Organizer: The Politics of Leadership in the Early Civil Rights Movement" in *Ella Baker and the Black Freedom Movement*, 170–209, has become a paradigmatic example of this critique.
73. Charlene Carruthers, *Unapologetic: A Black, Queer, and Feminist Mandate for Radical Movements* (Boston: Beacon Press, 2018), 70–71.
74. Here my analysis is guided by Erica R. Edwards, *Charisma and the Fictions of Black Leadership* (Minneapolis: University of Minnesota Press, 2012).
75. Edwards, *Charisma*, ix.

CHAPTER 3

Good Cops?

Peter Pihos

> Negroes talk frequently about the "good cop" who, while fully enforcing the law, treats them as fellow human beings.
>
> —PRESIDENT'S COMMISSION ON LAW ENFORCEMENT
> AND THE ADMINISTRATION OF JUSTICE,
> *Task Force Report: The Police* (1967)

In summing up the perspective that informs their critical 2018 handbook of "copspeak," *Police: A Field Guide*, scholars Tyler Wall and David Correia assert, "There are no bad apples; there are no good cops; there are just cops, specialists in the use of violence, fabricating order."[1] This claim, that "there are no good cops" (like its vulgar vernacular cousin, All Cops are Bastards, or ACAB), does not address the moral standing of individual officers. Rather, it moves observers away from thinking of or about the individual to focus instead on the institution and how it structures American society. As Black Lives Matter Movement (BLMM) co-founder Patrisse Khan-Cullors argues, "Police . . . meant harm to our community, and the race or class of any one officer, nor the good heart of an officer, could [not] change that. No isolated acts of decency could wholly change an organization that became an institution that was created not to protect but catch, control, and kill us."[2] Informed by abolitionist perspectives first articulated in 1997 by organizations such as Critical Resistance, many BLMM organizers argue that the police function not to protect but to dominate Black people.[3] From this perspective, the police institution cannot be reformed.[4] There are no good cops.

Critiques of the police are not new. Historian Simon Balto has shown that in Chicago, for instance, Black protest targeted police practices throughout the twentieth century.[5] Although conflict with police was a staple of everyday life for Black, Latino, and poor white youth throughout the preceding decades, a broad-based social movement politics focused on police violence only emerged after Chicago police officers who were detailed to State Attorney Edward V. Hanrahan's special anti-gang squad assassinated local Black Panther leader Fred Hampton Jr. on December 4, 1969. In the aftermath of Hampton's murder, a politically diverse spectrum of Chicagoans directly challenged racism in the Chicago Police Department (CPD) while seeking to curtail police brutality and demanding a transformation in Black communities' relationship to policing.[6] An organized group of rank-and-file Black Chicago police officers, members of the Afro-American Patrolmen's League (AAPL), were among the key protagonists in the struggle against the CPD during the 1970s. Buoyed by the large numbers of Black officers in the CPD compared to other cities, the AAPL would become the country's largest and most influential group of rank-and-file Black officers.[7] Embracing Black Power, they became a model for other Black officers across the country.[8]

If Black police officers directly confronting state violence were rare in the 1960s and 1970s, today they are non-existent. For many police abolitionists, this absence makes sense. After all, they often describe policing in functional, rather than historical, terms. In activist and educator Mariame Kaba's words, "when you see a police officer pressing his knee into a Black man's neck until he dies, that's the logical result of policing in America."[9] Or, as the abolitionist lawyer Derecka Purnell articulates, "I knew the origins of [prisons, police, and prosecutors] and that they were working according to their design."[10] Abolitionists and scholars see police as politically monolithic; police institutions are not themselves the site of meaningful struggle.[11] Activists view black and white police similarly with little hope for transformation. "Policing," Geo Maher submits, "is racist no matter who is doing the legwork."[12] Indeed, scholars like James Foreman Jr. and Keeanga-Yamahtta Taylor, among others, have shown that since the 1970s, Black police leaders have played an important role in overseeing, if not pushing, the development and implementation of militarized and punitive policing.[13] Both historic and contemporary studies of rank-and-file Black police officers note their conformity to departmental norms and practices.[14]

This chapter offers a different understanding of the history of police institutions. It begins by highlighting the fracture and politicization of the Chicago Police Department in the 1960s. In that decade, Black Power and other radical social movements became locked in an escalating dialectic of repression and resistance with an increasingly right-wing Chicago Police Department.[15] This conflict created political space for the mobilization of Black rank-and-file officers, in part because of their presence in the police department as a product of desegregation. During those years, the Afro-American Patrolmen's League formed part of a social movement that embraced political ideas and strategies that remain popular within the BLMM today. The League's deployment of patriarchal masculinity and police reform contrasts sharply with contemporary organizers' embrace of queer Black feminist ideas and abolition. Nevertheless, the BLMM echoes the efforts of the League and its allies in the early 1970s to champion grassroots empowerment and community-centered knowledge to politicize questions of public safety. These shared features are central to understanding the continuities in Black struggles against state violence.

Seeing these similarities between Black patrolmen's challenge to their own police department five decades ago and the BLMM's efforts raises important questions about what has changed. Closer examination of the politics internal to police institutions provides a helpful vantage point for understanding the creation of the impenetrable and politically homogeneous police departments that the BLMM confronts today. Despite the many continuities that historians have identified in policing over the course of the twentieth century, urban politics and urban institutions—including police departments—have changed dramatically since the 1960s.[16] In its final sections, this chapter reexamines two elements of this shift that changed the internal dynamics of police institutions: the rise of Black Police executives and the unionization of police officers. Both had the effect of marginalizing the League and cutting off avenues for advancing dissident politics from within the Department. Amid the political, economic, and social crises of the 1980s, Black police executives and Chicago's newly certified police union effectively eliminated the AAPL's ability to dissent internally and consolidated a punitive hegemony within the Department. As such, this story reveals some of the important conditions under which police themselves created politically impermeable institutions in opposition to the League's activism.

The Fracturing of American Police Departments in the 1960s

Conflicts over policing in American cities during the 1960s revealed the competing, and often clashing, interests inside police departments.[17] In many cities, police organizations entered openly into politics in order to both contest top-down managerial reforms that sought to control the discretion of officers on the beat and resist moderate accountability reforms proposed by civil rights activists. White officers, mostly of Irish descent, dominated these organizations. Relying on racist tropes that blamed their cities' growing Black populations for crime and disorder, local police leaders in Philadelphia and New York, especially, fought relatively liberal mayors and police chiefs over civilian reviews of police brutality.[18] Organizations like Philadelphia's Fraternal Order of Police (FOP) demanded "get tough" policies that demonized social welfare provisions and promoted the need to control Black residents. "Police have an amazing political power," Cleveland's liberal Black mayor Carl B. Stokes concluded in 1973, "a power that has mushroomed in the last few years with the advent of the big-city crime scare."[19]

Chicago's largely white police organizations did not develop the strong political voice found in Philadelphia or New York. At the beginning of the 1960s, the Chicago Patrolmen's Association, then the leading organization for rank-and-file officers, rebelled against the imposition of a new internal discipline system proposed by liberal reform police superintendent O. W. Wilson and demanded union recognition. While Mayor Richard J. Daley used his tight bonds with organized labor to head off these efforts, the goals articulated remained alive into the 1970s in other organizations, including Chicago's own FOP.[20] Unlike their counterparts in Philadelphia and New York, Chicago patrolmen's organizations received support from their mayor, Richard J. Daley—his role in quashing police unionization efforts notwithstanding. Elected in 1955, Daley maintained tight control over the city in the face of civil rights challenges, and in the 1960s embraced an increasingly reactionary law-and-order politics that Chicago police officers cheered. Following the West Side uprising in response to Martin Luther King Jr.'s assassination in 1968, Daley ordered his police superintendent to instruct officers to "shoot to kill any arsonist or anyone with a Molotov cocktail in his hand," which made him a hero to white police officers nationwide.[21] In New York, where Mayor John Lindsay had condemned Daley's approach, police officers picketed city hall, chanting, "We want Daley; Lindsay must go."[22] Police organizations in Chicago also spoke out in support of their mayor's belligerent directive.

If Black officers made up seventeen percent of the force by the mid 1960s, they nonetheless emerged as the most dynamic political force among the rank-and-file, openly opposing the law-and-order politics of Mayor Daley and mainstream police organizations. In creating the Afro-American Patrolmen's League a month after the King uprising, Black officers justified the need for a Black police organization by referencing their colleagues' racism. Around 2:00 p.m. on July 12, 1968, standing under the green line elevated train on 63rd Street before a crowd of two hundred, including undercover CPD Red Squad and FBI operatives, they declared, "We disagree categorically with the position of the Fraternal Order of Police supporting 'Stop and Frisk,' and their position supporting the order to 'shoot to kill' or maim looters during civil disorders."[23] Over the next decade, these Black officers continued to challenge racialized law-and-order politics.

None of the men who started the League had joined the police department as activists. They had envisioned public employment as a viable path to middle-class financial security and saw working in the police department as among the best public jobs, but they encountered racism in multiple forms as part of their work. During the first half of the 1960s, liberal reform police superintendent O. W. Wilson vastly expanded the number of Black officers and clamped down on outright racial chauvinism within the CPD.[24] Nonetheless, segregation in the organization remained into the 1970s, and racist policies and practices stymied Black officers' advancement within the force.[25] Moreover, many of their fellow rank-and-file officers were openly racist. An observational study in 1966 concluded that 72 percent of officers in Chicago and Boston were "prejudiced" or "highly prejudiced" against Black people. The numbers were even worse among those who patrolled Black neighborhoods.[26]

If being a police officer allowed Black Chicagoans access to the middle class, the tradeoff was playing a role in managing urban inequality. As AAPL Executive Director Renault Robinson notes, economic vulnerability and the desire for respect shaped Black officers' behavior. "Black policemen . . . operate out of the fear of losing their jobs; out of the vague hope of being promoted or rewarded by the establishment; out of their love for the luxury of big expensive cars, good living and the apparent authority their badges and guns give them in the black community."[27] Some Black officers adopted the behavior patterns of white officers, developing reputations for brutality and harboring prejudices against other Black people.[28] Many concluded, according to Robinson, "it is better (or at least seems safer) to join the oppressive force, rather than oppose it."[29]

During the first years the AAPL founders were on the force, CPD adopted more aggressive strategies for policing Black neighborhoods, flooding them with task force officers and employing widespread implementation of stop-and-frisk, despite the protest of civil rights organizations.[30] Black youth resisted police harassment on the street, sometimes using physical confrontation to oppose the authority of a state that had little regard for their well-being.[31] Police often intensified their repression in response. Even supporters of the reformist superintendent, O. W. Wilson, recognized that the full-spectrum of police brutality—from verbal abuse to casual violence to murder—persisted under his reign.³² Affected by the claims and activities of the Civil Rights and Black Power Movements, and in the crucible of this conflict over policing, the League's founders began to question how they could remain in solidarity with struggles for equality even as they held onto the economic security and status that their jobs as police officers provided. Like many other Black professionals of this era, they sought transformation by embracing the tenets of Black Power.³³

Unapologetically Black (Cops)

League members sought to reframe the structural position of Black police officers, describing their mission in their first press release as "elevat[ing] the black policeman in the black community to the same image-status enjoyed by the white policeman in the white community; that is a protector of the citizenry and not a brutal oppressor." Rather than subordinating racial solidarity to their occupational role, the League sought to harmonize them by rooting their jobs in an embrace of Black solidarity. They began with their identities as Black men: "We are husbands, fathers, brothers, neighbors and members of the black community. Donning the blue uniform has not changed this."³⁴ Highly gendered notions of Black masculinity reverberated with the men's conception of policing, as was the norm in this era. Yet even through these patriarchal notions, the men shifted focus away from the individual officer and toward the creation of political solidarities capable of sustaining a new police role for Black officers.

The League's critique of the CPD rested on their understanding of its role in sustaining the unequal distribution of power in Chicago. In writing about the AAPL's form of Black Power, historian Beryl Satter argues that its "most radical aspect . . . was its drive to analyze institutional racism and violence—that is, its unveiling of the 'white power structure.'"³⁵ According to this analysis, police behavior created the conditions by which Black Chicagoans became victims of violence. As AAPL Executive Director Renault Robinson explains in a 1971 *Chicago Defender* column, selective law enforcement targeting Black people led police to believe that all Black people were suspicious, which just reinforced profiling and the indiscriminate targeting of Black youth as gang members. At the same time, the purposeful absence of adequate resources reduced Black communities to a state of abjection in the face of serious violent crime, forcing them to request the assistance of the hostile police force. As Robinson describes, "They send in the Task Force or just the regular police officer, only he's very vicious and when you complain about police brutality the Police Department remarks, 'You people ask for service and our help and when you get it you complain about the service we give you—what do you want?'"[36] Black vulnerability to violence led them to request police intervention, which, in turn, replicated and amplified that violence; then, the police blamed Black people both for their vulnerability and for highlighting their vulnerability.

League officers echoed their Black Power contemporaries in describing the nature of power in America. For example, they argued that policing was crucial to the production of urban racial inequality.[37] As Robinson writes in the *Chicago Defender* in 1970, "The role of the white policeman from the beginning until now has been to keep Black[s] in line, no matter what they have to do . . . to accomplish it."[38] Moreover, they deployed Black Power's openly confrontational tactics against their own institution—a confrontational militancy that seems unimaginable today. Picture rank-and-file Black police officers today holding a press conference in uniform outside the apartment where a shotgun-wielding fellow officer killed a Black woman and denouncing their fellow officers as having "complete disregard for black life"—the image beggars belief.[39] While contemporary Black officers have on occasion spoken out about racism in policing in recent years, they do not challenge their superiors and fellow officers as directly or persistently as the League did in the 1960s.

Like BLMM activists today, League members contested the notion that individual moral disposition made some Black officers "good cops." As Renault Robinson argues in a different 1970 column, "decent Black men" working for the CPD were powerless "as individuals to do anything about the overall situation." Indeed, if Black officers failed to keep other Black people in their place, Robinson notes, it could result in their police supervisors criticizing, punishing, or even removing them from the force.[40] While they insisted police officers should treat Black people with respect, League members sought to ensure this by organizing collectively with other Black people for political control of police power. Their strategy followed the generally pragmatic trajectory of Black Power in Chicago, pointing to what historian Jeff Hegelson has identified as the "conflict between the sense that Chicago had failed black people . . . and the idea that the institutions of the city could be reformed to deliver greater equality for all."[41] League officers sought not to abandon engagement with the police institution, but to transform it. Could they alter the structure of policing, even as they sought to deal with the conditions it produced?[42]

For League members, Black Chicagoans could only solve this problem of unequal power through collective action. Echoing Stokely Carmichael (in 1966 when he served as SNCC chairman in Mississippi), Robinson argues, "The only reason white police continue to brutalize black people is that black people let them do it. The only reason white people will stop beating and killing black people is that people stop them."[43] Drawing on ideas of communal Black solidarity, they sought to establish a new basis of police authority. Robinson writes: "Organized Black policemen represent Black police power. Organized Black police power, with the Black community behind it represents a real threat to the power structure's control over the lives of Black people."[44] With Black police officers in the lead, Black communities could take political control over their lives. They proposed transformative change from within.

The League quickly grew, with 270 officers signing up in the first three months.[45] Their position shook the police department, leading to tense relations with other officers. Harassment by whites became routine, and even some "Veteran brothers"—as an article in the League's newsletter puts it—criticized what they perceived as the organization's confrontational approach.[46] Supervisory personnel sought to make an example of League members, transferring them involuntarily and disciplining them for minor infractions. "Don't come to work with a button missing because [internal investigators] will frame you," Robinson notes.[47] By the fall of 1969, CPD brass strategized in secret meetings about how to get rid of the League. Such efforts went furthest in the case of Robinson, who not only saw his work conditions downgraded drastically, but also faced discipline and was even arrested by fellow officers on numerous occasions. His superiors recommended his termination from the department.[48]

Repression by police administrators, especially the effort to fire Robinson, ironically facilitated the League's acceptance by Chicago's Civil Rights and Black Power activists. By harassing League members, the CPD reproduced the grounds for critique leveled by the League and other critics. When officers arrested Robinson on trumped-up driving charges in September 1969, community groups issued a statement decrying "the repressive tactics being demonstrated against the Afro-American Patrolmen's League."[49] Following Robinson's suspension from the CPD in 1970, Reverend Jesse Jackson held a meeting during which Robinson made a dramatic show of relinquishing his gun, badge, baton, cap, department gas mask, and blue riot helmet, telling the audience, "I have always seen myself as your representative. It was you who gave me this gun and badge. Now I surrender them to you for safekeeping. If I ever get them back, it will only be because of you."[50] In this obvious performance, Robinson showed that he was a good cop, on the League's terms, by refusing to stay silent about police racism and brutality. He also realized that only an organized political movement could succeed in pressuring the department on his behalf.

Movement Echoes: 1968–1974 and 2014–2020

From 1968 to 1974, the League assumed an insurgent posture toward the CPD, much like the BLMM would do almost five decades later.

The organization relied upon a strategy of using its officers' positions inside the department to maintain its legitimacy even as it challenged the department in terms similar to other liberal and radical critics. This insider's posture is one significant difference between the League and its allies and BLMM in their aims and orientation. In contrast to many (though not all) contemporary BLMM organizers who identify as abolitionists seeking to defund the police in favor of building other social programs, movements in Chicago in the 1970s focused primarily on ways to democratize the police.[51] Similarly, the masculinist and patriarchal character of the League's ideology, especially in its early years, contrasts sharply with the Black queer feminism many BLMM organizers embrace.[52] Nonetheless, the movements share what social movement scholars describe as a repertoire of contention, a shared set of actions that involve directly confronting police officials by highlighting the harm caused by police violence.[53] They also share a style of movement building focused on grassroots engagement of those affected by police violence, creating collective knowledge to contest police lies known today as "copaganda."[54] Finally, both share a sensibility about the political nature of policing.

The press, particularly the *Defender*, tracked the League's adoption of the confrontational tactics and language developed by Black Power activists. In highlighting the use of such tactics by the BLMM today, philosopher Christopher Lebron notes the long tradition of directly shaming the oppressor that traces back at least as far as Frederick Douglass and Ida B. Wells.[55] Examples of such League actions abound. When, in April 1969, white patrolman Martin Anderson shot through a closed door and killed Linda Anderson, a Black nineteen-year-old mother of two whose husband was serving in Vietnam, the League held a press conference in front of Anderson's apartment. Showing the damage done by the shotgun, the League upbraided the department's "complete disregard for black life."[56] A few days after December 4, 1969, when police officers murdered Fred Hampton in a predawn raid, the AAPL held a press conference at Holy Angels Catholic Church, where Howard Saffold comprehensively critiqued police evidence and described the killings as "obviously a political assassination."[57]

By the early 1970s, Robinson had a weekly column in the legendary Black newspaper the *Chicago Defender*, which he used to attack the Chicago police as racist, publishing articles about the political control of the CPD with titles like "Racist Power Is Black's Downfall."[58] Transgressing the ethic of the thin blue line, Robinson used his columns to accuse and identify fellow police officers who abused Black women, giving their names and star numbers. For example: "Officer Rafferty's favorite pastime is beating and kicking, and cursing black women in his district."[59] Nor did League officers respect departmental hierarchies: when the police superintendent held a series of community meetings in which he refused to take questions directly from the audience, three League members showed up in uniform with bullhorns and took over the meeting, allowing audience members to use the bullhorns to speak back to the police brass.[60]

Like the BLMM today, the League and its allies challenged police efforts to "improve" their relationship to Black communities. For example, they criticized the CPD's community-relations programs as smoke and mirrors. Such programs had begun in the early 1960s, and police officials leaned on them in moments of crisis to frame conflict over policing as a problem of communication rather than a contest of power. Even on these limited terms, police community-relations programs failed because they did not offer genuine dialogue. Instead, they insisted that residents passively recognize what Robinson described as attempts "to sell the police image to the public" and to "accept the department as it is," when in fact the police policy toward Black Chicagoans was the problem itself: "Unless the legitimate grievances relating to the police are confronted by the police administration frankly and effectively, improvement of police-community relations will be impossible."[61] Robinson concluded that, without offering Black people any power or control over policymaking, such programs would never succeed.[62]

Anti-brutality activists believed they could prevail only if they had power to control policing. The 1969 murder of Fred Hampton catalyzed organizers in Chicago to focus more on the police. Their campaign to hold accountable Cook County State's Attorney Edward V.

Hanrahan, whose office supervised and covered up the raid, and the police officers who killed Hampton highlighted how the police and other state institutions worked together to cover up malfeasance.[63] Similarly, the BLMM conducted a similar form of investigation and public education in the aftermath of the murders of Trayvon Martin (2012), Michael Brown (2014), Sandra Bland (2015), Freddie Gray (2015), and Eric Garner (2014) nationally, and in Chicago, they amplified cases such as Dominique (Damo) Franklin Jr. (2014), Rekia Boyd (2012), and Laquan McDonald (2014). In both eras, the active pursuit of justice led activists to probe the workings of state institutions, and the success of those institutions in deflecting calls for justice led organizers to a deeper understanding of the workings of state power. Ideas about justice, whether through greater democratic control or abolition, emerged from these pragmatic efforts to seek accountability.

Both movements, half a century apart, focused on transforming Chicago's institutions through grassroots organizing. As Ruth Wells, the coordinator of Citizens Alert, the liberal police watchdog organization that grew directly out of efforts related to Hampton's murder, said when reflecting on the past half-decade of activism in 1975, "It may take a long time to organize, motivate, educate and put people into motion. But nobody yet has demonstrated any shortcut which works."[64] Citizen's Alert's campaign to open police board meetings and democratize the board's composition was one such effort. The AAPL's Police Brutality Complaint and Referral Service provided aid to victims of police violence and, in the process, gathered more information about people's experience with the police, which would inform future legal and political efforts, rather than relying solely on the fragmentary information the government provided. Similarly, in recent campaigns, such as #NoCopAcademy, created in September 2017, organizers invested in community knowledge and mobilized public witnesses against the building of a $95 million-dollar police training facility.[65]

In both eras, these campaigns forced police and the state to publicize and justify their actions and decisions that in earlier years would have required no explanation. Both movements accomplished this by leveraging grassroots organizing to challenge key power-brokers in the criminal justice system. Each movement defeated an incumbent Democratic state attorney: Edward V. Hanrahan in 1972 and Anita Alvarez in 2016. Both prosecutors had covered up a police murder on the pretext that the deceased (Fred Hampton and Laquan McDonald, respectively) had been a threat to police, and both officials symbolized the complicity of Democratic politicians and criminal legal institutions in creating police impunity. Both faced elections after activists had politicized the broader question of the police's role and accountability; in each, social movements shaped electoral politics and then led a campaign against the incumbent. In 1972, multiple organizations, from the Urban League to the Alliance Against Repression (an umbrella organization), Operation PUSH, the Black Panthers, and the AAPL, joined together to defeat Hanrahan.[66] Likewise, in 2016, BYP100, Assata's Daughters, Fearless Leading by Youth, #LetUsBreathe, Black Lives Matter Chicago, and We Charge Genocide were successful in their campaign to say #ByeAnita.[67]

Political and legal challenges to the Chicago Police Department in the early 1970s forced a new equilibrium during the latter half of that decade. Control of the police department remained in the hands of city hall, and social movement organizing largely dissipated. Yet at the same time, new liberal legal arrangements that constrained the police incorporated movement demands. Lawsuits brought by Fred Hampton's family, the AAPL, the Department of Justice, and the Alliance to End Repression resulted in a series of landmark court decisions that recognized police wrongdoing and placed new limitations on police action. The city paid Fred Hampton's family millions of dollars in a wrongful death suit.[68] The federal district court held the CPD liable for spying on citizens' political activities, revealed its Red Squad files, and ordered it to close its spying operation.[69] The federal court also held the CPD liable for discrimination in hiring and promotions and ordered the implementation of a stringent affirmative action program. It also concluded that the CPD had retaliated against AAPL members for their activity and ordered it to pay back wages and punitive damages to those it had targeted, including Robinson.[70] Even as the federal district court ordered the CPD to meet its affirmative action quotas, the size of the police department began to shrink: among other factors, a massive contraction in available federal dollars resulted in a more than 10 percent reduction in the CPD workforce.[71] These changes—the restriction of police authority, the implementation of affirmative action, and the diminution of the overall size of the police force— did not mean that policing ceased to be oppressive. Indeed, perhaps the largest scandal in Chicago police history, involving Commander John Burge's torture of more than a hundred Black suspects—most of whom were convicted of crimes they did not commit—was ramping up.[72] Even so, policing remained contested, and fiscal retrenchment limited its expansion.[73]

Transformations

The belligerent defender of police impunity, Mayor Daley, died on December 20, 1976, at the same time as the police department's authority came under new limits and shrank in size, creating what appeared to be a more open political terrain for achieving Black political power and influence over policing. Yet, in the dozen years between Richard J. Daley's death and his son Richard M. Daley's consolidation of power in city hall, the possibilities for transformative change in policing disappeared almost entirely. Although many changes reshaped policing during these years, there were two key events that constrained political dissent from within the police department. First, in 1981, Chicago police reached an agreement with the city to allow officers to vote for an exclusive collective bargaining representative. Second, in 1983, following the triumph of Harold Washington as the city's first Black mayor, Black supervisory personnel came to run the police department. The political valence of these events was very different: the League staunchly opposed unionization while it supported Washington's hiring. Nonetheless, the political context in which these events transpired would result in the reduction of political dissent expressed by the League.

During this interregnum, vestiges of the elder Daley's political coalition remained formidable. Nonetheless, insurgent mayoral candidates twice defeated the machine: Daley-protégé-turned-machine-antagonist Jane Byrne prevailed in 1979, and Congressman Harold Washington was elected mayor in 1983. Given the AAPL's despised status under Mayor Daley, the organization played a surprising role in both mayoral coalitions: the League had become a salient enough symbol of Black opposition to the political status quo that less than two months after Jane Byrne's inauguration in 1979, she showed up at an AAPL awards ceremony. *Tribune* columnist Vernon Jarrett marveled, "Who would have predicted that in 1979, Chicago would have a mayor who would even listen to a suggestion from Renault Robinson?"[74] Byrne, however, soon recognized that the old Daley regime remained useful for governing, and she coddled its racist elements. While Washington always remained close with Black rank-and-file officers, *both* mayoral tenures reduced the capacity for political opposition both within and outside the police department. In this context, the League's conception of a political solidarity between Black officers and the communities they policed became a fleeting dream.

Byrne's lasting impact was her recognition of Chicago FOP Lodge 7 as the exclusive collective bargaining agent for police officers. Mayor Daley had preferred "handshake deals" to real negotiations. As Byrne sought to assemble a winning political coalition in 1979, she cultivated support from public employees by promising to pass a collective bargaining ordinance.[75] In 1981, Byrne agreed to a representation election for police officers.[76] Despite their long-standing battles with each other, both the CPD administration and the League had fought unionization.[77] The League knew that the FOP was racist and would ignore the concerns of Black officers about hiring and promotion.[78] They warned members that they would be forced to pay dues to a union that would likely fight the affirmative action decree they had won in federal court.[79] Nonetheless, CPD leadership's ham-fisted efforts to encourage officers not to choose an exclusive bargaining representative drove the white rank-and-file toward support for the FOP, which prevailed by a substantial margin.[80]

FOP's victory harmed the League in two ways: first, the FOP joined the Reagan administration to fight the affirmative action consent decree that the League had won in 1976.[81] Using dues paid at least in part by Black officers, the FOP lobbying efforts weakened court-ordered affirmative action and, once Washington became mayor, would obstruct his efforts at voluntary affirmative action as well.[82] When hundreds of League members initially refused to join the union and tried to withhold "fair share" payments, the FOP charged them with misconduct, which could potentially lead to their termination. League stalwarts held out until 1983, when they finally paid "under protest."[83] The FOP destroyed the financial well-being of the League by eliminating their access to dues checkoff, which allowed for membership fees to be withdrawn directly from officers' paychecks.[84] In 1984, League president Edgar Gosa wrote to members: "[We've] had to tighten our belts, dig deeply into our pockets and make do with what we have."[85] Unionization did not completely kill the AAPL, but it radically narrowed its base in the department and constricted its financial resources, leading to a period of dormancy. Black officers today remain captive to a hostile FOP.[86]

The FOP's negative impact goes well beyond dismantling affirmative action and disabling Black officers' political capacity, however. Since winning its first contract, the FOP's primary focus has been obscuring and obstructing police accountability. In its first contract following the 1981 election, the FOP won almost no financial improvements for officers; rather, their only major success was in adopting an officer's "Bill of Rights," which provided extraordinary due process protections for police in internal investigations. These would be further strengthened in subsequent agreements.[87] Similarly, far from funding efforts to improve salaries or benefits for officers and their families, union dues have overwhelmingly been used to fund legal representation for officers accused of misconduct ($2.3 million, or 40 percent of dues in 2018).[88] The FOP has also played an aggressive public relations role in police shootings, consistently falsifying or misleading reporters about crucial details to obscure police accountability.[89] Perhaps most detrimental has been the FOP's continued promotion of law and order narratives: paraphrasing the arguments of a FOP attorney defending officer Jason Van Dyke (who murdered Laquan McDonald), a *Chicago Sun-Times* reporter wrote, "Police officers now are much more aware of the possibility they could face criminal charges for their efforts to fight crime."[90] The FOP portrays any restrictions on police discretion as a threat to public safety, and it is the credibility of this framing, rather than FOP's strength in traditional areas of labor organizing, that provides the primary source of its power.

If the FOP's victory weakened the AAPL's capacity as a workplace organization, the rise of Black police executives muted Black rank-and-file officers' criticisms of the leadership. This was bitterly ironic because the League's greatest victory—Harold Washington's election as mayor in 1983—had facilitated it. During the run up to the election, the FOP president declared that 92.5 percent of the ten thousand union members favored Washington's Republican opponent, but Black officers worked tirelessly for Washington's victory.[91] Once in office, white intransigence limited the avenues available to Fred Rice, Washington's appointee as police superintendent, to institute major changes to police tactics. When Rice and Mayor Washington tried to cut the number of police officers, redistribute the police patrol so that Black neighborhoods got equal service, or create a focused gang-violence prevention program, the anti-Washington majority obstructed them.[92] Within the Department, Rice faced opposition from both white supervisory officers and the FOP to his efforts to root out racism and impose greater fairness. They challenged his efforts to diversify the command staff and implement affirmative action.[93] At the same time, white recalcitrance made criticism of the Chicago Police Department by Black rank-and-file officers much more difficult. Not only were both groups of Black officers aligned in favor of increased opportunities for Black and Latino officers, and female officers of all groups, but they also both opposed the sabotage undertaken by white officers and politicians. Yet, while the Black rank-and-file officers' interests aligned with their Black supervisors on these issues, Black command staff showed little to no more interest than their white predecessors in their Black subordinates' desire to remake the relationship between policing and politics. Moreover, with Black people in power both in city hall and the police department, the League's ideas about Black Power lost some of their salience.

Ultimately, the distance between the League's critiques and the politics of Black police leaders resonated in how they sought to reform the department. Superintendent Rice saw racism as a problem of personnel and professionalism, and inequalities in policing as tactical and technical, not political. As such, he sought to better regulate but not fundamentally change policing and disavowed the institution's political character.[94] While Rice had faced racism at work for three decades, he did not embrace the League's vision of policing. Instead, he focused on navigating the color line to rise up the ranks. Now in charge, he believed that such pluralist representation, embodied in the rise of Black officers into the supervisory ranks, could produce dramatic changes. As scholar Keeanga-Yamahtta Taylor and James Forman Jr. have both shown, however, Black leadership only brought more aggressive and punitive policing, and with a Black superintendent in charge, the CPD became more politically impenetrable.[95]

The Chicago police in the 1980s turned to managing the emerging new forms of urban inequality, characterized by geographically concentrated poverty and labor market exclusion.[96] Black vulnerability to homicide was a key indicator of inequality and a reflection of the failure of state social provision.[97] Policing became the modality through which successive city administrations managed the impact of these political-economic changes. Beginning in the mid-1980s, the war on drugs provided the rhetorical justification and political logic by which police came to deal with problems of urban poverty and dispossession.[98] Unlike the growing power of the police union, which was rooted in longstanding racial antagonisms, Chicago's Black police executives followed others across the country in mobilizing racial solidarity to implement discriminatory and punitive police policies. As Washington's second Black Police Superintendent, Leroy Martin, explained in 1988, "I've got to make arrest after arrest after arrest until I break the backs of the street peddlers."[99] The harmful social problems, particularly unsafe schools and housing, homelessness, and unemployment, which drug warriors argued aggressive drug policing would address, only deepened as their harsh tactics intensified.[100]

No Good Cops

BLMM arguments that highlight the monolithic and functional character of policing are in part the product of this dismal history. Although BLMM organizers ground their claims in the longer history of policing, much of their rhetorical power derives from the nature of a contemporary police institution whose impermeability was reinforced by these transformations at the end of the twentieth century. Sustained organizing by the AAPL and others did not produce new or more equitable relations between the police institution and Black people; rather, changes to the CPD in the 1980s fortified the institution against accountability and muted criticism at the very moment when the Department shifted tactics to embrace more draconian intrusions into neighborhoods of concentrated poverty. Aggressive policing of drugs became the primary mode of governing the city with few alternatives in sight.

The disavowal of political struggle by Black police executives and the explicitly anti-egalitarian political project of the FOP both constricted the political space available to rank-and-file Black officers to side with the communities they purportedly served. Understanding this history helps to explain the character of abolitionist demands of and to police institutions today. As of this writing, the Chicago FOP is an openly proud bulwark of right-wing militancy, run by John Catanzara, an avowed "Blue Lives Matter" supporter currently on paid leave due to misconduct allegations.[101] Activists who challenge the police continue to endure poor treatment from David Brown, the CPD's sixth Black superintendent out of the last ten, and will likely face the same from Brown's successor. During the summer of 2020, cameras documented police officers pushing, clubbing, punching, or kicking BLMM demonstrators; the challenges to police violence were met by the very violence they critiqued.

Understanding the history of Chicago's Afro-American Patrolmen's League, their efforts to reform policing, and their subsequent marginalization, shows the ways in which, through internal changes brought about in the 1970s and 1980s, the police department became monolithic and impenetrable, foreclosing any possibility of political solidarity between police officers and the communities they police. During the 1960s, such political space opened as police leaders sought to modernize their departments and respond to changes in the social geography and political economy of urban life. In that moment, all Black people suffered from institutional and systemic racism in obvious ways dictated by Jim Crow. Today, the political and social landscape has shifted. The class composition of cities—divided ever more sharply between rich and poor—and the radicalized character of police institutions, which have co-opted the language of representation to mask the preservation of inequality, make the emergence of any such political faction within police departments exceedingly unlikely. Under these conditions, there can be no good cops.

NOTES

1. David Correia and Tyler Wall, "Response (Book Review Forum on Police: A Field Guide By David Correia And Tyler Wall)," *Society + Space*, October 30, 2018, https://www.societyandspace.org/articles/response-by-david-correia-and-tyler-wall.
2. Patrisse Khan-Cullors and asha bandele, *When They Call You a Terrorist: A Black Lives Matter Memoir* (New York: St. Martin's Press, 2017), 186.
3. Barbara Ransby, *Making All Black Lives Matter: Reimagining Freedom in the Twenty-First Century* (Berkeley: University of California Press, 2018), 15–18. Of course, not all individuals engaged in activities identified with the Black Lives Matter Movement or sympathetic to BLMM identify as abolitionists. For a genealogy of abolition, see Angela Y. Davis, et al., *Abolition. Feminism. Now.* (Chicago: Haymarket Books, 2022), 34–52.
4. For example, Mariame Kaba, "Yes, We Mean Literally Abolish the Police," in *We Do This 'Til We Free Us: Abolitionist Organizing and Transforming Justice*, ed. Tamara K. Nopper (Chicago: Haymarket Books, 2021).
5. Simon Balto, *Occupied Territory: Policing Black Chicago from Red Summer to Black Power* (Chapel Hill: University of North Carolina Press, 2019).

6. Balto, chap. 7; Peter C. Pihos, "'Police Brutality Exposed': Chicago, 1960–1974," *Radical History Review* 141 (October 2021): 128–50.
7. W. Marvin Dulaney, *Black Police in America* (Bloomington: Indiana University Press, 1996), 74–75.
8. Black professionals across occupations embraced Black Power during these years. See Joyce M. Bell, *The Black Power Movement and American Social Work* (New York: Columbia University Press, 2014). The AAPL's efforts bear no resemblance to contemporary "copaganda," such as the efforts of police officers to perform solidarity with the BLMM in the immediate aftermath of Derrick Chauvin's murder of George Floyd on May 25, 2020. See Peter C. Pihos, "Challenging Copaganda," *The Abusable Past* (blog), December 20, 2021, https://www.radicalhistoryreview.org/abusablepast/challenging-copaganda. The sporadic examples today of Black officers who have blown the whistle on their colleagues only faintly resemble the organizing of the AAPL to build organizational power within the police department.
9. Kaba, "Yes, We Mean Literally Abolish the Police," 14.
10. Derecka Purnell, *Becoming Abolitionists: Police, Protests, and the Pursuit of Freedom* (New York: Astra House, 2021), 110.
11. One notable exception is Christopher Lowen Agee, *The Streets of San Francisco: Policing and the Creation of a Cosmopolitan Liberal Politics, 1950–1972* (Chicago: University of Chicago Press, 2014).
12. Geo Maher, *A World Without Police: How Strong Communities Make Cops Obsolete* (New York: Verso, 2021).
13. Keeanga-Yamahtta Taylor, *From #BlackLivesMatter to Black Liberation* (Chicago: Haymarket Books, 2016), chap. 3; James Forman Jr., *Locking Up Our Own: Crime and Punishment in Black America* (New York: Farrar, Straus and Giroux, 2017), chaps. 3, 5, 6.
14. For an overview of contemporary research, see Devin W. Carbado and L. Song Richardson, "The Black Police: Police Our Own," *Harvard Law Review* 131, no. 7 (May 2018): 1979–2025. Previous important studies include Harold F. Gosnell, *Negro Politicians: The Rise of Negro Politics in Chicago* (Chicago: University of Chicago Press, 1935), chap. 12; and Nicholas Alex, *Black in Blue: A Study of the Negro Policeman* (New York: Appleton-Century Crofts, 1969).
15. The phrase "dialectic of repression and resistance" is taken from Donna Murch, *Living for the City: Migration, Education, and the Rise of the Black Panther Party in Oakland, California* (Chapel Hill: University of North Carolina Press, 2010), 143. For a similar dynamic, see Timothy J. Lombardo, *Blue-Collar Conservatism: Frank Rizzo's Philadelphia and Populist Politics* (Philadelphia: University of Pennsylvania Press, 2018), chap. 2.
16. For an account that identifies important continuities in the Chicago Police Department's anti-Black practices and policies from the start of the Great Migration through the 1970s, see Balto, *Occupied Territory*.

17. Agee, *The Streets of San Francisco*.
18. Michael W. Flamm, "'Law and Order' at Large: The New York Civilian Review Board Referendum of 1966 and the Crisis of Liberalism," *Historian* 64, no. 3–4 (2002): 643–65; Lombardo, *Blue-Collar Conservatism*.
19. Carl B. Stokes, *Promises of Power: A Political Autobiography* (New York: Simon and Schuster, 1973), 174.
20. Megan Marie Adams, "The Patrolmen's Revolt: Chicago Police and the Labor and Urban Crises of the Late Twentieth Century" (PhD diss. University of California, Berkeley, 2012), chaps. 1 and 3.
21. Adam Cohen and Elizabeth Taylor, *American Pharaoh: Mayor Richard J. Daley: His Battle for Chicago and the Nation* (Boston: Back Bay Books, 2001), 455.
22. Hervey A. Juris, "The Implications of Police Unionism," *Law and Society Review* 6 (1971): 240.
23. Statement reproduced in full in Renault Robinson, "Black Police: A Means of Social Change" (master's thesis, Roosevelt University, 1971), 15; Afro American Police League Papers Box 54, Folder 73, Chicago History Museum (hereafter, AAPL Papers).
24. Justin McCrary, "The Effect of Court-Ordered Hiring Quotas on the Composition and Quality of Police," *American Economic Review* 91 (2007): 324, fig. 1A; Peter C. Pihos, "Policing, Race, and Politics in Chicago" (PhD diss., University of Philadelphia, 2015), 39–47.
25. "Cops' Spirits Low Over Car Changes," *Chicago Defender*, July 22, 1974, 4. The League's victorious lawsuit against the department successfully proved these charges of discrimination. Pihos, "Policing, Race, and Politics in Chicago," chaps. 6–7.
26. Donald J. Black and Albert J. Reiss Jr., "Section I: Patterns of Behavior in Police and Citizen Transactions," in *Studies of Crime and Law Enforcement in Major Metropolitan Areas, vol. 2* (Ann Arbor: University of Michigan, 1967), 135, tbl. 25.
27. Renault A. Robinson, "Black Cop's Dilemma," *Chicago Defender*, September 26, 1970, 2. Cf. Ralph's claims that in a particular case Black officers' self-interest made it difficult to expose police torture. Laurence Ralph, *The Torture Letters: Reckoning with Police Violence* (Chicago: University of Chicago Press, 2020), 57–100.
28. Balto, *Occupied Territory*, 117–20.
29. Renault A. Robinson, "Black Cop's Dilemma," 2.
30. Balto, *Occupied Territory*, 160. For an example, see National Association for the Advancement of Colored People, "Press Release," June 15, 1965, 1, Roger Baldwin Foundation, American Civil Liberties Union Papers Series V, Box 79, Folder 9, Hanna Holborn Gray Special Collections Research Center, University of Chicago.
31. Andrew J. Diamond, *Mean Streets: Chicago Youths and the Everyday Struggle for Empowerment in the Multiracial City, 1908–1969* (Berkeley: University of

California Press, 2009), 254–55. Such actions were, to use Robin Kelley's language, a type of infrapolitics. Robin D. G. Kelley, *Race Rebels: Culture, Politics, and the Black Working Class*, repr. ed. (New York: Free Press, 1996), chap. 1.

32. Edwin C. Berry, "Testimony before the Citizens' Committee to Study Police Community Relations," Nov. 23, 1966, 6, Chicago Urban League Papers, Series II, Box 242, Folder 2442, University of Illinois Chicago Special Collections and University Archives.
33. Bell, *Black Power Movement*; Elizabeth Todd-Breland, *A Political Education: Black Politics and Education Reform in Chicago since the 1960s* (Chapel Hill: University of North Carolina Press, 2018).
34. Quoted in Robinson, "Black Police," 15–16.
35. Beryl Satter, "Cops, Gangs, and Revolutionaries in 1960s Chicago: What Black Police Can Tell Us about Power," *Journal of Urban History* 42, no. 6 (November 2016): 1111.
36. "Beware the 'Big Trick,'" *Chicago Defender*, July 17, 1971, 4.
37. Tera Agyepong, "In the Belly of the Beast: Black Policemen Combat Police Brutality in Chicago, 1968–1983," *Journal of African American History* 98, no. 2 (2013): 253–76; Satter, "Cops, Gangs, and Revolutionaries," 1110–34.
38. "Afro Cops Know System," *Chicago Defender*, April 9, 1970, 8.
39. "Black Police Unit Seeks to Ban Shotguns," *Chicago Tribune*, July 4, 1969, A1.
40. "Brutality Boosts Blacks' Fear," *Chicago Defender*, March 26, 1970, 20.
41. Jeffrey Hegelson, *Crucibles of Black Empowerment: Neighborhood Politics from the New Deal to Harold Washington* (Chicago: University of Chicago Press, 2014), 239.
42. Audre Lorde, *Sister Outsider: Essays and Speeches* (Berkeley: Crossing Press, 2007), 123.
43. "Who's to Blame for Cop Brutality," *Chicago Defender*, July 10, 1971, 3.
44. "Racist Power is Black's Downfall," *Chicago Defender*, April 16, 1970, 10.
45. Afro-American Police League of Chicago, "Initial Supporting Pledges Received as of 12 October 1968," n.d., AAPL Papers, Box 68.
46. "Together We Stand," *Grapevine*, March 1970, 2, AAPL Papers, Box 64, Folder 8. See also, The HistoryMakers Video Oral History Interview with Howard Saffold, June 5, 2002, Section A2002_091_001_004, https://www.thehistorymakers.org/biography/howard-saffold-39.
47. "Report of Proceedings Taken of a Speech Given by Renault Robinson," February 3, 1971, 27, AAPL Papers, Box 54.
48. *United States of America vs. City of Chicago*, 73 C 2080, "Cross Examination of George Sims" (May 15, 1975), Vol. 34-A, 5814, National Archives and Records Administration, Chicago Branch, Record Group 118-93-0019, Selected Case Files, 1972–1976.
49. Duke McNeil, "Press Statement," September 19, 1969, AAPL, 3-8.

50. Robert McClory, *The Man Who Beat Clout City* (Chicago: Swallow Press, 1977), 74.
51. Balto, *Occupied Territory*, 240–46.
52. Ransby, *Making All Black Lives Matter*; Charlene A. Carruthers, *Unapologetic: A Black, Queer, and Feminist Mandate for Radical Movements* (Boston: Beacon Press, 2018).
53. Sidney G. Tarrow, *Power in Movement: Social Movements and Contentious Politics*, 3rd ed. (Cambridge: Cambridge University Press, 2019), 98–105.
54. Pihos, "Challenging Copaganda."
55. Christopher J. Lebron, *The Making of Black Lives Matter: A Brief History of an Idea* (New York: Oxford University Press, 2017), chap. 1.
56. "Black Police Unit Seeks to Ban Shotguns," *Chicago Tribune*, July 4, 1969, A1.
57. "Afro Cops Begin Own Death Quiz," *Chicago Defender*, Dec. 10, 1969, 3.
58. Renault Robinson, "Racist Power Is Black's Downfall," *Chicago Defender*, April 16, 1970.
59. Renault Robinson, "The Black Watch," *Chicago Defender*, April 1, 1972, 26.
60. Thomas Powers, "Summerdale Recalled: Police Crisis Worst in 12 Years," *Chicago Tribune*, May 10, 1972, 1.
61. Renault Robinson, "Says Police Public Image a Failure," *Chicago Defender*, July 24, 1971, 4.
62. Renault Robinson, "U.S. Can Solve Crisis," *Chicago Defender*, December 12, 1970, 16.
63. Pihos, "'Police Brutality Exposed.'"
64. Ruth Wells, "Law Enforcement in the Minority Community," 1975, 4, Alliance to End Repression Papers, Box 17, Folder 39, Chicago History Museum (hereafter Alliance).
65. Benji Hart, "How #NoCopAcademy Shook the Machine," *Chicago Reader*, April 26, 2019, https://www.chicagoreader.com/chicago/how-nocopacademy-shook-the-machine/Content?oid=69862164.
66. Alliance to End Repression, "Draft Statement and Resolution on Hanrahan Election," June 13, 1972, Alliance, Box 3, Folder 25. On this campaign, see Pihos, "Policing, Race, and Politics in Chicago," 189–93.
67. Carruthers, *Unapologetic*, 129–30; Ransby, *Making All Black Lives Matter*, 143–44.
68. Jeffrey Haas, *The Assassination of Fred Hampton: How the FBI and the Chicago Police Murdered a Black Panther* (Chicago: Lawrence Hill Books, 2010).
69. Bud Schultz, "A Notable Reversal: Holding the Chicago Red Squad Accountable," in *The Price of Dissent: Testimonies to Political Repression in America* (Berkeley: University of California Press, 2001).
70. Robert McClory, *The Man Who Beat Clout City* (Chicago: Swallow Press, 1977).
71. McCrary, "Effect of Court-Ordered Hiring," 318–53.

72. Andrew S. Baer, *Beyond the Usual Beating: The Jon Burge Police Torture Scandal and Social Movement for Police Accountability in Chicago* (Chicago: University of Chicago Press, 2020).
73. My argument that court orders and fiscal retrenchment limited police power during the 1970s contrasts with the work of some recent scholars who see in the era a definitive turn toward repression. See, for example, Heather Ann Thompson, "Why Mass Incarceration Matters: Rethinking Crisis, Decline, and Transformation in Postwar American History," *Journal of American History* 97, no. 3 (December 2010), 703–34; and Elizabeth Hinton, *From the War on Poverty to the War on Crime: The Making of Mass Incarceration in America* (Cambridge: Harvard University Press, 2016).
74. Vernon Jarrett, "A Mayor Who's Learned to Listen," *Chicago Tribune*, Jun. 22, 1979, B3.
75. Lawrence Muhammad, "Supt. O'Grady Isn't the Only Cop Who's Worried," *Chicago Defender*, Mar. 3, 1979, 3.
76. The representation election was a complex affair with multiple entities vying to be the sole bargaining agent. The League criticized them all as racist. See Adams, "The Patrolmen's Revolt," 112–26.
77. David Axelrod and Robert Enstad, "Byrne Approves Teamsters Joining Race to Unionize Cops," *Chicago Tribune*, July 30, 1980, C1; Phillip J. O'Connor, "Black Cops Beginning 'No Union' Vote Drive," *Chicago Sun-Times*, September 21, 1985, AAPL Papers Box 58, Folder 430.
78. Howard Saffold and Sherman Williams to Officer, August 1980, AAPL Papers, Box 58, Folder 430.
79. Afro-American Police League to Members, November 1980, AAPL Papers Box 58, Folder 430.
80. Adams, "The Patrolmen's Revolt."
81. Matt L. Rodriguez to Constance M. Davis, Apr. 23, 1993, 5, in Illinois Advisory Committee to the United States Commission on Civil Rights, "Police Protection of the African American Community in Chicago," September 1983, 56.
82. Illinois Advisory Committee to the United States Commission on Civil Rights, 33–34.
83. Robin P. Charleston and Marvin Gittler, April 8, 1983, AAPL Papers, Box 58, Folder 430.
84. Joseph T. Mildice to Howard Saffold, April 12, 1976, AAPL Papers Box 61, folder "Dues Deduction Letters, AAPL, 1976."
85. Edgar Gosa, "The President Speaks," *The Grapevine*, March 1984, 1, AAPL Papers Box 64, Folder 8.
86. William Lee, "Black Rookie Cop Says He's Leaving Police Union over Criticism of Kneeling Officers," *Chicago Tribune*, July 3, 2020, https://www.chicagotribune.com/news/breaking/ct-black-officer-leaves-cop-union-20200703-dizisd6dwncoji4sxdexrdthjm-story.html.

87. Adams, "The Patrolmen's Revolt," 64–70, 123–24; Maya Dukmasova, "From Soldier to Worker," *Chicago Reader*, June 10, 2020, https://www.chicagoreader.com/chicago/cops-union-history-fraternal-order-of-police/Content?oid=80542709.
88. Fraternal Order of Police Chicago Lodge No. 7, "Form 990" (2018), https://projects.propublica.org/nonprofits/display_990/362467755/10_2019_prefixes_34-36%2F362467755_201812_990O_2019103016799457.
89. Yana Kunichoff and Sam Stecklow, "How Chicago's 'Fraternal Order of Propaganda' Shapes the Stories of Fatal Police Shootings," *Chicago Reader*, February 3, 2016, https://www.chicagoreader.com/chicago/fraternal-order-of-police-shootings-propaganda-pat-camden/Content?oid=21092544.
90. Dan Mihalopoulos, "Has There Been Enough Change a Year after the McDonald Video Release?," *Chicago Sun-Times*, November 23, 2016, https://chicago.suntimes.com/2016/11/23/18335047/has-there-been-enough-change-a-year-after-mcdonald-video-release.
91. "Election Plot Uncovered in Police Dept.," *Philadelphia Tribune*, April 8, 1983, 1.
92. Peter C. Pihos, "The Local War on Drugs," in *The War on Drugs: A History*, ed. David A. Farber (New York: New York University Press, 2021), 131–58.
93. Philip Wattley and Lynn Emmerman, "87 Top Cops Given New Posts," *Chicago Tribune*, December 3, 1983, 1. Rice described the people he transferred as "saboteurs." The HistoryMakers Video Oral History Interview with Fred Rice, Jr., June 27, 2002, Section A1993_005_001_004, https://www.thehistorymakers.org/biography/fred-rice-jr.
94. Max Felker-Kantor, *Policing Los Angeles: Race, Resistance, and the Rise of the LAPD* (Chapel Hill: University of North Carolina Press, 2018).
95. Taylor, *From #BlackLivesMatter to Black Liberation* (Chicago: Haymarket Books, 2016), chap. 4; James Forman Jr., *Locking Up Our Own*, chaps. 4–6.
96. On employment, see Joel Rast, *Remaking Chicago: The Political Origins of Urban Industrial Change* (Dekalb, IL: Northern Illinois University Press, 1999), 88, tbl.8; Gregory D. Squires et al., *Chicago: Race, Class, and the Response to Urban Decline* (Philadelphia, PA: Temple University Press, n.d.), 29–37. On concentrated poverty, see William Julius Wilson, *The Truly Disadvantaged: The Inner City, the Underclass, and Public Policy* (Chicago: University of Chicago Press, 1987), 49–56.
97. Lisa L. Miller, "What's Violence Got to Do with It? Inequality, Punishment, and State Failure in US Politics," *Punishment and Society* 17, no. 2 (2015): 184–210.
98. Pihos, "The Local War on Drugs."
99. Art Petacque, "Martin Explains Drug War," *Chicago Sun-Times*, March 9, 1988.
100. Carolyn R. Block and Antigone Christakos, "Chicago Homicide from the Sixties to the Nineties: Major Trends in Lethal Violence," in *Trends, Risks,*

and *Interventions in Lethal Violence: Proceedings of the Third Annual Spring Symposium of the Homicide Research Working Group*, ed. Carolyn R. Block and Richard Block, 1995, 17–50; David Farber, *Crack: Rock Cocaine, Street Capitalism, and the Decade of Greed* (New York: Cambridge University Press, 2019).

101. Jeremy Gorner, "New Police Union President John Catanzara Rode a Wave of Controversy to Popularity with Fellow Officers," *Chicago Tribune*, May 13, 2020, https://www.chicagotribune.com/news/criminal-justice/ct-fop-president-catanzara-profile-20200513-x4e37d4gijadbjacvc2x55shau-story.html.

CHAPTER 4

"We May Have to Defend Ourselves"

Black Women and Campaigns against Police Sexual Violence during the Civil Rights and Black Lives Matter Eras

Althea Legal-Miller

The Civil Rights Movement (CRM) of the 1960s and contemporary organizing under the umbrella of Black Lives Matter (BLM) both evolved out of the need to continue the Black liberation struggle. Nationwide protests and policy reform efforts to end widespread police abuse and violence that pervade Black communities constitute core aspects of these social movements. Indeed, as one of the longest-standing sites of the Black Freedom Struggle in American history, abuse of power and violence in everyday policing practices has often come to exemplify the magnitude of state-sponsored indifference to the rights and lives of Black people.

Exceptional instances of police violence often spark mass protests and rebellions, with the victimization of Black men and boys frequently galvanizing national attention and driving the discourse. Yet Black women have always been at the forefront of efforts to expand the public conversation on police violence, making deliberate interventions to expose police brutality as part of a system of racialized gender oppression. As leaders in anti-police brutality activism, in both the CRM and BLM Movement, Black women have used their positions at the intersection of race, gender, and class oppression, among other factors, to highlight the specific vulnerabilities of Black women and girls to state violence. Within social movements committed to the elimination of deep and persistent patterns of racism, Black women have ensured and continue to ensure that police violence against Black women and girls remains legible to activists, policy makers, and the media. In short, Black women's organizing has broadened the discourse on the scope of police brutality to include the largely uncharted territory of systemic sexual violence.

Through two case studies, this chapter explores the extent, the determination, and the creativity of Black women's activism to expose and resist sexual violence by police. It traces a fifty-year period, juxtaposing two campaigns led by Black women against police sexual violence, to provide a pathway for analyzing continuity and change during the CRM and BLM eras. The first case examines the police accountability efforts of Dorothy Height, president of the National Council of Negro Women (NCNW), who between 1963 and 1964 coordinated efforts to expose and mobilize a national response to sexual violence by law enforcement officers against women and girls participating in Civil Rights protests. The second study surveys the activism of Grace Franklin and Candace Liger, two Oklahoma City-based artists who combined art and social action to launch an advocacy and accountability campaign following the 2014 arrest of Oklahoma City police officer Daniel Holtzclaw for multiple sexual assaults against thirteen Black women. A chronological overview of these campaigns, fifty years apart, demonstrates Black women's extensive mobilization to address sexist and racist systems of policing, often in local contexts but also in national settings. The chapter explores how these campaigns utilized media, the civil rights establishment, and coalition building with liberal white women's organizations, revealing both the possibilities and limitations of these approaches. It concludes that Black women's organizing and advocacy for victim-survivors of police sexual violence is rooted in their own intersectional experiences, which holds the capacity to deepen understandings of police brutality along the axes of gender, race, and class.[1]

Policing and the Civil Rights Movement

The histories of chattel slavery that subjected Black women to rape, forced pregnancies, and other gender-specific violations, which enslavers, "slave" patrollers, and other white colonialists legitimatized through stereotypes and pseudo-scientific justifications, unleashed enduring myths about Black women's deficient sexual standards, licentious behavior, and animal-like capacity for sex.[2] In the century following legal emancipation, state-sponsored police forces continued to rely on the historical precedent of using sexual violence to destabilize Black activism, Black advancement, and Black women. For instance, police officers were among the white vigilantes who sexually assaulted and raped Black freedwomen during post–Civil War riots and attacks. In resistance, Black women invoked their rights to bodily autonomy and integrity under post-emancipation authority, reporting sexual violators to federal officials and testifying in courts and at congressional hearings.[3] Historian Adriane Lentz-Smith explains that, as the statutory strands of white supremacy were woven into a codified political economy at the turn of the twentieth century, Black women remained "potent" targets of sexualized forms of violence that served to fortify Jim Crow.[4]

Under the enforcement of Jim Crow segregation, the daily occurrence of interracial sexualized violence against Black women and girls included white police officers as perpetrators of street harassment, lewd and indecent behavior, solicitation of sex, kidnapping, and rape.[5] For examples, in July 1942, three uniformed white male police officers in Little Rock, Arkansas, told teenager Rosa Lee Cherry to either enter their police car or go to jail. They drove her to an uninhabited railroad embankment where they sexually molested her. In October 1946, two white male police officers in Richmond, Virginia, coerced Nannie Strayhorn into accepting a ride back to her house. Instead of taking her home, however, the officers took her to a remote area outside of town where they raped her multiple times at gunpoint.⁶ In 1949, two uniformed white male police officers in Montgomery, Alabama, forced Gertrude Perkins into the backseat of their patrol car and drove her to a desolate area, dragged her behind a building, and similarly raped her multiple times at gunpoint.⁷ In September 1961, two uniformed white male police officers in Birmingham, Alabama, pulled over Creola Rivers in her car and demanded to see her driver's license, which she could not produce. The officers took her to the backseat of their patrol car, instructed her to lie down on the floor, and drove her to a secluded wooded area where one of the officers raped her while the other watched, gun in hand. When a Black man inadvertently advanced toward the officers, they quickly left with Rivers, driving her to another location where the second officer raped her. She later testified that during the rape, she "thought of another Negro woman who was found dead one night by the railroad tracks and . . . knew the same thing could happen to [her]."⁸ In January 1962, two white male police officers in Clarksdale, Mississippi, arrested and detained teenager Bessie Turner for suspected theft. The officers made Turner lie face down on the concrete floor of an interrogation room, with one of them ordering her to pull her dress up and panties down before proceeding to whip her with his belt across her back and buttocks. Next, they instructed her to "turn over and open up your legs and let me see how you look down there," and then lashed her genitalia.⁹ In most of these cases, the police officers avoided any sanction, and none were convicted. So many more attacks were never reported due to the victim-survivor's obvious fear of retribution. In the absence of justice, these known cases remind us that Black women and girls courageously undertook the risks associated with disclosing police sexual violence and allowed their testimonies to be integrated into a wider program of political action in the hopes that doing so would protect Black communities.

The testimonies of sexually violated Black women and girls provided the brutal raw material that Black community organizers used to push for Black protection and white prosecution. In 1944, for example, the Montgomery branch of the National Association for the

Advancement of Colored People (NAACP) and their field investigator Rosa Parks formed the Committee for Equal Justice in response to the abduction and gang rape of a Black woman, Recy Taylor, by white men in Abbeville, Alabama. When the local sheriff resisted NAACP calls to prosecute Taylor's assailants, the Committee raised funds for legal assistance and utilized Parks's fieldwork and experience with interracial rape cases to launch a press and letter-writing campaign pressuring Alabama governor Chauncey Sparks to order a criminal investigation. Consequently, a special grand jury took up Taylor's case, although they ultimately did not indict the men. Still, local Committee for Equal Justice chapters and partner organizations emerged nationwide to expose the frequency and ubiquity of sexual violence, providing organizational insights and movement infrastructures that campaigns in the 1960s would leverage in their fight against law enforcement officers who sexually harassed and brutalized civil rights workers.[10]

The CRM amplified demands for police accountability, but as Black resistance intensified, so too did police violence against Black women, who made up the majority of local activists organizing behind the scenes and working on the front lines.[11] As the "backbone" of the CRM, direct action protests brought police into greater contact with women and girls engaged in mass public assemblies and confrontational protests, which marked them for persistent and conspicuous state-sponsored and -condoned violence.[12] Indeed, as historian Charles Payne reminds us, Black women's civil rights work generated some of the "most violent" reprisals, as breaking the movement's back ostensibly meant breaking women through public spectacles of force, as well as clandestine sexual brutalities.[13]

The camera and its ability to capture police violence became an important tool of the CRM. For instance, in 1963, images depicting law enforcement's use of high-powered fire hoses and snarling dogs on nonviolent, often young, protesters in Birmingham, Alabama, provided the nation and the world irrefutable evidence of Jim Crow's brutality. Martin Luther King Jr. believed that visual media held the potential to "imprison" police violence in a "luminous glare" that rendered it "impotent" when denied "stealth" and the ability to "remain unobserved."[14] However, as one of the longstanding "preferred weapons" of political subjugation, sexual violence could not be corroborated in ways that photographs and broadcast media facilitated.[15] Therefore, as thousands of Black women and girls participated in direct-action protests that resulted in actual imprisonment, the reach of the camera's vigilant eye did not extend into semi-occluded carceral spaces. Indeed, in stealth and without visual challenge, law enforcers used sexual terror to discipline and punish women and girls through a multitude of abuses, including sexual intimidation and threats, forced groping and fondling, internal examinations and strip searches, forced nudity, sexual assaults, and rape.

The nonviolence training used extensively during the CRM did not explicitly include preparation against sexual violence. A set of "dos" and "don'ts" compiled by John Lewis during the Nashville Student Movement in 1960 to facilitate nonviolent protest included, "Do be friendly and courteous at all times," "Do remember the nonviolent teachings of Jesus Christ, Mohandas Gandhi, and Martin Luther King," and "Don't strike back or curse if abused."[16] When King, quoting Gandhi, explained that Black protesters were as ready to go to jail for freedom as is the "bridegroom [who] enters the bedchamber," the unfortunate analogy did not consider the state agents who entered the jail cells of Black women and girls.[17] Indeed, the high-minded oratory of the sort offered by Gandhi and King failed to address the low-down indignities regularly visited upon women and girls and exposed gendered oversights in the preparation of activists for direct-action protests.

Historian Danielle McGuire has noted that stories of police sexual violence against civil rights workers "rarely reached a mass audience," but reports of sexual abuse on the front lines of the freedom struggle circulated within and among Black communities and in the Black press.[18] Black women and girls imprisoned for their CRM activities shared harrowing experiences of sexual assault, with one such testimony reporting that police placed Black women and girls in the custody of "drunken trustees," who took them to the cells of male prisoners, where they were "mistreated and molested."[19] Other testimonies described cell breaches where police officers allowed predatory white men into cell blocks to "walk around and stare" at incarcerated Black women and girls, which epitomized the continued presumption of unfettered sexual access to Black women's bodies.[20] One group of jailed female activists, organized by Marion King, the wife of the Albany Movement's vice president, Slater King, resisted the voyeurism and sexual threat that white men posed by preparing women and girls to arm themselves with homespun ammunition—hardened, stale cornbread saved from their evening meal. "We may have to defend ourselves tonight," Marion King warned.[21] Alongside women's asserted right to use violence in self-defense (demonstrating how nonviolent direct action and armed self-defense were not mutually exclusive), the survival of sexual assault and rape also exemplified resistance.[22]

Empowered by decades of organizing strategies that challenged racial terrorism in southern jurisdictions, Black women and girls used their bold denunciations of sexual violence by police to expose a racist and patriarchal Jim Crow culture thoroughly reliant on Black women's sexual domination. Police brutality had long been endemic in Black communities, but as Black women's and girls' activism dramatically increased the frequency and intensity of police interactions, their experiences of intersectional oppressions, as well as a political tradition of anti-violence organizing, ensured their place at the forefront of framing the range and scope of anti-Black police brutality. Just as Rosa Parks and many more Black women conducted on-the-ground investigations into reports of interracial sexual violence, Dorothy Height, president of the National Council of Negro Women, would travel to the South from her base in Washington, DC, and use her political and public platform to investigate charges of sexual violence against women and girls on the frontlines of the Black Freedom Struggle.

The Height Campaign, 1963–1964

Mary McLeod Bethune founded the NCNW in 1935 to centralize Black women's groups—including sororities and clubwomen—and leverage their combined power to push federal institutions to act on behalf of race and gender equality. For Bethune, the representation of Black women "at the highest levels of government" served a central mission of enhancing their collective professional and political power.[23] When Dorothy Height became the president of NCNW in 1957, she continued this work but also steered the Council toward more direct involvement in the burgeoning CRM by the early 1960s.[24] Compelled to coordinate the public testimonies of movement women and girls who bravely disclosed experiences of retaliatory sexual assaults by law enforcement, Height initiated a pioneering institutional effort to end civil rights-related sexual violence as a weapon of police repression.

For Height and her NCNW civil rights team, preserving and protecting the integrity of women's activism during a period of heightened Black insurgency and vicious police backlash required nothing less than national organizing. First, Height built a coalition with twenty-four presidents of women's groups to investigate the treatment of female protesters by police and guards in southern jails. The alliance produced a comprehensive report that documented firsthand accounts of rape, sexual assault, body cavity searches, sexual humiliation, and forced nudity in front of male prisoners and officers.[25] Next, Height and key leaders from women's organizations, including Jeanne Noble, a professor at New York University and president of Delta Sigma Theta, set about organizing press conferences and media appearances to raise public awareness about state repression through sexual violence.

In June 1963, Height and Noble appeared on the popular New York radio station WNEW to share the firsthand testimonies they had gathered on the sexually abusive nature of civil rights policing. Height revealed to the public that police and prison guards had committed rape and other "indignities" to "discourage" women and girls from "participating in social protest movements."[26] Height and Noble spoke candidly about multiple forms of police sexual abuse, although simultaneously aware that discussions involving Black protest required careful orchestration to appeal to mainstream white audiences. In hopes of insulating Black women and girls from historically persistent charges of Black promiscuity that are, to use activist and scholar Angela Y. Davis's apt words, "conjured up" when violence and terror against Black women require "a convincing explanation," Height and Noble vividly set the scene of a battle between respectable women and girls "peaceably demonstrating" and sexually barbarous law enforcement officers.[27] Narratives of routinized sexual humiliation by police and prison guards, such as the denial of menstrual products that forced incarcerated activists to improvise with cloths and rags, and on occasion, share used sanitary napkins, illustrated the dramatic contrast between Black virtue and white vulgarity.[28] Recognizing the potency of having "perfectly coiffured, immaculately dressed, quietly dignified, and stoically nonviolent" women and girls participating in protests, Height and Noble harnessed the politics of respectability to discredit claims by police that female demonstrators in police custody had to be given "vaginal" searches to prevent the "smuggling [of] dope into the penitentiary."[29] First and foremost, they identified "unsanitary and unmedical" internal exams as punitive and abusive, but they also tactically emphasized that criminal activity had not led to the arrests of women and girls. Rather, those incarcerated were "housewives and their daughters, products of stable homes, [and] good churchwomen" in pursuit of moral goals. Within the context of respectability politics, Height wielded these middle-class signifiers to nullify the legitimacy of body cavity searches against this particular population.[30] Further, the radio broadcast afforded Height and Noble the strategic opportunity to foreground gender as the basis for mobilizing women across racial lines and eliciting broad-based liberal support. "One thing we could do as women," Height declared, "[is] speak out and work toward the elimination of these horrible atrocities that seemed to be vented against women and girls." Noble added, "As a woman I can think of no greater indignity than rape . . . or sexual exposure." In defiant resistance, Noble concluded that retaliatory sexual violence against CRM participants is "not going to work."[31]

Almost one month prior to Height's and Noble's WNEW radio broadcast, images of Black children attacked by police officers, dogs, and fire hoses in Birmingham had elicited the sympathies of the white press, public, and political elites, including President John F. Kennedy. Despite Height's sharp distinction between women and girls imprisoned for civil rights activity versus criminal activity, the white public appeared hostile and suspicious of allegations of sexual violence by law enforcement. Indeed, white listeners flooded WNEW with abusive messages, threats of violence, and criticisms of inappropriate content. In addition, the white press almost universally deemed the sexual abuse claims of civil rights activists as unnewsworthy and speculative, replicating a protracted history since enslavement of white southerners' common refusal to recognize the rape of Black women.[32]

As advocates for racial justice, the Black press in the 1960s, as in previous generations, shared a stake in promoting civil rights and used their editorial voices to challenge dominant white-controlled journalism. Height described white journalists' silence on perceived litigious issues as a "complete blackout," but she also maintained that women and girls were simply not believed.[33] Accordingly, a media-savvy Height looked to the Black press and a rising celebrity-focused journalism to raise public awareness about state-sponsored sexual violence. As Height explained, if a Black star like Lena Horne could be "linked," no matter how tangentially, to testimonies given by victim-survivors of law enforcement sexual violence, then the Black press might be more inclined to print them. The strategy worked, and articles bolstered by headlines such as "[Dick] Gregory Hits Jail Abuses" and "Lena Horne Going to Jackson, Miss." appeared in publications like the *Crusader* and the *New York Amsterdam News* to inform Black communities how police and custodial officers abused demonstrators.[34] Firsthand accounts from women and girls "fondled and manhandled" and subjected to routine narrative violence revealed the predatory ecology of jails, with one article printing quotes from teenage girls reporting the things said to them by police officers: "You sure have pretty breasts, you B—-h! Nobody has a prettier can than n*gger women. You sure have some pretty legs, you n*gger whore.... I wish I could get you alone for an hour.... You n*gger whores, what are you out there parading for?"[35] Crucially, in the absence of photographic evidence, the Black press used graphic quotes (including redacted obscenities) to embody a gritty realism intended to convey accuracy and proof. As a performance of power, sexual violation enacted on gendered bodies both reinforced and derived potency from white supremacy as a patriarchal system. For Height, an effective Civil Rights response had to include and recognize gender.

As the only woman selected to serve on the elite "Big Six" committee of Civil Rights leaders, Height unequivocally framed the protection of women and girls as a Civil Rights objective on par with voting rights and the desegregation of public facilities.[36] When male Civil Rights organizers sidelined Height in their refusal to appoint a woman to speak at the 1963 March on Washington, she learned a crucial lesson: "If we did not demand our rights," Height explained, "we were not going to get them."[37] In the aftermath of the March on Washington decision, Height recalled that she adopted a "much more aggressive" stance on women's advocacy and the navigation of, as she put it, "sexism" in male civil rights leadership.[38]

In the month following the March on Washington, Height received a request from the Student Nonviolent Coordinating Committee (SNCC) to join grassroots efforts to investigate charges of law enforcement abuses against three hundred children jailed for participating in Civil Rights demonstrations in Dallas County, Alabama. Height and her civil rights team soon arrived in Selma to launch their investigation, joining locals at a mass meeting attended by "a great many women and very few men," including among them dozens of Black girls incarcerated only weeks earlier.[39] At the close of the mass meeting, girls of twelve to sixteen years old remained behind to talk with Height about experiences "they didn't or couldn't say to men."[40] For almost an hour, girls shared firsthand accounts of jailhouse sexualized violence, revealing that guards constantly threatened them with sexual assault.[41] One report relayed the threats of a warden to let male prisoners into their cells "if they didn't behave," thereby forcing girls to "huddle together at night, taking turns staying awake to keep watch in case the guards came in to harass them."[42] Such mass meeting testimonies bolstered Height's already comprehensive documentation on police sexual violence and the establishment of a climate conducive to impunity. In the tradition of movement activism, Height sought to leverage the evidence she had compiled and disseminated to demand federal intervention.

At Height's behest, Hyman H. Bookbinder, former special assistant to the secretary of commerce, alerted Lee Calvin White, assistant special counsel to the president, to her concerns about civil rights–related police brutality and her disappointment with the Kennedy administration's apathy toward the sexual violence "visited upon civil rights prisoners, especially women."[43] Bookbinder cautiously suggested that President Kennedy might "appoint a special committee of inquiry," but Burke Marshall, assistant United States attorney general for the civil rights division, stepped in to reject the idea out of hand, claiming that the allegations were "too vague . . . [for] a special committee," preferring instead to arrange a meeting with law enforcement officers.[44] As mass CRM protests continued to spread around the country, meeting escalating acts of violent resistance from white supremacists, President Kennedy shifted his gradualist, "quiet the flames" approach—a viewpoint he had initially appointed Marshall to facilitate—to a more proactive role that included open criticism of "repressive police action."[45] Yet the Department of Justice (DOJ) did not deem Height's petition for the protection of women, as they put it, "serious" enough to warrant federal intervention, which compelled her to rethink the enormity of the work ahead and the scale of the response necessary.[46]

In the wake of the dead-end she had met at the federal level, Height undertook the work of building broader coalitions with liberal, majority-white women's organizations. In March 1964, Height and NCNW arranged an interracial and interfaith Atlanta-based conference with the Young Women's Christian Association (YWCA), the National Council of Catholic Women (NCCW), the National Council of Jewish Women (NCJW), and Church Women United (CWU), with the remit to produce a civil rights "charter" to protect "women and girls in an era of social change."[47] The development of a charter attempted to consolidate the plethora of national faith-based women's associations, which Height brought together under a newly formed umbrella entity named the Women's Inter-Organizational Committee (WIC). The establishment of WIC did not afford Height and other

Black women the level of autonomy that separate Black women's organizations provided, but as a broad multiracial and multifaith coalition, it held potential as a powerful moral and social force for human rights and equality. During the conference's opening session, Height explicitly announced the urgency of the work that lay ahead. She not only positioned the safety of women and girls involved in Civil Rights work as a *right* in and of itself, but she also argued for its prioritization alongside the right to vote and the integration of public accommodations.[48] Through gendered human rights appeals, Height attempted to persuade the seventy-five mostly white and middle-class women in attendance that a "womanly approach would prove more effective . . . than that which might be evoked from men."[49] By positioning gender as WIC's central organizing principle, Height used the familiar discourse of female reformers and clubwomen as a means of securing delegates' commitment.

However, the WIC conference did not meet Height's radical expectations. While women and male representatives communicated both shock and outrage at the sexual brutality of law enforcement, Height and NCNW did not move the coalition much beyond a commitment of solidarity and support for local organizing. Invited by the WIC to share his organizational expertise, attorney Norman Amaker of the NAACP demurred, "the most someone outside can really do is boost morale and make [jailed protesters] feel that they are not alone—this can be done most effectively by mobilizing the women of the community."[50] He classified jail-based sexualized violence as a local issue solely under the purview of local women, even though Civil Rights activists campaigned nationally against police brutality in general. Donald L. Hollowell, a prominent Atlanta civil rights attorney, agreed: "It [would] be much more effective for a local official to be faced by a local group of women."[51] Reverend John B. Morris, the executive director of the Episcopal Society for Cultural and Racial Unity, called for white women to position themselves "near the front lines" of civil rights by adopting a "subtle, behind-the-scenes" approach. Amid the male voices advocating for the tempering of Height's and other Black women's organizing vision, representatives from majority-white women's organizations continued to pledge their support for bringing women together, but they had "no plans for inter-racial meetings" or institutional partnerships.[52] Instead, "privately-organized" interracial teams of Northern women would be deployed to the South to "keep watchful eyes and hearts" with the aim to "encourage humane police treatment."[53] In the absence of sufficient interest from either the Civil Rights establishment or majority-white women's groups to protect Black women and girls from sexual violence perpetrated by police, an "educational and cultural enrichment" program replaced Height's original goal to formulate a robust anti sexual violence charter and create infrastructure capable of advancing prevention efforts.[54]

Using her national prominence, Height importantly articulated women's investment in their own roles as protectors but also steered critical debates about who bore responsibility for safeguarding Black women and activist communities. Indeed, the civil rights and women's organizations that Height brought together held the requisite platforms to raise police sexual violence as a potential national priority. However, with only tepid commitments from key stakeholders, securing the integral workings of the local and the national to deliver what Black women had defined as a pivotal objective of the freedom struggle proved insurmountable. Despite the shortcomings, however, Height's campaign broadened the discourse on civil rights and expanded the Movement's conception of freedom by forcing a spotlight on police sexual violence, thereby adding to the blueprint of freedom struggles which future generations of Black women activists would utilize and expand.

Policing in the Era of Black Lives Matter

Over half a century since the mass CRM, BLM demands that American society reconsider how it values Black lives in an era where racially gendered and sexualized myths about Black women persist, and police sexual violence remains foremost among gender-specific forms of police brutality.[55] To date, there are no official federal statistics documenting the number of rapes and sexual assaults committed by police officers.⁵⁶ However, studies on police sexual misconduct based on samples garnered from media coverage, criminal convictions, and civil cases, reveal that sexual violence against women by law enforcement officers persists in the twenty-first century. For example, according to the Cato Institute, national data from public complaints filed against police officers from 2009 to 2010 identified police sexual violence as the second most common complaint, behind excessive force. The Cato Institute's research uncovered that of the 618 police officers with sexual misconduct complaints against them, 354 involved rape, sexual assault, and sexual battery.⁵⁷ Similarly, research from Bowling Green State University revealed that police departments across the United States charged law enforcement officers with forcible fondling 636 times, and with forcible rape 405 times, between the years 2005 and 2013.⁵⁸ In 2015, the Associated Press published the results of their year-long investigation on police decertification for serious sexual misconduct. Using records obtained from forty-one states over a period of six years, the AP found that approximately one thousand police officers had their licenses or certificates revoked for a range of sexual violations and crimes, with over half decertified for sexual assault, rape, sodomy, sexual extortion, and sexually gratuitous body searches.⁵⁹ Research studies based on complaints and media reports reveal that male officers perpetrate 99.1 percent of investigated cases of police sexual violence, and half are committed while those officers are on duty.⁶⁰

With only one-third of rapes and sexual assaults reported in general, the rate of reporting for sexual crimes perpetrated by law enforcement is arguably much lower.⁶¹ Fear of retaliation remains a key barrier to reporting crimes committed by the police to the police, but at the same time, many law enforcement agents do not accept and investigate accusations from victims even when they do come forward.⁶² A 2007 United Nations committee report identified women of color in the United States as specific targets for law enforcement sexual violence, in part because of racial biases against believing Black women.⁶³ In sum, racial discrimination in policing dramatically heightens Black women's and girls' vulnerability to police sexual violence. Still.

Black Lives Matter, as a social/political movement, has increased national and international scrutiny of police brutality, but some have critiqued the movement's unilateral focus on police killings to the exclusion of police sexual violence.[64] Black women remain unseen all too often in the national conversation about police brutality, even as police routinely rape and assault them.[65] As community organizer and writer Ahmad Greene-Hayes highlights, "police officers can be killers, but they can also be rapists."[66] In recent years, amid BLM protests, Black women activists have demanded attention to and action against police sexual violence.

The OKC Artists for Justice Campaign, 2014–2015

Between December 2013 and June 2014, Daniel Holtzclaw, a white-passing/presenting Oklahoma City police officer, raped and sexually brutalized at least thirteen Black women, with investigating officers admitting the possibility of more victims.[67] Holtzclaw's sexual violence came to light during BLM protests over the police killings of Michael Brown and Eric Garner in 2014, which prompted increased national scrutiny on anti-Black police violence. Yet Holtzclaw's indictment on thirty-six felony counts including rape, sexual battery, indecent exposure, stalking, and forcible oral sodomy against Black women initially attracted little media attention or support from anti-violence groups. Only a few grassroots organizers, Twitter users, and bloggers—predominately Black women—highlighted the Holtzclaw case as a compelling example of public indifference to Black women as victims of police violence.[68] The case also epitomized Black women's position at the intersection of race, gender, and class oppression, as Holtzclaw did not target all the Black women he encountered but selected those with prior or recent criminal-system involvement, outstanding traffic tickets, and open warrants. In particular, Holtzclaw sought to victimize women marginalized by criminal histories of sex work and controlled-substance use, intentionally targeting women already deemed less credible in society.[69] The fact that Black women's intersectionality played a role in his predatory behavior was further underscored by the fact that he targeted Black women within Oklahoma City's predominantly Black and high-poverty northeast neighborhoods.

In Oklahoma, a state that ranks among the highest for female incarceration but the lowest for women's mental health and economic security, Black women are especially vulnerable to surveillance and punishment by police as enforcers of white supremacy.[70] Not unlike the racially sexualized verbal abuse from police officers to Black women and girls incarcerated for Civil Rights protests in the 1960s, Holtzclaw's victim-survivors also endured narrative violence rooted in white heteropatriarchal power. Indeed, Shandegreon Hill, whom Holtzclaw first assaulted while she was handcuffed to a hospital bed, testified that he questioned her about "the type of baby daddies" she had and remarked, "Ha-ha, you've never sucked a white dick before."[71] Yet another woman testified that Holtzclaw commented, "Damn, you got a big ass" while masturbating in front of her.[72] As scholar Evette Dionne Brown emphasizes, Black women are "defined and labelled by our body parts" as a means of reinforcing racialized patriarchy.[73] Certainly, Holtzclaw's racialized references to Black women's sexual histories and bodies during the course of his assaults constituted an effort to shame and silence them. Also, the multiple marginalities of race, gender, class, and criminalization embodied by these Black women empowered Holtzclaw to systematically engage in sexual torture against women he knew he could all too easily discredit. Indeed, almost none of the victim-survivors of Holtzclaw's sexual violence reported him until detectives from Oklahoma City's sexual-assault unit—their investigation aided by Holtzclaw's patrol-car GPS system—approached them. As legal scholar Jasmine (Philips) Sankofa argues, the considerable societal barriers associated with reporting sexual assault are exacerbated when state agents are the perpetrators.[74] Holtzclaw's teenaged rape victim-survivor identified her quandary clearly when she said, "What's the good of telling the police? What kind of police do you call on the police?"[75] She understood, unambiguously, the power of the Blue Code of Silence.

On October 1, 2014, Grace Franklin and Candace Liger, two Oklahoma City-based artists and Black women, responded to the lack of public knowledge about the Holtzclaw case by founding OKC Artists for Justice—an organization that mobilized local artists to use their art as awareness-building tools to raise the profile of the Holtzclaw case and advocate for the victim-survivors. Through artistic expressions, founding members, mostly comprising Black women artists, used performance and visual art, such as poetry, dance, painting, and writing, to broaden the conversation around police brutality to include sexual violence perpetrated by law enforcement. For Franklin, activism functioned as an extension of her creativity, so as a group, OKC Artists for Justice developed a communal artistic language demanding that "socially, economically, spiritually, artistically, individually, and collectively, black women matter."[76] Ebony Iman Dallas, artist and OKC Artists for Justice board member, used painting to counter dominant messaging that Black women's "lives are not worth fighting or prosecuting for."[77] Franklin and Liger understood how the simultaneity of Black women's historical devaluation and experiences of policing uniquely informed by race, gender, and class held the potential to broaden the vision of BLM struggles. Evocative of Height's leadership rooted in the belief that, for Black women, the intersection of multiple oppressions proved advantageous in devising strategies to protect and empower marginalized women (and other oppressed people), Franklin declared: "We are black women. It could have been us. We are both artists who speak about the power of women and the need for each woman to protect the other. We live what we write about. We had to speak up. We have to be a catalyst for change."[78] Furthermore, as Black women, the one thing they could do, echoing Dorothy Height's efforts fifty years earlier, was to generate visibility and stand with the victim-survivors to demand police accountability.

The campaigns of Height and OKC Artists for Justice are emblematic of Black women's leadership in challenging gendered state violence and demanding protection for Black women and girls. Yet both are also reflective of their times. For Height, constraints of respectability politics drew sharp distinctions between a spectrum of women and girls imprisoned for civil rights activity on one end, and those serving time for "criminal" activity on the other. Height and other

Black Civil Rights leaders sought to strategically destabilize stereotypes that fostered and justified anti-Black violence by cultivating social performances of civil rights protesters that aligned with predefined norms of civility.[79] In contrast, fifty years later, the politics of respectability did not impose the same restraints. In fact, the OKC Artists for Justice campaign grew out of a specific opposition to respectability politics that seemed to compel the unapologetic advocacy of Black women deemed by dominant culture to exist outside the norms of feminine propriety and respectability. Holtzclaw's victim-survivors were the women that, as Liger explained, represented "the [under]belly of society . . . that nobody would care about," which seemed to disqualify them as worthy symbols of police injustice.[80] As theorists Edward S. Herman and Noam Chomsky argue regarding victims' dichotomous representation in media, "worthy victims" will be humanized through rich "detail and context" that generates interest and sympathy, while the minimal humanization of "unworthy victims" provokes little emotional resonance.[81] As a case in point, Oklahoma City police detectives launched their investigation into Holtzclaw only hours after, to use the prosecution's telling words, "he messed up" by sexually assaulting Jannie Ligons, a fifty-seven-year-old daycare manager and grandmother with no criminal record or outstanding warrants.[82]

Holtzclaw's defense strategy relied on discrediting most of his accusers by focusing on their past criminal histories, drug use, and delays in reporting their assaults to the police. Two of Holtzclaw's victim-survivors testified while in pretrial custody (one of them had been arrested for a drug relapse in violation of a court-ordered rehabilitation program) and appeared for the duration of their court appearance in orange jumpsuits, shackled in leg and handcuffs.[83] Franklin later recalled that the juxtaposition of having victim-survivors in prison garb with Holtzclaw in his "wonderfully tailored suit" unquestionably impacted jurors' perceptions of credibility.[84]

Through OKC Artists for Justice's insistence that communities organize around the Holtzclaw survivors with indignation and fervor, details and context about the case circulated via the group's Twitter account, @OKCARTISTS4JUSTICE, and Facebook page. They also organized community meetings, encouraged the wearing of teal (the awareness color for sexual violence), organized exhibitions and performances, and submitted artistic outputs for publication, such as Liger's poem on the Holtzclaw case entitled "For Pseudo-Gardeners."[85] Despite their efforts, the Holtzclaw trial began with a virtually empty courtroom. Nevertheless, with limited support during the first week, Franklin and Liger live-tweeted the proceedings from inside the courtroom, scheduled volunteers in morning and afternoon shifts to occupy the public gallery, and organized protesters outside the courthouse with signs that read "Black Women Matter" and "Stop Police Terror in Our Community."[86]

OKC Artists for Justice attempted, as Height had done, to mobilize majority-white women's organizations to support their campaign, but as they had fifty years earlier, Franklin and Liger also faced coalition conflicts. Indeed, anti-rape and women's organizations—including the local YMCA—declined their requests for support in order to preserve mutually beneficial partnerships with law enforcement.[87] Franklin and Liger also attempted to tap into the organizational power of the Black Church but, as Pastor Jesse Jackson Jr. of the East 6th Street Christian Church in Oklahoma City admitted, supporters were slow to rally around women who "aren't little old church ladies," implying that they did not meet the standard of *worthy* victim.[88]

Amid OKC Artists for Justice's tireless local efforts, the pre-trial selection of an all-white jury suddenly launched the Holtzclaw trial into the national spotlight. With the case now reframed as a traditional civil rights issue (namely racial discrimination in jury selection) that seemed to demand immediate political and media scrutiny, Civil Rights leaders (men) became the most visible commentators on the case. President of the Oklahoma City NAACP, Garland Pruitt, for example, expressed the organization's "disappointment" that the jury contained no people of color.[89] However, Black women seized back control of the Holtzclaw narrative from the mainstream media and the Civil Rights establishment, using Black feminist approaches to uncompromisingly (re)center Black women and police sexual violence. With assistance from OKC Artists for Justice, Black women's organizations with national platforms worked, as Height had done, to ensure that awareness around the case remained amplified.

One of the earliest national accounts, Black Women's Blueprint (BWBP), cited the Holtzclaw case in their report, *Invisible Betrayal: Police Violence and the Rapes of Black Women in the United States* (2014), compiled for the United Nations Committee Against Torture. Following their summary of the case, BWBP called for the US Department of Justice (DOJ) to open an independent federal investigation into the issue of sexual violence by police against Black women, and into the Holtzclaw case specifically.[90] As they did when confronted with Height's federal-level demand for investigation and protection, the DOJ took no action. Nonetheless, Farah Tanis, the BWBP executive director, leveraged age-old traditions of Black women's organizing to connect at the local level and provide on-the-ground support by organizing a "National Justice Ride for Black Women"—a caravan that took supporters to Oklahoma City to stand with Holtzclaw survivors and rally for justice with hundreds of activists and artists.[91] Similarly, legal theorist Kimberlé Crenshaw of the African American Policy Forum engaged liberal media outlets to raise awareness about the Holtzclaw case, which included an appearance on *Democracy Now!* (alongside Franklin and Liger), uploading a video to *For Harriet* entitled "Why Everyone Should Care About the Daniel Holtzclaw Trial," and recording a guest spot on the *This Is Hell!* podcast.[92] Barbara Arnwine of the Transformative Justice Coalition, in collaboration with Crenshaw, Franklin, and Liger, also organized "Days of Visibility" events to sustain media interest and awareness. One such event included the creation of a "Twitter Storm" (a sudden spike in Twitter activity) using the hashtags #SayHerName and #BlackWomenMatter to share stories of sexual assault and opinions on why the Holtzclaw case mattered. OKC Artists for Justice, for their part, urged supporters to share poems, reflections, songs, and artwork on Facebook and Twitter to demonstrate that Holtzclaw's predation was not an anomaly.[93]

In December 2015, the jury found Holtzclaw guilty of eighteen of the thirty-six charges of sexual assault involving eight of the thirteen women who came forward, and the presiding judge subsequently sentenced him to 263 years in prison. Following the verdict, prominent civil rights attorney Benjamin Crump (who filed a federal civil lawsuit against Oklahoma City and Holtzclaw on behalf of several victim-survivors) publicly thanked OKC Artists for Justice and its founders for "helping to tell America about the biggest rape case that none of [us] had heard about."[94] After the verdict and sentencing, OKC Artists for Justice redirected their efforts toward community education for women of color, specifically focusing on prevention where possible, and victim-survivors' responses to sexual assault.[95] Fifty years after Height and NCNW exposed the largely unpublicized sexual violence of law enforcement officers against civil rights protestors, OKC Artists for Justice continues to demonstrate the sustained legacy of Black women's local organizing in ways that reflect their experiences of intersectionality and their determination to empower women and girls.

Conclusion

In May 2020, the protracted extrajudicial execution of George Floyd by a white Minneapolis police officer sparked a resurgence of BLM mass protests and reform efforts across the United States. Under sustained pressure from activists, the Democratic-controlled House of Representatives passed the George Floyd Justice in Policing Act, first in June 2020 and later in March 2021.[96] Although the bill stalled in the Republican-controlled Senate, it is significant that, as proposed, it contains a provision to prohibit federal law enforcement officers from engaging in any sexual acts with individuals under arrest, in detention, or in custody, regardless of consent.[97] In March 2022, lawmakers passed the Closing the Law Enforcement Consent Loophole Act (as part of the Consolidated Appropriations Act of 2022), finally closing a legal loophole which had allowed approximately one hundred thousand law enforcement officers across all federal agencies to claim "consent" as a defense to prosecution for unlawful sexual contact with detainees.[98] Black Lives Matter is critically impacting both public discourse and policy on police violence and misconduct; this era of Black women's police accountability activism represents the accumulation of decades of Black women organizing in defense of themselves.

The sexual violation of Black women and girls by law enforcement agents propelled Dorothy Height and the NCNW and then Grace

Franklin, Candace Liger, and the OKC Artists for Justice, as Black women, to the frontlines of police accountability leadership. Dorothy Height, assessing her police sexual-violence civil-rights work some forty-five years later, commented: "African American women ... seldom do what we want to do, but we always do what we have to do. We believe in getting things done.... We had ... suffered, and we understood the issues, and we believed that we could make a change if we worked at it."[99] Indeed, the intersectionality of Black women's identities and the experiences of multiple oppressions grounded two campaigns more than fifty years apart and demonstrated the persistence of the challenges both faced with media and coalition building. However, where Height's campaign strove to raise awareness of the abuse sustained by "perfect" or "worthy" victims of police sexual violence, OKC Artists for Justice's efforts signal a progressive move beyond strategies mobilized during the CRM. Society has changed somewhat, even if Black women's vulnerability to sexual violence at the hands of law enforcement has not. As the OKC Artists for Justice campaign reveals, contesting respectability politics opens the way for more comprehensive and effective organizing against police violence for all Black lives, and so the work continues.

NOTES

1. The hyphenation of "victim-survivor" draws on Rahila Gupta's argument that while the term "survivor" is important because it recognizes the agency of women it nevertheless focuses on individual capacity. Gupta further argues that feminist politics needs to reclaim the term "victim" because it recognizes the enormity of the system and its brutalizing potential. See Rahila Gupta, "'Victim' vs 'Survivor': Feminism and Language," *Open Democracy*, June 16, 2014, https://www.opendemocracy.net/5050/rahila-gupta/victim-vs-survivor-feminism-and-language.
2. For an interpretive framework on the instrumental role of state-sponsored violence, particularly sexual violence, against Black women, see Angela Y. Davis, *Women, Race and Class* (New York: Random House, 1981); and Patricia Hill Collins, *Black Feminist Thought: Knowledge, Consciousness, and the Politics of Empowerment*, 2nd ed. (New York: Routledge, 2000).
3. Hannah Rosen, *Terror in the Heart of Freedom: Citizenship, Sexual Violence, and the Meaning of Race in the Postemancipation South* (Chapel Hill: University of North Carolina Press, 2009); and Crystal N. Feimster, *Southern*

Horrors: Women and the Politics of Rape and Lynching (Cambridge: Harvard University Press, 2009).

4. Adriane Lentz-Smith, "'The Laws Have Hurt Me': Violence, Violation, and Black Women's Struggles for Civil Rights," The Women's Issue, special issue of *Southern Cultures* 26, no. 3, (Fall 2020): 47.
5. Danielle L. McGuire, *At the Dark End of the Street: Black Women, Rape, and Resistance—A New History of the Civil Rights Movement from Rosa Parks to the Rise of Black Power* (New York: Alfred A. Knopf, 2010); and Susan K. Cahn, *Sexual Reckonings: Southern Girls in a Troubling Age* (Cambridge: Harvard University Press, 2007), 108.
6. McGuire, *At the Dark End*, 29.
7. McGuire, *At the Dark End*, 53.
8. "Eighteen Affidavits from Alabama," *New South: Police Practice in Alabama* 19, no. 6 (Atlanta, GA: Southern Regional Council, June 1964): 6.
9. "Full Text Affidavit Sworn by Miss Bessie Turner," 1962, SNCC Papers on Microfilm 1959–1972, Subgroup A, Series 8, File 3, Reel 13, Manuscript Division, Library of Congress, Washington, DC.
10. McGuire, *At the Dark End*, 3–39.
11. Laurie B. Green, "Challenging the Civil Rights Narrative: Women, Gender, and the 'Politics of Protection,'" in *Civil Rights History from the Ground Up: Local Struggles, a National Movement*, ed. Emilye Crosby (Athens: University of Georgia Press, 2011), 56; and Tiyi Morris, *Womanpower Unlimited and the Black Freedom Struggle in Mississippi* (Athens: University of Georgia Press, 2015), 3-4.
12. Historian William Chafe's 1980 statement (based on his research on Greensboro, North Carolina) that women formed "the backbone" of the freedom movement is widely accepted and frequently cited in historical and popular accounts of the Civil Rights Movement. See Green, "Challenging the Civil Rights Narrative," 56.
13. Charles M. Payne, "Men Led, But Women Organized: Movement Participation of Women in the Mississippi Delta," in *Women in the Civil Rights Movement: Trailblazers and Torchbearers, 1941–1965*, ed. Vicki L Crawford, Jacqueline Anne Rouse, and Barbara Woods (Bloomington: Indiana University Press, 1993), 4.
14. Martin Luther King Jr., *Why We Can't Wait* (New York: Signet Books, 1964), 39. Historian Leigh Raiford uses King's metaphor to explore the vital yet contentious role of photography in twentieth-century Black freedom movements. Leigh Raiford, *Imprisoned in a Luminous Glare: Photography and the African American Freedom Struggle* (Chapel Hill: University of North Carolina Press, 2011).
15. Lentz-Smith, "'The Laws Have Hurt Me,'" 47.
16. Bruce J. Dierenfield, *The Civil Rights Movement*, rev. ed. (Harlow, England: Pearson Longman, 2008), 57.

17. Martin Luther King Jr., *Stride toward Freedom: The Montgomery Story*, 1st ed. (New York: Harper and Row, 1958), 103.
18. McGuire, *At the Dark End*, 164.
19. "Panel of Young Women Who Have Been in Jail: Inter-Organization Women's Committee - Atlanta, Georgia - Sunday Evening, March 15, 1964," 1964, Collection 1, National Council of Negro Women Papers (hereafter cited as NCNW Papers) Series 19, Box 8, File 3, National Archives for Black Women's History (hereafter cited as NABWH), Mary McLeod Bethune Council House, Washington, DC, 3.
20. Annette Jones White, "Finding Form for the Expression of My Discontent," in *Hands on the Freedom Plow: Personal Accounts by Women in SNCC*, ed. Faith S. Holsaert et al. (Urbana: University of Illinois Press, 2010), 112.
21. White, "Finding Form," 112.
22. Regarding Black self-defense in the Civil Rights Movement, Emilye J. Crosby explains that it was neither the opposite of nonviolence nor the equivalent of violence. See Crosby, "'This Nonviolent Stuff Ain't No Good. It'll Get Ya Killed': Teaching about Self-Defense in the African-American Freedom Struggle," in *Teaching the American Civil Rights Movement: Freedom's Bittersweet Song*, ed. J. B. Armstrong (New York: Routledge, 2002), 160.
23. Joyce Ann Hanson, *Mary McLeod Bethune and Black Women's Political Activism* (Columbia: University of Missouri Press, 2003), 168.
24. Rebecca Tuuri, *Strategic Sisterhood: The National Council of Negro Women in the Black Freedom Struggle* (Chapel Hill: University of North Carolina Press, 2018), 5.
25. McGuire, *At the Dark End*, 159.
26. "WNEW Radio Exclusively Reveals Reports of Indignities to Girl Freedom Demonstrators in Southern Prisons," June 6, 1963, Radio Transcript, CORE Papers, Series 3, Reel 22, Frames 219–29, microfilm, University of California, Berkeley.
27. Angela Y. Davis, "Rape, Racism and the Capitalist Setting," *Black Scholar* 9, no. 7 (1978): 25; and "WNEW Radio."
28. "WNEW Radio."
29. Marisa Chappell, Jenny Hutchinson, and Brian Ward, "'Dress Modestly, Neatly . . . as If You Were Going to Church': Respectability, Class and Gender in the Montgomery Bus Boycott and the Early Civil Rights Movement," in *Gender and the Civil Rights Movement*, ed. Peter J. Ling and Sharon Monteith (New Brunswick, NJ: Rutgers University Press, 2004), 69; and "WNEW Radio."
30. "WNEW Radio"; and Anne Karro, "Confidential: File Submitted by Anne Karro," 1964, Collection 6, Polly Speigel Cowan Papers, Series 1, Sub-series 2, File 11, NABWH, Mary McLeod Bethune Council House, Washington, DC, 2.
31. "WNEW Radio."
32. "WNEW Radio."

33. Dorothy Height, oral history with author, Washington, DC, digital voice recorder, April 9, 2009.
34. "Gregory Hits Jail Abuses," *Crusader* 1, no. 10, February 13, 1964, 3, Sub-series D, Box 1, Hosea L. Williams Papers, AARL04-004, Auburn Avenue Research Library on African-American Culture and History, Atlanta, GA; and Sara Slack, "Lena Horne Going to Jackson, Miss.," *New York Amsterdam News*, June 8, 1963, 1–2.
35. "Gregory Hits Jail Abuses," 3; and Slack, "Lena Horne," 2.
36. The Big Six comprised Martin Luther King Jr., James Farmer, John Lewis, A. Philip Randolph, Roy Wilkins, and Whitney Young. "Opening Session: Inter-Organization Women's Committee - Atlanta, Georgia - Sunday Afternoon," March 15, 1964, Collection 1, NCNW Papers, Series 19, Box 8, File 3, NABWH, Mary McLeod Bethune Council House, Washington, DC.
37. Dorothy Height, "'We Wanted the Voice of a Woman to Be Heard': Black Women and the 1963 March on Washington," in *Sisters in the Struggle: African American Women in the Civil Rights-Black Power Movement*, ed. Bettye Collier-Thomas and V. P. Franklin (New York: New York University Press, 2001), 89.
38. Height, "We Wanted the Voice," 89.
39. Polly Cowan, "WIMS Book Material - Chapter 1," Collection 6, Polly Speigel Cowan Papers, Series 1, Sub-series 2, File 8, NABWH, Mary McLeod Bethune Council House, Washington, DC, 17.
40. Polly Cowan, "Selma, Alabama - October 4–5, 1963," Collection 6, Polly Speigel Cowan Papers, Series 1, Sub-series 2, File 11, NABWH, Mary McLeod Bethune Council House, Washington, DC, 1963, 2.
41. Dorothy Height, *Open Wide the Freedom Gates: A Memoir* (New York: Public Affairs, 2005), 158.
42. Cowan, "Selma, Alabama," 2; and Height, *Open Wide*, 159.
43. "Hyman H. Bookbinder to Lee C. White," July 18, 1963, Burke Marshall Papers, Box 31, John F. Kennedy Presidential Library, Boston, Massachusetts.
44. "Memorandum to Lee C. White," July 25, 1963, Burke Marshall Papers, Box 31, John F. Kennedy Presidential Library, Boston, Massachusetts.
45. Thomas Hilbink, "The Profession, the Grassroots, and the Elite: Lawyering for Civil Rights in the Direct Action Era," in *Cause Lawyers and Social Movements*, ed. Austin Sarat and Stuart A. Scheingold (Stanford, CA: Stanford University Press, 2006), 60; and John F. Kennedy, Radio and Television Address on Civil Rights, June 11, 1963, https://www.jfklibrary.org/archives/other-resources/john-f-kennedy-speeches/civil-rights-radio-and-television-report-19630611.
46. "Hyman H. Bookbinder to Lee C. White," July 18, 1963, Burke Marshall Papers, Box 31, John F. Kennedy Presidential Library, Boston, Massachusetts.
47. "Conference on the Treatment of Women and Girls Engaged in Civil Rights Activities at the Hands of Law Enforcement Officers," March 1964, Collec-

tion 1, NCNW Papers, Series 19, Box 8, File 2, NABWH, Mary McLeod Bethune Council House, Washington, DC.
48. "Opening Session: Inter-Organization Women's Committee - Atlanta, Georgia - Sunday Afternoon, March 15."
49. "Report of Police Brutality Conference - Atlanta, Georgia - March 1964," Collection 1, 1964, NCNW Papers, Series 19, Box 8, File 3, NABWH, Mary McLeod Bethune Council House, Washington, DC, 1.
50. "Planning Session: Inter-Organization Women's Committee - Atlanta, Georgia - Saturday Evening, March 14, 1964," 1964, Collection 1, NCNW Papers, Series 19, Box 8, File 3, NABWH, Mary McLeod Bethune Council House, Washington, DC, 1.
51. "Planning Session," 1.
52. "Planning Session," 1.
53. "Wednesdays in Mississippi," 1964, Collection 1, NCNW Papers, Series 19, Box 12, File 15, NABWH, Mary McLeod Bethune Council House, Washington, DC, 1. The plan to send interracial teams of Northern women to the South to foster local activism resulted in the creation of the "Wednesdays in Mississippi" project in 1964. Although NCNW assumed sponsorship, Northern women organized visits to Mississippi through individual networks and relied upon the contacts of local and national organizations, including Womanpower Unlimited and the League of Women Voters, respectively. See Morris, *Womanpower Unlimited*, 120–27.
54. McGuire, 164.
55. Andrea J. Richie, "Law Enforcement Violence against Women of Color," in *Color of Violence: The INCITE! Anthology*, ed. INCITE! Women of Color against Violence (Durham, NC: Duke University Press, 2016), 149.
56. Andrea J. Ritchie, *Invisible No More: Policing Violence against Black Women and Women of Color* (Boston: Beacon Press, 2017), 109.
57. David Packman, "2010 NPMSRP [National Police Misconduct Statistics and Reporting Project] Police Misconduct Statistical Report – Draft," *The Cato Institute*, April 5, 2011, https://www.policemisconduct.net/2010-npmsrp-police-misconduct-statistical-report.
58. Eliott C. McLaughlin, "Police Officers in the US Were Charged with More Than 400 Rapes over a 9-Year Period," *CNN*, October 19, 2018, https://edition.cnn.com/2018/10/19/us/police-sexual-assaults-maryland-scope/index.html.
59. Matt Sedensky and Nomaan Merchant, "Hundreds of Officers Lose Licenses over Sex Misconduct," Associated Press, November 1, 2015, https://apnews.com/fd1d4d05e561462a85abe50e7eaed4ec/ap-hundreds-officers-lose-licenses-over-sex-misconduct.
60. Philip M. Stinson, John Liederbach, Steven L. Brewer, and Brooke E. Mathna, "Police Sexual Misconduct: A National Scale Study of Arrested Officers," *Criminal Justice Policy Review* 26, no. 7 (2015): 673, 676.

61. Ritchie, *Invisible No More*, 110.
62. Samuel Walker, Dawn Irlbeck, and Police Professionalism Initiative, *Driving while Female: A National Problem in Police Misconduct* (Omaha: Department of Criminal Justice, University of Nebraska at Omaha, 2002), 2, https://samuelwalker.net/wp-content/uploads/2010/06/dwf2002.pdf.
63. Andrea J. Richie and Joey L. Mogul, "In the Shadows of the War on Terror: Persistent Police Brutality and Abuse of People of Color in the United States," *DePaul Journal for Social Justice* 1, no. 2, art. 3 (2008): 220.
64. Ritchie, *Invisible No More*, 123.
65. Kimberlé W. Crenshaw, Andrea J. Ritchie, Rachel Anspach, Rachel Gilmer, and Luke Harris, *Say Her Name: Resisting Police Brutality against Black Women* (New York: African American Policy Forum and Center for Intersectionality and Social Policy Studies, 2015).
66. Darnell L. Moore, "While We Focus on Shootings, We Ignore Victims of Police Sexual Assault," *MIC*, March 23, 2015, https://www.mic.com/articles/116216/the-type-of-police-brutality-no-one-is-talking-about.
67. Daniel Holtzclaw's father is white, and his mother is Japanese. The term white-passing/presenting emphasizes Holtzclaw's ability to access white-passing/presenting privilege (whether temporarily or situationally) as a person perceived by some as phenotypically white. Scholars on US multiracial identity have argued that biracial individuals of white and East Asian ancestry have experienced increased opportunities in the late twentieth and early twenty-first centuries to embrace a white racial identity, particularly if there is an observable approximation to a European American phenotype. See G. Reginald Daniel, Laura Kina, Wei Ming Dariotis, and Camilla Fojas, "Emerging Paradigms in Critical Mixed Race Studies," *Journal of Critical Mixed Race Studies* 1, no. 1 (2014): 38, n.37.
68. An early report on Holtzclaw's sex crimes came from writer Kirsten West Savali, who placed the case in the larger context of protests over the police killings of Michael Brown and Eric Garner. See Ritchie, *Invisible No More*, 105–6.
69. Democracy Now! Staff, "When Cops Rape: Daniel Holtzclaw and the Vulnerability of Black Women to Police Abuse," Democracy Now!, December 15, 2015, https://www.democracynow.org/2015/12/15/daniel_holtzclaw_convicted_of_serial_rape.
70. Victoria Law, "Why Are So Many Women Behind Bars in Oklahoma?" *The Nation*, September 29, 2015, https://www.thenation.com/article/why-are-so-many-women-behind-bars-in-oklahoma. In 2013, the state of Oklahoma incarcerated more women per capita than any other state, with 127 out of every 100,000 women in prison. The national average was 63 per 100,000 women. See "Fact Sheet: Trends in U.S. Corrections," The Sentencing Project, 2013, https://sentencingproject.org/doc/publications/inc_trends_in_corrections_fact_sheet.pdf.

71. Jessica Testa, "The 13 Women Who Accused a Cop of Sexual Assault, in Their Own Words," BuzzFeed News, December 10, 2015, https://www.buzzfeed.com/jtes/daniel-holtzclaw-women-in-their-ow#.itxNjpYw0.
72. Testa, "The 13 Women."
73. Evette Dionne Brown, "BDSM, Gazes and Wedding Rings: The Centering of Black Female Pleasure and Agency in Beyoncé," in *The Beyoncé Effect: Essays on Sexuality, Race, and Feminism*, ed. Adrienne M. Trier-Bieniek (Jefferson, North Carolina: McFarland, 2016), 188.
74. Jasmine (Phillips) Sankofa, "Mapping the Blank: Centering Black Women's Vulnerability to Police Sexual Violence to Upend Mainstream Police Reform," *Howard Law Journal* 59, no. 3 (2016): 656.
75. The harrowing testimony of this unnamed teenager included reliving the moment that Holtzclaw pulled down her shorts and raped her on her mother's front porch. See *Crimesider* Staff and Associated Press, "Witness Credibility a Focus in Ex-officer's Sex Abuse Trial," *CBS News*, December 2, 2015, https://www.cbsnews.com/news/witness-credibility-a-focus-in-ex-officers-daniel-holtzclaw-sex-abuse-trial.
76. Ebony Iman Dallas, "OKC Artists for Justice Founders See Activism as Extension of Creativity," *Oklahoman*, December 3, 2015, https://eu.oklahoman.com/story/entertainment/2015/12/03/okc-artists-for-justice-founders-see-activism-as-extension-of-creativity/60706132007.
77. Ebony Iman Dallas, Marie Casimir, and Jeanette R Davidson, "Contemporary Women of the African Diaspora: Identity, Artistic Expression, and Activism," in *African American Studies*, 2nd ed., ed. Jeanette R. Davidson (Edinburgh: Edinburgh University Press, 2021), 198–99.
78. Dallas, "OKC Artists for Justice."
79. From the late nineteenth century, middle-class Black women in the Baptist Church and Convention movement used the politics of respectability to counter racist stereotypes and advance an agenda of racial equality. See Evelyn Brooks Higginbotham, *Righteous Discontent: The Women's Movement in the Black Baptist Church, 1880–1920* (Cambridge, MA: Harvard University Press, 1993).
80. African American Policy Forum Staff, "Stand Up for Justice for the OKC 13: Visibility and Accountability Beyond the Holtzclaw Verdict," African American Policy Forum Webinar, Vimeo, January 19, 2016, https://vimeo.com/149680328.
81. Edward S. Herman and Noam Chomsky, *Manufacturing Consent: The Political Economy of the Mass Media* (New York, Pantheon Books, 1988), 35.
82. Molly Redden, "Police Officials Were Investigating Daniel Holtzclaw before Final Attack, Suit Claims," *Guardian*, December 11, 2015, https://www.theguardian.com/us-news/2015/dec/11/daniel-holtzclaw-questions-police-chiefs-rape-oklahoma.
83. Molly Redden and Lauren Gambino, "Oklahoma Officer's Trial Defense Attacks Credibility of Vulnerable Black Women," *Guardian*, November 27,

2015, https://www.theguardian.com/us-news/2015/nov/27/oklahoma-officer-daniel-holtzclaw-trial-defense-attacks-credibility-of-vulnerable-black-women.

84. Democracy Now! Staff, "When Cops Rape."
85. For Candace Liger's poem, see Candace Liger, "A Poem on Holtzclaw: 'For Pseudo-Gardeners,'" NonDoc, December 14, 2015, https://nondoc.com/2015/12/14/a-poem-on-holtzclaw-for-pseudo-gardeners.
86. Laura Eastes, "Advocacy Groups Call for Action as Holtzclaw Faces Sentencing," *Oklahoma Gazette*, January 20, 2016, https://www.okgazette.com/oklahoma/advocacy-groups-call-for-action-as-holtzclaw-faces-sentencing/Content?oid=2959565.
87. Ritchie, *Invisible No More*, 125.
88. Jessica Lussenhop, "Daniel Holtzclaw Trial: Standing with 'Imperfect' Accusers," *BBC News Magazine*, November 13, 2015, https://www.bbc.co.uk/news/magazine-34791191.
89. DiversityInc Staff, "All White Jury for White Cop Charged with 36 Counts of Rape against Black Women," *DiversityInc*, November 11, 2015, https://www.diversityinc.com/all-white-jury-for-white-cop-charged-with-36-counts-of-rape-against-black-women.
90. Black Women's Blueprint, Yolande M. S. Tomlinson, and Women's All Points Bulletin, "Invisible Betrayal: Police Violence and the Rapes of Black Women in the United States," Black Women's Blueprint, September 22, 2014, https://enforcerapelaws.org/wp-content/uploads/2015/07/invisible-betrayal-final.pdf.
91. Eastes, "Advocacy Groups Call"; and Ritchie, *Invisible No More*, 125.
92. Democracy Now! Staff, "When Cops Rape"; For Harriet Staff, "Why Everyone Should Care about the Daniel Holtzclaw Trial," YouTube, December 9, 2015, https://www.youtube.com/watch?v=jui1R84h4nY; and This Is Hell! Staff, "#SayHerName Gives a Voice, and Power, to Black Women Brutalized by Police Violence," *This Is Hell!*, episode 851, May 30, 2015, https://www.thisishell.com/interviews/851-kimberl-crenshaw. Kimberlé Crenshaw coined the term "intersectionality," and her work is foundational in critical race theory.
93. Kirsten West Savali, "African American Policy Forum Demands Justice for Holtzclaw Survivors," *The Root*, January 19, 2016, https://www.theroot.com/african-american-policy-forum-demands-justice-for-holtz-1790853951.
94. Redden, "Police Officials Were Investigating."
95. Eastes, "Advocacy Groups Call."
96. The George Floyd Justice in Policing Act passed in the House almost entirely along party lines in 2021, with most Republicans opposed to the legislation. The bill did not pass in the Republican-controlled Senate, and is unlikely to be reconsidered in the Congress that convened on January 3, 2023. See "H.R.1280 - 117th Congress (2021-2022): George Floyd Justice in

Policing Act of 2021," March 9, 2021, https://www.congress.gov/bill/117th-congress/house-bill/1280.

97. Between 2006 and 2018, twenty-six federal officers charged with unlawful sexual conduct with detainees had prosecutors drop their cases or received jury acquittals following a consensual sex defense. See Albert Samaha, "Congress Has Closed the Loophole That Allowed Federal Officers to Claim Sex with a Detainee Is Consensual," BuzzFeed News, March 16, 2022, https://www.buzzfeednews.com/article/albertsamaha/congress-close-police-consent-loophole-law.

98. Samaha, "Congress Has Closed the Loophole." Although the Closing the Law Enforcement Consent Loophole Act establishes funding incentives for state and local authorities if similar laws are enacted, the bill only applies to law enforcement officers at the federal level. See "H.R.2172 - 117th Congress (2021-2022): Closing the Law Enforcement Consent Loophole Act of 2021," October 19, 2021, https://www.congress.gov/bill/117th-congress/house-bill/2172.

99. Height, oral history with author.

CHAPTER 5

Revolts of the Black Athletes

Race, Sport, and Activism from the Civil Rights Movement to Black Lives Matter

Scott N. Brooks and Aram Goudsouzian

"I am more than an athlete," proclaimed Natasha Cloud. On the court, Cloud was the floor general of the WNBA champion Washington Mystics. Off it, Cloud used her voice to amplify the plight of the powerless. In 2019, for instance, she organized a team-wide media blackout to concentrate press attention on gun reform in Washington, DC. Then, in the summer of 2020, after the high-profile deaths of Ahmaud Arbery, George Floyd, and Breonna Taylor, she declared her disillusion with America's democratic ideals. How, she asked in a *Players' Tribune* article, could Black people face such violence and injustice in the twenty-first century? How could so many others remain silent? She soon announced via Instagram that she would sit out the upcoming WNBA season: "I have a responsibility to myself, to my community, and to my future children to fight for something that is much bigger than myself and the game of basketball. I will, instead, continue the fight on the front lines for social reform, because until Black lives matter, all lives can't matter."[1]

The year 2020 represented a new peak in activism among Black athletes. Cloud followed in the footsteps of Maya Moore, the WNBA superstar who sat out two seasons while helping to secure the release of a wrongfully imprisoned man. Fellow WNBA players Renee Montgomery and LaToya Sanders also skipped the 2020 season to focus on social justice issues. Young NBA stars such as Jaylen Brown, Malcolm Brogdon, John Wall, and Bradley Beal joined Black Lives Matter (BLM) demonstrations. In the mostly white and conservative bastion of NASCAR, Bubba Wallace rolled out a custom BLM paint scheme on his car at a Virginia race. In the NHL, players formed a "Hockey Diversity Alliance" to address the sport's history and legacies of racism. College football players spoke out against racially insensitive coaches, stadium names, and Confederate memorials that glorified white supremacists on their campuses. As professional leagues planned to resume play amid the COVID-19 pandemic, Black athletes—including Kyrie Irving in the NBA and Odell Beckham Jr. in the NFL—were outspoken critics who decried human exploitation for profit. Meanwhile, basketball megastar LeBron James helped start "More Than a Vote," an organization that combats voter suppression.[2]

Racial protest then ground professional sports to a halt. The NBA had been staging its playoffs in a "bubble" at Disney World in Orlando, Florida, as a caution against COVID-19. But on August 26, 2020, the Milwaukee Bucks boycotted their playoff game against the Orlando Magic. The police in Kenosha, Wisconsin, had recently shot a Black man, Jacob Blake, and during the protests that ensued, a white gunman had killed two protestors, shooting them with an AR-15 before driving himself home. Demanding concrete action from the NBA to address systemic racism in America, the Bucks chose to stay in their locker room. When the players from the Magic figured out what was happening, they too walked off the court. Then the referees left. In one of the year's most resonant images from the sports world, all that remained was an empty arena, with the NBA logo at center court and, along one sideline, the words "Black Lives Matter."[3]

After the Bucks' boycott, more athletes professed support. The league postponed more playoff games. When the Washington Mystics refused to play, the WNBA also canceled games. Baseball's Milwaukee Brewers followed the Bucks' lead by sitting out their next game.

In tennis, Naomi Osaka delayed her semifinal match in the Western and Southern Open. Ten Major League Soccer teams refused to take the field. To resume play, NBA team owners agreed to concessions, such as using arenas as voting centers and establishing social justice committees. Athletes had forced the sports world to confront racial injustice.[4]

Black athletes' voices and actions in the summer of 2020 echoed LeBron James's February 2018 response to conservative radio host Laura Ingraham: "We will definitely not shut up and dribble." Ingraham had blasted him for criticizing President Donald Trump, and James had remained defiant. Their exchange highlighted the distinct place of sports within racial politics. On one hand, Black athletes have earned great attention and praise for their activism. James, for instance, has enhanced his status as a cultural icon by investing in urban education, highlighting Black voices in media content, and supporting political causes. On the other hand, sports are no more immune to white supremacy than any other realm in American life. Professional team owners and college sports administrators remain overwhelmingly white and male, while athletes in the revenue-generating sports are mostly Black. Also, in a politically polarized environment, cultural conservatives reject the athletes' political engagement, often in explicitly racist and sexist ways.[5]

Modern media technology, including social media, allows athletes to communicate their viewpoints more openly than ever, putting them in direct conversation with fans and media members. Their voices garner a spectrum of responses, from support and praise on one end to ridicule and hatred on the other. This is not new—sport is perhaps the quintessential space for society to confront and engage in conversations about racism, sexism, ableism, and other forms of oppression. This contemporary surge in sports activism recalls the "Revolt of the Black Athlete" of the late 1960s, even as this new activism is more inclusive—Black women, gay and straight, are visible leaders, and they highlight issues that include gender violence, pay equity, and reproductive justice. In this essay, we illuminate the current moment in sports activism by placing it into its historic and social context, employing the analytical frames of both sports historians and critical race studies scholars.[6]

We aim to accomplish four tasks. First, we situate the original Revolt of the Black Athlete in the triumphs and tensions of sports amid the Civil Rights Movement (CRM) of the 1960s. By the era of Black Power, athletes had launched a significant challenge to white expectations of their cultural styles and political stances. Second, we discuss the mass marketing of Black athletes in the 1970s, 1980s, and 1990s, with a particular focus on professional basketball. The commercial possibilities of this era served to contain athletes' expression as political actors but also built a mass-media platform for African Americans within the sports world. Third, we add the lens of critical race theory to sports, illustrating intersectional differences in Black athletes' treatment and their responses. We discuss the uneven use of gender testing, and we employ women's tennis champion Serena Williams as a case study to examine the racism that modern Black women athletes must endure. The global media has magnified the disrespect, hyper-surveillance, and narrative manipulation that Williams confronts.

Fourth, we explain the forces that shaped our current moment in sports activism. Like their counterparts in the 1960s, today's athletes have undergone a process of political hopes and persistent frustrations. They have exploited a popular culture that opened doors for Black athletes, while using new means of mass communication to put forth their messages. With an awareness of the racist and gendered barriers that plague the sports world and the nation at large, these athletes have lent their voices and put their bodies on the line. The Revolt of the Black Athlete has begun anew.

In 1963, the year of the infamous campaigns in Birmingham, Alabama, and the historic March on Washington, A. S. "Doc" Young published *Negro Firsts in Sports*. While chronicling pioneers of athletic achievement, from jockey Isaac Murphy to baseball entrepreneur Rube Foster to cyclist Major Taylor, the Black journalist Young boasted that he lived in the Golden Age of Black Sports. Baseball's integrationist hero Jackie Robinson stood upon a foundation laid by boxer Joe Louis and Olympian Jesse Owens, projecting dignity and democratic ideals. Willie Mays earned more public goodwill than Martin Luther King Jr. Track star Wilma Rudolph won plaudits not only for her three gold medals from the 1960 Olympics, but also for her feminine grace. Golfer Charlie Sifford entered the privileged, white world of the PGA tour in 1961. As Young wrote, "the great Negro sports stars are, perhaps, more responsible for the ever-rising tide of pride among Negroes than any other group of professionals. For they dwell in a world characterized by a more nearly ideal Americanism than any other group." In Young's eyes, Black athletes were smashing old barriers and garnering new respect, not only for themselves as athletes, but also for the entire race.[7]

Six years later, at the height of the Black Power era, Harry Edwards published *The Revolt of the Black Athlete*. The young sociologist rejected the assumptions within *Negro Firsts in Sports*. Where Young had promoted athletics as a vehicle of racial progress, Edwards argued that sports more accurately reflected the racism in American life. Drawing upon his personal experiences, he chronicled the abuses of Black college athletes. He celebrated outspoken stars such as Bill Russell and Muhammad Ali, who had forced sports fans to confront racial hypocrisies. Most importantly, he explained the roots, course, and impact of the Olympic Project for Human Rights, a movement led by Edwards that called for Black athletes to boycott the 1968 Olympics in Mexico City. Although the boycott never materialized, sprinters Tommie Smith and John Carlos, clad in black gloves and socks, raised their fists from the medal stand, embodying the militant spirit of a new generation of Black athletes. Reflecting on his goals fifty years later, Edwards said that he had sought "to stridently challenge and demonstrably prove the fallacy of prevailing definitions portraying the character of race relations in American sport, to establish as unimpeachable fact that Negroes had no more 'made it' in sport than in any other sector of American society." As he saw it, Black athletes, like other African Americans, had the right and duty to serve as activists for racial equality.[8]

Together, the chronicles by Doc Young and Harry Edwards illustrate a tension in sport history: does Black athletic success represent progress toward racial equality, or does it highlight the racism that defines the African-American experience? How can they do both? The books further foreground an important thread in the Black Freedom

Struggle—the evolving political consciousness of Black athletes in the Civil Rights and Black Power eras. Black athletes served as public symbols of American democracy, particularly in the context of the Cold War, and their presence buttressed the myth of sports as a "level playing field." Yet they also challenged that myth, spotlighting racism both on and off the field, while demanding public consideration as authentic individuals.

Jackie Robinson was a key pioneer in this epic story. He was not necessarily the best Black ballplayer of his era, but he contradicted racial stereotypes in ways that made him the perfect icon. He was college educated, a World War II veteran, and faithfully married. Although proud and combative, he respected Brooklyn Dodgers president Branch Rickey's demands that he turn the other cheek when harassed by opponents and fans, staying silent even when his white teammates threatened to boycott his rookie season in 1947. During his playing career, Robinson earned a folk-hero status among African Americans, the respect of his teammates, and the admiration of many white baseball fans. While paving the way for more Black players in the major leagues, he won a World Series and election to the Hall of Fame.[9]

As the CRM emerged—protesting racial segregation, embracing the tactic of nonviolence, and casting the Black struggle as patriotic—Robinson embodied the promise of Black citizenship. The Cold War promoted American democracy to the world, yet this same society perceived and feared a Black threat to American order. Robinson had to adhere to a liberal construction of his Blackness: as a disciplined worker, as nonthreatening to racist sexual mores, and as an anti-Communist patriot who could counter Soviet propaganda critiquing America's racialized democracy. Robinson's 1949 testimony before the House Un-American Activities Committee showcased the paradox of the Black athlete. Star singer and actor (and former Princeton football player) Paul Robeson, a leftist enamored with the Soviet Union, had questioned whether African Americans would bear arms for a nation that oppressed them. Called to testify, Robinson denounced Jim Crow and criticized the media's tendency to employ Black celebrities as spokesmen for the whole race. He also insisted that African Americans would "do their best to help their country stay out of war; if unsuccessful, they'd do their best to help their country win the war—against Russia or any other enemy that threatened us."[10] In the aftermath, Robeson's public status plummeted while Robinson won commendations from civic groups, reporters, and fans. The message was clear: Black athletes could be celebrated public figures as long as they reassured whites of Black faith in American democracy.[11]

Various Black athletes followed in Robinson's footsteps, forging images as respectable integrationists. In 1960, at the Olympic Games in Rome, the humble and affable decathlete Rafer Johnson carried the American flag during the opening ceremony. "We thought Rafer represented the best in Americanism," stated one official.[12] In those same Olympics, Wilma Rudolph won gold medals in the 100-meter, 200-meter, and 4×100-meter relay races. Even more than Johnson, the media cast Rudolph as a symbol of American achievement in an international competition against Communist enemies. They highlighted that she had overcome a childhood disability, ran with grace, and subscribed to a conventional femininity to present her as emblematic of American opportunity. Rudolph herself carefully adhered to gendered norms: her coach, Ed Temple, insisted that his dominating Tennessee State Tigerbelles be "ladies" while beating their opponents. Rudolph accordingly refused to race against men and, after one victory, asked a friend for a mirror and comb before appearing on the medal stand. Her admirers in the press saw her as evidence of racial progress along multiple valences: as Doc Young notes in *Negro Firsts in Sports*, Rudolph was "the first Negro woman athlete to draw worldwide praise for her beauty . . . and this is indisputable proof that 'things are getting better' for Negroes!" Rudolph operated within the Black "politics of respectability," using style and restraint to win respect.[13]

In the early 1960s, the civil rights campaigns to dismantle segregation all showcased brave, resilient Black activists who demanded equal access to the institutions of American democracy and beyond. Martin Luther King Jr., a figure of international significance, envisioned such protests as stirring the national conscience and leading to remedial measures. As Doc Young would argue, sports already provided a "level playing field"—the rules, records, statistics, and titles were otherwise meaningless. In this frame, athletics provided an important cultural arena to appreciate Black excellence, to read Blacks as non-threatening, and to foster interracial goodwill. Baseball heroes such as Willie Mays and Ernie Banks soothed racial anxieties with their exuberant personalities. Tennis champion Althea Gibson was a quiet paragon of achievement. Reporters lauded heavyweight boxing champion Floyd Patterson for his resilience, integrity, and introspection. Athletes had a unique, non-threatening forum to claim racial progress.[14]

Some stars, however, consciously defied the political and cultural expectations laden upon Black athletes. Although they had distinct ideologies and adopted different approaches, each possessed an athletic prowess that guaranteed them a status and voice. The Black Freedom Struggle inspired them to deploy their fame for political ends. Athletes such as Bill Russell, Jim Brown, and Muhammad Ali emerged as sport's pioneers of the Black Power Movement. They emphasized pride in Blackness, urged Black unity and self-determination, spotlighted Black struggles for justice beyond the South, and adopted more international outlooks.

Between 1957 and 1969, Bill Russell won five MVP awards and eleven NBA titles with the Boston Celtics. He was the first African American coach of a major team sport and won his last two titles as a player-coach. The media cast him as the team-oriented winner, and his Celtics squad as racial integration in action. Yet Russell threw himself into political action when his conscience demanded it. In 1961, he led a boycott of an exhibition game in Kentucky after a hotel coffee shop refused to serve his Black teammates. In 1964, he accused the NBA of instituting a racial quota system that limited rosters to only four or five African Americans. He also got involved in the Movement: he joined the NAACP and advocated for equitable resources in Boston Public Schools, and he attended the 1963 March on Washington and conferences at the White House. He further defied stereotypes of grinning, happy-go-lucky Black athletes by scowling and refusing to sign autographs. For all that, he paid a price:

in his 1966 autobiography *Go Up for Glory*, Russell revealed how he had long faced an onslaught of racist slurs and bigoted reporters. He received streams of hate mail, and long after he had brought championships to the city of Boston, some Boston reporters still refused to give him his due. His family once found their home robbed and trashed, with "NIGGA" spray-painted on one wall and human feces under his bed covers. Despite all this, Russell continued to insist on his dignity and rights.[15]

If Russell reflected the Black Power Movement's efforts to spotlight racism and Jim Crow in the North, Jim Brown, Russell's counterpart in professional football, embodied its celebration of Black pride and an assertive Black masculinity. The running back, an awe-inspiring combination of power and speed, led the NFL in rushing yards in eight of his nine seasons, and his team, Cleveland Browns, won the 1964 NFL title. Unlike Russell, who straddled a line between liberal and radical, Brown's racial activism sprung from a fundamental conservatism rooted in individual self-determination. While demanding recognition of his individual worth, he attacked his league's racist patterns. For instance, each team had either six or eight African American players, to avoid race mixing in hotel accommodations on road trips. Brown advocated for fair treatment for his Black teammates and helped engineer the firing of legendary coach Paul Brown. The football star had the clout to force sports fans to see him on his own terms, as his own man, on and off the field.[16]

Brown asserted his independence within the Black Freedom Struggle. In his 1964 memoir *Off My Chest*, he defended the politics of the Nation of Islam. He organized the Negro Industrial and Economic Union (later called the Black Economic Union) to launch Black-owned businesses, and he retired in 1966, in his athletic prime, to pursue a film career in Hollywood. Perhaps the central theme in the football star's life was his assertion of his manhood. His aggressive masculinity was part of his public image as a football and movie star, but it also had a dark edge: at various points, Brown faced allegations of domestic abuse. He nevertheless stands as one of sport's pioneers in the Black Power Movement.[17]

More than any other figure, Muhammad Ali danced at the crossroads of sports, race, and politics. Born Cassius Clay, the boxer won gold at the 1960 Rome Olympics. His brash pronouncements ("I am the Greatest!"), dashing looks, fluid style, and confident persona won international press attention, but few anticipated what came next. In 1964, he shocked the sports establishment by knocking out heavyweight champion Sonny Liston. "Eat your words!" he exclaimed to the press. He soon revealed that he had joined the Nation of Islam and had been renamed Muhammad Ali. He inspired both reverence and disgust. As he established himself as one of history's heavyweight kings, Ali sought to be "a new kind of Black man," unfettered by whites' expectations of humility and deference.[18]

Ali possessed the fierce courage and race pride of Jackie Robinson, but he presented a very different image. He played a trickster hero, keeping reporters off balance with humorous rhymes, outrageous boasts, and quick shifts in personality, almost like his moves in the ring. He juggled with gender: he was the heavyweight champion of the word, the ultimate expression of manhood, yet called himself "pretty." Most important, he promoted the Nation of Islam's doctrines about racial separation, the evil nature of whiteness, and the shortcomings of nonviolent protest and liberal politics. Instead of appeasing mainstream white opinion, he openly challenged it. Then, in 1967, he refused to serve in the Vietnam War, famously uttering, "Man, I ain't got no quarrel with them Vietcong." At the peak of his career, he was convicted of draft evasion, which he appealed and had overturned, and he served as a lightning rod for both the anti-war and Black Power movements. To many whites, he was an unpatriotic, entitled braggart who deserved this punishment. To many African Americans, he embodied the pride of a new generation. Harry Edwards called him a "warrior-saint."[19]

Russell, Brown, and Ali forecast the great shift in the racial meaning of sports: the Revolt of the Black Athlete. The philosophy of Black Power insisted upon self-determination: African Americans should control their own institutions rather than seek entrance into white society. Harry Edwards organized athletes for the Olympic Project for Human Rights, which not only sought to boycott the 1968 Olympic Games in Mexico City but also demanded the restoration of Ali's title, the exclusion of apartheid South Africa from the Olympics, and the boycotting of segregated sporting institutions such as the New York Athletic Club. Some prominent athletes, such as UCLA center Lew Alcindor, chose not to participate in the games in Mexico City. Many others attended meetings and voiced support, although they ultimately competed. Yet when Tommie Smith and John Carlos raised their black-gloved fists in what the media construed as the Black Power salute from the medal stand in Mexico City, they were staking out for themselves a new role as athlete-activist—unapologetically rejecting the racism that had hindered their full participation in American life while also representing America to the world, using the literal platform on which they stood.[20]

This new generation of athletes, standing on the shoulders of the Civil Rights generation that had integrated college campuses and athletic arenas, and coming of age themselves in the Black Power Movement, asserted itself through sports activism. Between 1967 and 1970, an estimated thirty-seven protests by Black athletes took place on college campuses, typically over racist exclusion or autocratic white coaches. Lew Alcindor converted to Islam and adopted the name Kareem Abdul-Jabbar, compelling the public to understand his spiritual journey as connected to his pride in his race and a global Blackness. Tennis star Arthur Ashe, once verbally restrained and politically moderate, demanded to compete in South Africa in 1973 and spoke out against apartheid. Curt Flood launched a legal challenge of baseball's reserve clause, arguing that his racial experiences informed his resistance of labor exploitation. As he insisted, "a well-paid slave is, nonetheless, a slave." The Revolt of the Black Athlete had made explicit the links that bound race to sport to politics. The legacies for the future were enduring, if ambiguous.[21]

Roughly half a century separates the original Revolt of the Black Athlete and the more recent one. The CRM of the 1960s left an impact, as Black culture integrated and then indelibly influenced sports, both on the playing fields and in public perception. In subsequent decades, the mass marketing of Black athletes built new national and global platforms. Yet from the 1970s into the new millennium, most Black athletes tended to avoid overt political engagement. These trends were obvious in the sport most intertwined with Black culture: professional basketball.

In the 1970s, in both the NBA and the rival American Basketball Association (ABA), Black men infused the game with the speed, bounce, and creativity that flourished on urban playgrounds. Fans and promoters sought this athleticism from Black men's bodies, even as they fretted about the status of whites in the sport. The media stigmatized these Black athletes as lazy, violent, cocaine-addicted "thugs."[22] The NBA changed its image in the 1980s, as illustrated by the high-flying forward Julius Erving. In the 1970s, while starring in the ABA, the goateed, Afro-wearing "Dr. J" seemed to embody Black urban style. When he joined the NBA's Philadelphia 76ers, however, he was promoted as an amazing athlete representing the emerging Black middle class. In one ad campaign from 1980, he was "Dr. Chapstick," charming a gaggle of adoring children while lauding the virtues of this product. He wore slacks and a stylishly comfortable jacket, like a cool suburban dad. "It has emollients," he told the kids, casually signaling his sophistication. Four years later, Coca-Cola doubled down on this middle-class image. In a commercial for its signature product, Coke cast Erving with Bill Cosby, whose image at the time was squeaky-clean—he held a doctorate and played Dr. Cliff Huxtable, a family doctor, on *The Cosby Show*. Erving and Cosby wore suits and ties in the television advertisement. They sat in a men's club with dark mahogany wood and leather couches. Praising Coke, they deadpanned: "Two out of two doctors agree."[23]

Even more than Erving, Earvin "Magic" Johnson represented the mass marketability of Black NBA stars. An astonishingly creative passer and magnificent team leader, he had a style ready-made for Hollywood. Bearing a megawatt smile, he led the Los Angeles Lakers to five NBA championships. Magic, moreover, had a ready-made foil in the white, Indiana-born Larry Bird, nicknamed "The Hick from French Lick," and his white teammates, Kevin McHale, Bill Walton, and Danny Ainge. The public perceived an explicit racial dynamic between them, which the media amplified. These Celtics had multiple white players as their primary stars and scorers—players painted by the media as gritty, blue-collar, and smart: code words for "white." By contrast, the "Showtime" Lakers played a fast-breaking style associated with a Black men's aesthetic and a majority-Black squad. Magic Johnson exuded affability and charisma. Like Cosby, he projected a type of Black masculinity that white audiences found reassuring.[24]

Professional men's basketball harnessed and sold Blackness, packaging athletes into exceptional icons of global capitalism. Then came Michael Jordan, who embodied basketball's crossover. From the mid-1980s through the 1990s, Jordan won two Olympic gold medals and delighted fans with his incredible talents while leading the Chicago Bulls to six NBA championships. Meanwhile, he dressed, fed, and energized white America: Jordan endorsed Nike sneakers, McDonald's burgers, Wheaties cereal, Ballpark franks, and Hanes underwear. He dunked on cartoon aliens in *Space Jam*. Gatorade commercials sang, "I want to be like Mike," and men, teens, and small kids all echoed the sentiment. From a marketing standpoint, if nothing else, "Air Jordan" was the perfect combination of Jackie Robinson's Black citizenship, Dr. J's coolness, and Magic's title-winning leadership.[25]

Jordan exemplified how Black athletes had become de-politicized since the Civil Rights and Black Power eras. He chose not to highlight racial wrongs, such as the police brutality and miscarriage of justice during the 1991–1992 Rodney King incident in Los Angeles that led to widespread rebellion. Most notoriously, in 1990, Jordan declined to endorse Harvey Gantt, an African American Democrat from his home state of North Carolina who challenged arch-conservative Jesse Helms for his Senate seat. "Republicans buy sneakers, too," he said. Although made as an offhand joke, his comment illustrated the distance between Jordan's corporate era and the Revolt of the Black Athlete. Jordan was a Black athlete in style, but he was socially and financially wedded to an America that accepted inequality as the price of success.[26]

As the century ended, and with it Jordan's heyday, a new generation signaled a transition in the image of Black basketball stars. Shaquille O'Neal, with both the Orlando Magic and Los Angeles Lakers, was a fun-loving giant who gave himself absurd nicknames, cut rap albums, and acted in commercials and movies. Yet he had a punishing on-court style and tore down rims with his ferocious dunks. Though not an overt activist, O'Neal also reclaimed his autonomy from corporate domination by leaving the major shoe companies to produce his own affordable shoes. In the marketing of Black athletes, O'Neal was a bridge figure between the Jordan era and the twenty-first century.[27]

Younger NBA players capitalized on Jordan's wide marketing acceptability, but in different ways, they projected a more explicit Black men's consciousness and used their capital accordingly. Allen Iverson, for example, brought back Ali's rejection of white cultural normativity. He played with astounding swagger, embracing the one-on-one style of playground ball. He wore jewelry, cornrows, tattoos, and hip-hop fashion. His formative teen years in the late 1980s and early 1990s were to the soundtrack of rap groups such as Public Enemy and NWA—a new type of protest music, "the voice of the street," for and by the disenfranchised and forgotten. Like rap, Iverson demanded authenticity and rejected assimilation. However, his scrapes with the criminal justice system for domestic abuse, drug possession, and violent public behavior generated bad press for the NBA. Throughout his professional career from 1996 to 2011, Iverson was both a transcendent star and a figure of controversy. Professional basketball had thrived on its ability to simultaneously market and contain Blackness. In the new millennium, as "AI" showed, this was a tricky balancing act.[28]

Elite Black athletes today continue to face racism on and off the playing field, mixing older forms of oppression with new ones. As sociological theorist Patricia Hill Collins notes, multinational corporations and modern media help serve the *new* racism, which cashes in on Black talent as cultural influencers while also pushing and controlling content that strategically emphasizes or de-emphasizes notions of racial difference and racial politics. Black bodies are both commodified and disrespected.[29]

In the NBA, for instance, the infamous 2004 brawl known as the "Malice in the Palace" began after a Detroit Pistons fan launched a cup of beer at Ron Artest of the Indiana Pacers. In the aftermath, the media once again coded the Black athletes as violent thugs. Longtime Black sports journalist David Aldridge reflected on the question of whether the media got the story right:

> Look, the majority of reporters, media in the NBA . . . whether they're covering the NBA, or the NFL, or baseball, or whatever, are white males. And those are the people that, especially, certainly in 2004, were setting the agenda in terms of, this is how we're going to view this incident. Right? And in the [Malice at the Palace] documentary, you see Bob Costas, who usually is a pretty thoughtful guy on many subjects, just going right to "thug."[30]

In the aftermath of this brawl, NBA authorities fretted that their league was too associated with Black stereotypes, even as it continued to rely on Black bodies. It sought a return to Michael Jordan's safer marketability. The NBA created a "dress code," mandating business casual attire for players when not in uniform.[31]

Over the last two decades, three consistent themes emerge when identifying the nature of racism that Black athletes face: acute disrespect, hyper-surveillance, and twisted narratives offered by peers and the media that center whiteness and Black deviance. At the same time, Black women, in particular, are given attention and their athlete activism is expressed intersectionally, addressing issues uniquely faced by Black women athletes that have been largely kept invisible because they do not fit with acceptable forms of masculinity.

Serena Williams provides an illuminating case study for examining how contemporary Black athletes' voices and bodies are interpreted and treated by the public, as well as the athletes' responses. The most accomplished tennis player in history, Williams has won twenty-three Grand Slam singles titles and spent 319 weeks as the number-one-ranked player on the women's tour. She consistently displays resilience—not only with her myriad comeback victories but also in recovering from injuries to keep winning—while simultaneously experiencing public disrespect, hyper-surveillance, and white victimization. It seems the more that she dominated on the court, dressed boldly, and spoke against injustice, the more vitriol she received.[32]

Williams has endured public racist objectification of her body by her contemporaries, as if she were sport's twenty-first-century equivalent of the Hottentot Venus. In exhibition matches, where tennis players sometimes jokingly do impressions of each other, players such as Carol Wozniacki, Novak Djokovic, and Andy Roddick have imitated Williams by stuffing towels in their clothes and sticking out their buttocks, trading on old stereotypes of Black female sexuality. In 2018, three Australian-rules football players donned blackface and dressed up as Serena Williams, Venus Williams, and Aliir Aliir, a Sudanese-born Australian football player. When they posted their photo on Facebook, it attracted worldwide negative media attention.[33]

Williams has embodied excellence in her sport yet has faced earnings suppression because her body does not conform to traditional white standards of beauty. For eleven years, Williams earned far less than Maria Sharapova, whom she dominated throughout their careers. Both Williams and Sharapova endorsed Nike. The company's Sharapova commercial was "I feel pretty," in which women, men, girls, and boys sing the song "I Feel Pretty" as she passes them. The implication—that Sharapova is universally pretty—is apparent. By contrast, the 2006 Nike ad for Williams, "Tennis Instructor," shows the transformation of a gaggle of teenaged girls at a tennis camp. In the commercial, the girls fawn over a tennis instructor who is a young blond man with long hair and light eyes; the girls then transform into Williams and gain her hitting power, speed, and quickness around the court. They hit balls at the instructor so powerfully that, eventually, he falls while trying to protect himself. According to these Nike campaigns, Maria Sharapova is a classic beauty, making her universally beloved, while Serena Williams is a superior athlete who dominates other non-Black women and poses a threat to white men.[34]

Williams has also faced hyper-surveillance by governing bodies, media, and fans, resulting in excessive "random" drug tests, fines, and match penalties. After her impressive comeback from a near-death experience in 2017 (from complications due to childbirth), the WTA admitted to target-testing Williams to see if she used illegal substances to hasten her return. Her athletic superstardom has not protected her from insinuations of menace, either. During the 2009 US Open, tournament director Jim Curley claimed that Williams protested a call in "a threatening manner," and the USTA and US Open fined her for a record total of $82,500, plus a two-year probation. In the 2018 US Open final, Williams, upset about a penalty warning from the umpire, broke a racquet and was given a point penalty. She addressed the penalty with the umpire, asking for clarification and strongly defending herself, and was assessed an additional point penalty, giving her opponent, Naomi Osaka, match point. Williams critiqued the obvious sexism and racism at work. She pointed out in later interviews that violent outbursts by white male tennis stars such as John McEnroe or Ilie Nastase (who both routinely threw and destroyed racquets) had never prompted such regulation, underscoring the double standard and villainization that Williams endured as a Black, female athlete.[35]

For two decades, Williams has stood atop the world of women's tennis. As the designer of her own clothing and jewelry lines, she has challenged American beauty standards. As a sports franchise co-owner, business investor, philanthropist, and film producer, she has fashioned powerful narratives of Black achievement. She remains a powerful advocate for herself and other women of color. In 2017, soon after giving birth to her first daughter, she penned a letter to her mother, which she posted on Reddit. In it, Williams recalls how detractors had called her a man and falsely accused her of drug use. "But mom," she writes, "I'm not sure how you did not go off on every single reporter, person, announcer and quite frankly, hater, who was too ignorant to understand the power of a Black woman." In this letter, Williams highlights her success and oppression, shaming racists and sexists in sport, celebrating different body types, and affirming the strength of Black motherhood and Black bodies. Her willingness not only to speak her truth but also to address the "haters" speaks to the historical moment—she is unapologetically a Black woman.[36]

In 2016, Professor Emeritus Harry Edwards spoke about athlete activism at the annual conference for the North American Society for the Sociology of Sport. Some audience members critiqued him for offering a weak gender analysis. In the aftermath, he apologized for excluding Black women from being full partners in the Olympic Project for Human Rights back in the late 1960s and for his failure to acknowledge the profound impact that women have had as leaders in athlete activism. He identified Wilma Rudolph, among other women, as critical to the wave of activism that took place in the 1950s and early 1960s. He pinpointed a new, modern movement of athlete activism that partners Black women and men.[37]

This new wave builds on the past but tailors it to the future. Like Jackie Robinson, Wilma Rudolph, Bill Russell, and Muhammad Ali in the Civil Rights era, Black athletes of the 2010s accumulated experiences and tools to confront social injustice and protest brutality beyond the personal treatment they suffered. They shared frustrations with fellow African Americans, understanding that their relative wealth did not protect them from racism. They saw how organizations such as BLM built political movements and raised grassroots awareness. Like John Carlos and Tommie Smith on the medal stand in 1968, they used their platform, expanded by social media, to call for racial justice through powerful symbols. In 2012, the Miami Heat posed for a team picture wearing hoodies to honor slain teen Trayvon Martin. In 2014, five players on the NFL's St. Louis Rams ran onto the field in the "Hands Up, Don't Shoot" gesture to protest the killing of Michael Brown, while NBA stars donned "I Can't Breathe" t-shirts after the murder of Eric Garner. In 2016, WNBA stars defied league authorities by wearing "Black Lives Matter" t-shirts to protest police brutality.[38]

Today's Black athletes fight power with power. As much as they can, they have been in direct conversation with political leaders, professional sports owners and commissioners, and university administrators. They realize that beyond symbols, their most powerful weapon has been their refusal to play—their refusal to entertain, to generate revenue, and to accept their prescribed roles. In 2014, a recording surfaced of racist comments by Donald Sterling, owner of the Los Angeles Clippers. When the Clippers and Golden State Warriors announced their plan to boycott their playoff game in protest, they forced the hand of the NBA's leadership, which banned and fined Sterling, forcing him to sell the team. In 2015, students at the University of Missouri protested a series of racist incidents and the lukewarm response of university president Tim Wolfe. Thirty football players threatened to boycott practices and games until Wolfe left his job. Wolfe resigned the next day.[39]

After the wave of police shootings in 2020, Naomi Osaka pulled out of a tournament to raise public concern about violence against Black people. "Before I am an athlete," she stated, "I am a Black woman, and as a Black woman, I feel as though there are much more important matters at hand that need attention, rather than watching me play tennis."[40] Fighting power has also meant using the power of sports organizations and leagues to elevate a message. Led by several players, the WNBA dedicated its 2020 season to Breonna Taylor and the #SayHerName campaign to raise attention to the police violence Black girls and women experience. Layshia Clarendon of the New York Liberty announced the league's dedication, adding that it was for "Black women who are so often forgotten in this fight for justice, who do not have people marching in the streets for them."[41]

In the recent history of sport and racial protest, perhaps no figure has galvanized political passions more than Colin Kaepernick. In the aftermath of the terrorist attacks on September 11, 2001, and especially after the start of a US Department of Defense program that paid professional sports leagues to put on patriotic displays in support of the military, the pre-game national anthem has become a ritual with significant political overtones. During the 2016 season, Kaepernick, the San Francisco 49ers quarterback, began kneeling during the anthem, saying that he did not do so to demonize the military or police but rather to protest the nation's racist brutality. Kaepernick's action won support from many people, including fellow NFL players who knelt in solidarity, but he also provoked a venomous backlash from conservatives, both in the media and among sports fans, who argued that he should "stick to sports."[42] It was a full circle moment. Kaepernick drew on the longer history of Black athletes in a radical political tradition. He consulted with Dr. Harry Edwards, wanting to learn from the leader of the Olympic Project for Human Rights and the author of *The Revolt of the Black Athlete*. Just as the 1968 protests on the Olympic medal stand had illustrated a larger cause, the kneeling Kaepernick symbolized the racial crisis of his generation—and how sports stars could serve the cause for justice.[43]

That same year, Donald Trump won the presidential election, further fueling racial tensions. At a rally in Huntsville, Alabama, in 2017, he ranted: "Wouldn't you love to see one of these NFL owners, when somebody disrespects our flag, to say, 'Get that son of a bitch off the field right now, out. He's fired. He's fired!'" Trump also sparred on Twitter with LeBron James and Stephen Curry, two NBA superstars who criticized his divisiveness, and he demanded an apology from ESPN sportscaster Jemele Hill, who had labeled him a white supremacist.[44]

In the Trump era, just as in the late 1960s and early 1970s, Black athletes surveyed the racial landscape from across a political divide, and they played central roles in shaping opinions on both sides of that gulf. Yet Black athletes were also winning greater influence than ever before. Companies had long histories of using their economic leverage to silence Black athletes: in the past, for instance, sneaker companies had dropped Latrell Sprewell and Dennis Rodman for violent or what they deemed aberrant behavior. But at the first Monday night football game of the 2018 season, as public outcry grew against the apparent blackballing of Kaepernick by the NFL, Nike launched a remix of its iconic "Just Do It" campaign, celebrating Kaepernick as an icon of courage for his willingness to protest for racial justice.[45]

By the end of the 2010s, Black athletes—men and women—had undergone a process similar to that of their counterparts in the 1960s, experiencing moments of both racial tension and activism. Both groups achieved new levels of cultural currency, while generating resentment at their success. Both expressed their identities and visions, while enduring a sharpened hostility. Both possessed new political hopes, while chafing at persistent racial frustrations. Lastly, both participated in the building of these movements, using their status and the tools available to them. So in the tumultuous year of 2020, activists again took to the streets demanding that Americans confront systemic racism. Many Black athletes dedicated themselves to social causes, joined protests, sponsored voter registration efforts, and spoke out against racial injustice. After the August 2020 shooting of Jacob Blake, this spirit of protest reached its crescendo, spearheaded by the Milwaukee Bucks withholding their labor from an NBA playoff game. As games in MLB, MLS, the NHL, the NBA and the WNBA were canceled or postponed, it was clear that a new Revolt of the Black Athlete was in full force.[46]

This activism translated into concrete change at a national level. In the most obvious and dramatic example, the Atlanta Dream of the WNBA shaped the political future of the entire United States. In July 2020, the Dream's co-owner, Georgia's Republican senator Kelly Loeffler, criticized the BLM Movement as "divisive" and "Marxist." In response, the WNBA players donned warm-up t-shirts proclaiming, "VOTE WARNOCK." Their endorsement of Raphael Warnock, an African American Democrat, not only defied their team owner but also elevated Warnock's candidacy for Loeffler's Senate seat. Donations to his campaign escalated, and his profile grew. The Dream kept supporting his campaign. He had been polling in fourth place, but the WNBA players' advocacy arrived at a critical moment in the election process. On January 5, 2021, Warnock beat Loeffler in a run-off election, giving the Democratic Party fifty seats in the Senate. With new vice president Kamala Harris providing the tiebreaking vote, the Democrats had majority control. The history-making election could not have happened without the activism of the Atlanta Dream players and their allies throughout the WNBA. Echoing Black athletes of the Civil Rights and Black Power era, they had insisted, through their words and actions, that they were more than athletes.[47]

NOTES

1. Natasha Cloud, "Your Silence Is a Knee on My Neck," *Players' Tribune*, May 30, 2020, https://www.theplayerstribune.com/articles/natasha-cloud-your-silence-is-a-knee-on-my-neck-george-floyd; Aaron Dodson, "Why Natasha Cloud Decided to Opt out of the 2020 WNBA Season," *Undefeated*, July 24, 2020, https://andscape.com/features/why-natasha-cloud-decided-to-opt-out-of-the-2020-wnba-season.
2. Sean Hurd, "Maya Moore, the Game-Changer," *Undefeated*, July 2, 2020, https://www.andscape.com/features/maya-moore-game-changer-jonathan-irons-epitome-of-using-your-platform; Morgan Campbell, "Hockey, Rocked by Racist Acts, Embraces Black Lives Matter Campaigns," *New York Times*, August 10, 2020; Pat Forde, "Out of Control," *Sports Illustrated*, August 15, 2020; Emmanuel Morgan, "More Than a Vote Is More Than a Statement for

LeBron James and Other Athletes," *Los Angeles Times*, July 30, 2020. The authors discussed using "M"NBA when referring to the men's NBA to align with the WNBA, but decided that this might confuse readers because the NBA is a recognizable brand. We support the idea of a name change for the men's league and use of the NBA for the whole umbrella, the WNBA and the men's NBA.

3. Ben Golliver, "Sports Come to a Halt," *Washington Post*, August 26, 2020; "In Photos: The Sports World Has Been Taking a Stand," CNN, October 1, 2020, https://www.cnn.com/2020/08/27/world/gallery/sports-protests.
4. "The Day They Didn't Play," *New York Times*, August 27, 2020; Sarah Jones and Chas Danner, "NBA Playoffs Will Resume, League and Players Announce New Social Justice Initiatives," *New York – Intelligencer*, August 28, 2020.
5. Devan Cole, "LeBron James: 'I Am More Than an Athlete,'" CNN, February 17, 2018, https://www.cnn.com/2018/02/17/politics/lebron-james-laura-ingraham-kevin-durant.
6. Ben Carrington, "The Critical Sociology of Race and Sport: The First Fifty Years," *Annual Review of Sociology* 39, no. 1 (2013): 379–98. See also Lucia Trimbur, "Taking a Knee, Making a Stand: Social Justice, Trump America, and the Politics of Sport," *Quest* 71, no. 2 (2019): 252–65.
7. A. S. "Doc" Young, *Negro Firsts in Sports* (Chicago: Johnson, 1963), 4–5.
8. Harry Edwards, *The Revolt of the Black Athlete*, 50th anniv. ed. (Urbana: University of Illinois Press, 2017), xxx.
9. Jules Tygiel, *Baseball's Great Experiment: Jackie Robinson and His Legacy*, expand. ed. (New York: Oxford University Press, 1997).
10. "Negroes Are Americans," *Life*, Aug. 1, 1949, 22.
11. Arnold Rampersad, *Jackie Robinson: A Biography* (New York: Alfred A. Knopf, 1997), 210–16; Damion L. Thomas, *Globetrotting: African American Athletes and Cold War Politics* (Urbana: University of Illinois Press, 2012), 23–36; Gerald Early, *A Level Playing Field: African American Athletes and the Republic of Sports* (Cambridge, MA: Harvard University Press, 2011), 23–69. On Robeson, see also Martin Bauml Duberman, *Paul Robeson* (New York: Alfred A. Knopf, 1989).
12. Thomas, *Globetrotting*, 113–22.
13. Jennifer H. Lansbury, *A Spectacular Leap: Black Women Athletes in Twentieth-Century America* (Fayetteville: University of Arkansas Press, 2014), 115–50; David Maraniss, *Rome 1960: The Olympics That Changed the World* (New York: Simon and Schuster, 2008). For Doc Young quotation see Young, *Negro Firsts in Sports*, 197. There is not yet an "adult" biography of either Rafer Johnson or Wilma Rudolph, although Rita Liberti and Maureen M. Smith's *(Re)Presenting Wilma Rudolph* (Syracuse, NY: Syracuse University Press, 2015) offers a critical reading of Rudolph as a symbol at the intersection of African American history, women and gender history, southern history, and the Cold War.

14. For a survey of Black athletes and the CRM, see Louis Moore, *We Will Win the Day: The Civil Rights Movement, the Black Athlete, and the Quest for Equality* (Santa Barbara, CA: Praeger, 2017). See also Lansbury, *A Spectacular Leap*; David K. Wiggins, *Glory Bound: Black Athletes in a White America* (Syracuse, NY: Syracuse University Press, 1997). On the CRM of the early 1960s, see, for instance, Taylor Branch, *Parting the Waters: America in the King Years, 1954–1963* (New York: Simon and Schuster, 1988).
15. Aram Goudsouzian, *King of the Court: Bill Russell and the Basketball Revolution* (Berkeley: University of California Press, 2010).
16. Jimmy Brown with Myron Cope, *Off My Chest* (New York: Doubleday, 1964).
17. Dave Zirin, *Jim Brown: Last Man Standing* (New York: Blue Rider Press, 2018).
18. David Remnick, *King of the World: Muhammad Ali and the Rise of an American Hero* (New York: Vintage Books, 1998); Jonathan Eig, *Ali: A Life* (Boston: Houghton Mifflin Harcourt, 2017).
19. Randy Roberts and Johnny Smith, *Blood Brothers: The Fatal Friendship between Muhammad Ali and Malcolm X* (New York: Basic Books, 2016); Leigh Montville, *Sting Like a Bee: Muhammad Ali vs. the United States, 1966–1971* (New York: Doubleday, 2017); Edwards, *Revolt of the Black Athlete*, 90.
20. Amy Bass, *Not the Triumph but the Struggle: The 1968 Olympics and the Making of the Black Athlete* (Minneapolis: University of Minnesota Press, 2002); Douglass Hartmann, *Race, Culture, and Revolt of the Black Athlete: The 1968 Olympics and Their Aftermath* (Chicago: University of Chicago Press, 2004); Kevin Witherspoon, *Before the Eyes of the World: Mexico and the 1968 Olympic Games* (DeKalb, IL: Northern Illinois University Press, 2014); Richard Hoffer, *Something in the Air: American Passion and Defiance in the 1968 Mexico City Olympics* (New York: Free Press, 2009). See also Tom Ratcliffe and Becky Paige, dirs., *The Stand: How One Gesture Shook the World* (Link Voices, 2020).
21. John Matthew Smith, *The Sons of Westwood: John Wooden, UCLA, and the Dynasty That Changed College Basketball* (Urbana: University of Illinois Press, 2013); Aram Goudsouzian, "From Lew Alcindor to Kareem Abdul-Jabbar: Race, Religion, and Representation in Basketball, 1968–1975," *Journal of American Studies* 51, no. 2 (May 2017): 437–70; Eric Allen Hall, *Arthur Ashe: Tennis and Justice in the Civil Rights Era* (Baltimore: Johns Hopkins University Press, 2015); Brad Snyder, *A Well-Paid Slave: Curt Flood's Fight for Free Agency in Professional Sports* (New York: Plume, 2007); and Early, *A Level Playing Field*, 70–109.
22. On basketball and Black style in the 1970s, see Walt Frazier and Ira Berkow, *Rockin' Steady: A Guide to Basketball and Cool* (Englewood Cliffs, NJ: Prentice-Hall, 1974); Pete Axthelm, *The City Game: From the Garden to the Playgrounds* (1970; Lincoln: University of Nebraska Press, 1999); and Rick Telander, *Heaven Is a Playground*, 4th ed. (1976; Chicago: Sports Publishing, 2013;). On

the NBA in the 1970s, see Theresa Runstedtler, *Black Ball: Kareem Abdul-Jabbar, Spencer Haywood, and the Generation That Saved the Soul of the NBA* (New York: Bold Type Books, 2023); Adam J. Criblez, *Tall Tales and Short Shorts: Dr. J, Pistol Pete, and the Birth of the Modern NBA* (Lanham, MD: Rowman and Littlefield, 2017); and John Feinstein, *The Punch: One Night, Two Lives, and the Fight That Changed Basketball Forever* (Boston: Little, Brown, 2002).

23. Vincent Mallozzi, *Doc: The Rise and Rise of Julius Erving* (Hoboken, NJ: Wiley, 2009). For the Chapstick ad, see "Chap Stick ad w/Julius Erving, 1980," posted by Chuck D's All-New Classic TV Clubhouse, Dec 9, 2017, https://youtu.be/Wbo5SNja_qY?si=t0WssXD5K3HwsHiB. For the Coke ad, see "1984 Coca-Cola Commercial," posted by Jason Harder, Jun 26, 2011, https://youtu.be/wakFNm2BWyo?si=kVU-uxahUN5k1vK6.

24. Larry Bird and Magic Johnson with Jackie MacMullan, *When the Game Was Ours* (Boston: Houghton Mifflin Harcourt, 2009); John Matthew Smith, "'Gifts That God Didn't Give': White Hopes, Basketball, and the Legend of Larry Bird," *Massachusetts Historical Review* 13 (2001): 1–30; Daniel Nathan, "'We Were About Winning': Larry Bird, Magic Johnson, and the Rivalry That Remade the NBA," in *Rivals: Legendary Matchups That Made Sports History* (Fayetteville: University of Arkansas Press, 2010), 69–108; and Jeffrey Lane, *Under the Boards: The Cultural Revolution in Basketball* (Lincoln, NB: Bison Books, 2007).

25. See David L. Andrews, ed., *Michael Jordan Inc.: Corporate Sport, Media Culture, and Late Modern America* (Albany, NY: SUNY Press, 2001); David L. Andrews, *Sport-Commerce-Culture: Essays on Sport in Late Capitalist America* (New York: Peter Lang, 2006); Henry Louis Gates, "Net Worth," *New Yorker*, June 1, 1998, 48–61; David Halberstam, *Playing for Keeps: Michael Jordan and the World He Made* (New York: Three Rivers Press, 2000); and Walter LaFeber, *Michael Jordan and the New Global Capitalism* (New York: Norton, 2002).

26. William C. Rhoden, *Forty Million Dollar Slaves: The Rise, Fall, and Redemption of the Black Athlete* (New York: Crown, 2006), 147–217. In addition, Jordan did not criticize Nike, his most prominent corporate sponsor, for its use of Asian sweatshops to produce sneakers and clothes.

27. Rebecca Mead, "A Man-Child in Lotusland," *New Yorker*, May 20, 2002, 48–67.

28. Scott N. Brooks et al., "What Is Happening to the Black American Athlete?," in *Modern Sport and the African American Experience*, 2nd ed., ed. Gary Sailes (San Diego, CA: Cognella Academic Publishing, 2016), 271–92; Shaun Powell, *Souled Out: How Blacks Are Winning and Losing in Sports* (Chicago: Human Kinetics, 2008); David Leonard, "The Real Color of Money: Controlling Black Bodies in the NBA," *Journal of Sport and Social Issues* 30, no. 2 (2006): 158–79.

29. Scott N. Brooks, Matt Knudtson, and Isais Smith, "Some Kids Are Left Behind: The Failure of a Perspective, Using Critical Race Theory to Expand the Coverage in the Sociology of Youth Sports," *Sociology Compass* 11, no. 2

(2017): 1–14; Patricia Hill Collins, *Black Sexual Politics: African Americans, Gender, and the New Racism* (New York: Routledge, 2005).

30. Etan Thomas, "David Aldridge: The Media Failed to Tell Full Malice at the Palace Story," *Basketball News*, August 21, 2021, https://www.basketballnews.com/stories/david-aldridge-the-media-failed-to-tell-full-malice-at-the-palace-story.

31. David J. Leonard, *After Artest: The NBA and the Assault on Blackness* (Albany, NY: SUNY Press, 2012); David Leonard, "The Real Color of Money: Controlling Black Bodies in the NBA, *Journal of Sport and Social Issues* 30, no. 2 (2006): 158–79. For a more historical look at the criminalizing of Black NBA athletes, see Theresa Runstedlter, "Punishing the Punch: Constructions of Black Criminality during the NBA's 'Dark Ages,'" *Journal of African American History* 104, no.3 (2019): 445–73.

32. Merlisa Lawrence Corbett, *Serena Williams: Tennis Champion, Sports Legend and Cultural Heroine* (Rowman and Littlefield, 2020); and Scott N. Brooks, "How to Become a Marketable Black Female Athlete: The Case of Serena Williams," in *Women in Sports: Breaking Barriers, Facing Obstacles*, ed. Adrienne N. Milner and Jomills Henry Braddock II (Santa Barbara, CA: Praeger, 2017), 77–100.

33. Chris Chase, "Caroline Wozniacki Imitates Serena Williams by Stuffing Towels in Her Top and Bottom," *USA Today*, December 10, 2012; Cindy Boren, "Australian Rules Football Club Apologizes after Players Dress in Blackface as Serena and Venus Williams," *Washington Post*, September 19, 2018; Soraya Nadia McDonald, "Serena Williams, With or Without a Baby, Has Always Been a 'Real Woman,'" *Undefeated*, September 2, 2017; and Stephanie A. Tryce and Scott N. Brooks, "'Ain't I A Woman': Black Women and Title IX," *Journal for the Study of Sports and Athletes in Education* 4, no. 3 (2013): 243–56. "Hottentot Venus" refers to South African Khoikhoi women who were exhibited as freak-show attractions in nineteenth-century Europe. Sara Baartman, a South African Khoisan and First Nations person from the Western Cape of South Africa, was part of an 1810 English exhibit showcasing human oddities. Baartman was featured nearly nude and was gawked at because some of her physical features (buttocks and genitalia) were supposedly large and abnormal. See Natasha Gordon-Chipembere, ed., *Representation and Black Womanhood: The Legacy of Sarah Baartman* (New York: Palgrave-Macmillan, 2011); and Clifton Crais and Pamela Scully, *Sara Baartman and the Hottentot Venus: A Ghost Story and a Biography* (Princeton, NJ: Princeton University Press, 2009).

34. Brooks, "How to Become a Marketable Black Female Athlete."

35. Kevin B. Blackistone, "Serena Williams May Be Singled Out for Drug Testing. The Question is Why," *Washington Post*, July 27, 2018; "Top-10 Williams Sisters Controversies," ESPN.com, September 7, 2004, https://www.espn.

com/sports/tennis/usopen04/news/story?id=1876882; Christopher Clarey, "Probation and Fine for Serena Williams's Tirade," *New York Times*, November 30, 2009; Brooks, "How to Become a Marketable Black Female Athlete"; Jim Cook, "John McEnroe: Serena Is Right, It Wouldn't Happen to a Man—But Opinion Is Divided," *Irish Examiner*, September 11, 2018.

36. "Serena Williams to Receive NAACP's Jackie Robinson Award for Her Decorated Tennis Career, Business Success, and Philanthropy," *Daily Mail*, February 23, 2023; and Serena Williams, "Serena Williams Wrote a Letter to Her Mother Today. Here It Is," *Washington Post*, September 19, 2017.

37. Harry Edwards keynote, "The Fourth Wave: Black Athlete Protests in the Second Decade of the Twenty-first Century," NASSS 2016, Tampa Bay, Florida, November 3, 2016; desiballer, "#SayHerName! Confronting Erasure and Rethinking Possibilities for a Democratic Future," *Tropics of Meta: Historiography for the Masses*, July 13, 2017, https://www.tropicsofmeta.com/2017/07/13/say-her-name-confronting-erasure-rethinking-possibilities-for-a-democratic-future; Harry Edwards keynote, NCAA Inclusion Forum, Indianapolis, April 19, 2023; Harry Edwards keynote, NCAA Inclusion Forum, Indianapolis, April 21, 2023.

38. Wesley Morris, "What We Talk about When We Talk about Hoodies," *Grantland*, June 22, 2012, https://www.grantland.com/features/trayvon-martin-miami-heat-talk-talk-hoodies/; and Steve Wulf, "Athletes and Activism: The Long, Defiant History of Sports Protests," *Undefeated* [now *Andscape*], December 30, 2019, https://www.andscape.com/features/athletes-and-activism-the-long-defiant-history-of-sports-protests.

39. Joseph Zucker, "Clippers Owner Donald Sterling Banned for Life from NBA for Racist Remarks," *Bleacher Report*, April 29, 2014, https://www.bleacherreport.com/articles/2042902-clippers-owner-donald-sterling-banned-for-life-from-nba-for-racist-remarks; and Elahe Izadi, "The Incidents that Led to the University of Missouri President's Resignation," *Washington Post*, November 9, 2015, https://www.washingtonpost.com/news/grade-point/wp/2015/11/09/the-incidents-that-led-to-the-university-of-missouri-presidents-resignation.

40. Saroya Nadia McDonald, "Naomi Osaka Made Sure Black Lives Mattered at the US Open," September 12, 2020, *Undeafeated*, https://www.andscape.com/features/naomi-osaka-made-sure-black-lives-mattered-at-the-us-open.

41. Leah Asmelash, "WNBA Dedicates Season to Breonna Taylor and Say Her Name Campaign," CNN.com, July 25, 2020, https://www.cnn.com/2020/07/25/us/wnba-season-start-breonna-taylor-cnn/index.html.

42. Kareem Abdul-Jabbar, "Kareem Abdul-Jabbar: Don't Tell Colin Kaepernick to 'Stick to Sports,'" *Hollywood Reporter*, August 1, 2017.

43. Howard Bryant, *The Heritage: Black Athletes, a Divided America, and the Politics of Patriotism* (Boston: Beacon Press, 2018).

44. Adam Serwer, "Trump's War of Words with Black Athletes," *Atlantic*, September 23, 2017, https://www.theatlantic.com/politics/archive/2017/09/trump-urges-nfl-owners-to-fire-players-who-protest/540897.
45. Sean Gregory, "Colin Kaepernick Hasn't Played an NFL Game in 2 Seasons, But He Just Keeps Winning," *Time*, September 4, 2018; Jill Avery and Koen Pauwels, "Brand Activism: Nike and Colin Kaepernick," *Harvard Business Review*, Case 519-046, December 17, 2018.
46. Jill Martin, Leah Asmelash, and David Close, "These Teams and Athletes Refused to Play in Protest of the Jacob Blake Shooting," CNN, August 28, 2020, https://www.cnn.com/2020/08/27/us/nba-mlb-wnba-strike-sports.
47. "'We Did That': Inside the WNBA's Strategy to Support Raphael Warnock—and Help Democrats Win the Senate," *Time*, January 7, 2021; Angele Delevoye, "The WNBA Influenced the Georgia Senate Race, New Research Finds," *Washington Post*, November 30, 2020; and Elizabeth Williams, "How the WNBA Helped Flip Georgia Blue," *Vox*, January 11, 2021.

CHAPTER 6
The Search for Truth and Justice
A Diasporic Black Freedom Struggle

Kishauna Soljour

In 1948, James Baldwin arrived in Paris, France. Reeling from the death of his best friend, who had committed suicide, and fleeing the police after a violent encounter at a restaurant, Baldwin left the United States for his survival.[1] He states, "I knew what was going to happen to me, I'd kill or be killed.... I left because I didn't think I could survive the race problems."[2] Despite escaping the vitriol of American racism and violence, Baldwin encountered a post-World War II France that maintained its own system of inequality. He bore witness to France's prejudiced treatment of its colonies and Africans living in Paris experiencing extreme poverty, dilapidated housing conditions, and exploitation.[3] He saw how racial injustice, police violence, and the resulting civic unrest have existed and persist globally. National histories dictate how the calls for truth and justice unfold.

France is home to almost seventy million people, three million of whom are Black.[4] Despite France's having a smaller Black population, the country's racial history has some synchronicity with America's, beginning in the 1700s when Black populations in the United States and France collaborated transnationally in the abolition movement, and reaching a critical fever with the twentieth century Civil Rights and anti-colonial movements.[5] Both countries experienced urban uprisings in 1968, and the migration of the Black Lives Matter Movement (BLMM) from America to France in 2016 resulted in protests against racial injustice in both countries in 2020.[6]

This chapter explicates the convergences and divergences in moments of protest across the Black Atlantic diaspora in the twentieth and twenty-first centuries. In order to highlight the uneven process of movement building between the United States and France, each section examines critical moments of continuity and discontinuity between generations of activists. The first section focuses on the relationship between the US Civil Rights Movement (CRM) and activism in France and tracks three turning points between 1947 and 1968 to cement a global liberation genealogy. The narrative begins in the post-war moment with the founding in 1947 of *Présence Africaine*, a quarterly cultural, political, and literary magazine. These literary works called attention to and documented connections between Black activists in the United States and France, but also signaled points of departure in terms of cultural identity, processes of immigration, and political agendas shaped by the histories and exigencies of their respective countries.

Another opportunity to forge transnational organizing alliances came at the meeting of the Congress of Black Writers and Artists in 1956. Convened at a moment when the global impact of the nascent CRM placed increasing pressure on the unifying elements of Western oppression of Black peoples, the Congress navigated the gray spaces within Cold War politics and international diplomacy. Despite this movement toward synchronization in Black Liberation struggles throughout the world, the section highlights the limited recognition of women in positions of leadership at the conference. The physical absence of Black women from the Congress podium and the sequestering of their voices to the margins of the conference proceedings underscores a critical shortcoming of the movement, namely its continued reliance on patriarchal gender norms even as it challenged racial ones. It is noteworthy, then, that American expatriate entertainer Josephine Baker played a critical role in transcending this gendered silencing within the CRM, crossing oceans and other divides to support activist efforts within both the United States and France.

The final point of convergence-divergence was the year 1968. During this tumultuous time, Dr. Martin Luther King Jr. was assassinated, and uprisings swept the United States; the Tet Offensive in Vietnam prompted a series of anti-war protests on US college campuses; and violent interactions between the police and protestors soured proceedings at the Democratic National Convention in Chicago. Activism in the United States propelled the Parisian May 1968 uprisings. A major turning point in the history of contemporary France, 1968 marks the political radicalization of a segment of French society. In most scholarly explorations of this moment of politicization, the actions of white French students and workers dominate the narrative.[7] This homogenizing of national protest efforts undercuts the reality that Black students and migrant workers were at the forefront of several movements in 1968. My analysis utilizes this transnational framework to examine the impact the words and actions of Black leaders within the CRM had on Afropean individuals, students, and workers. Ironically, employing a global and diasporic lens to examine the grassroots activism in 1968 Paris reveals important truths about the protests there.

The second half of this chapter plots the development of the BLMM in the United States and its movement to France in 2016. Contextualizing efforts against inequality and police brutality in both countries, this chapter argues that protest, in all forms, remains a defining feature of the transnational Black experience. This section highlights direct-action and the use of social media as complementary tools for twenty-first century activists on both sides of the Atlantic. More importantly, as an evolution within this global movement, women and LGBTQ+ activists are at the center of organizing efforts in both the United States and France. Born in response to incidents of racist vigilante and police violence in Sanford, Florida, and Ferguson, Missouri, the BLMM in the United States called attention to the nature of racism in policing and the continuing struggle for Black freedom in America. These issues and the activism they spawned were not confined to Florida or Missouri, or even to within the United States. Rather, activists in France leveraged #BlackLivesMatter (#BLM) to build their own movement that would focus racially conscious attention on issues of police brutality in a society that had traditionally ignored them.

Grounded in a new geography and history, French activists transformed the organizing momentum of the US BLMM to meet uniquely French challenges: in responding to these popular uprisings, the metropole sought to maintain the status quo by literally erasing the category of race. Black France countered by organizing a mass movement that would reclaim the word "Noire" to describe their racial identity, thereby demanding that France own its own brand of racism.[8] In the search for truth and justice on both sides of the Atlantic, protest movement strategies and messages have proven both mutually constitutive and historically distinct.

Présence Africaine: Identifying with Blackness

In the wake of World War II, France grappled with a new set of challenges in its effort to keep its colonial empire unified. As migration patterns to France began to shift in 1945, so too did legislative priorities, and France established its modern immigration infrastructure.[9] Historians of contemporary France acknowledge these years as the largest period of mass immigration in the country's history.[10] In managing these population inflows, the government deliberately privileged the in-migration of those it deemed "most assimilable"— migrants from other parts of Europe—while categorizing African immigrants as largely unassimilable and undesirable. Accordingly, the immigration infrastructure developed in France to increasingly restrict Black migration, while the government also adopted progressively more punitive policies toward Black migrants already in the country.[11] Throughout the period, prospective Black migrants were categorized almost exclusively as students or workers—people with temporary visas and whose belonging was tenuous.[12] When the success of anti-colonial movements worldwide precipitated the fall of "the empire," France turned its energies toward the metropole to spur domestic industrial growth and production, a redirection of governmental priorities that, ironically, relied heavily on immigrant labor. Accordingly, then, government officials focused on monitoring migrants' presence through local agencies and policing, meticulously scrutinizing and surveilling immigrant communities in police records.[13] Nevertheless, the newly arrived Black French population found ways to resist.

For example, two years after World War II ended, Alioune Diop published the first edition of *Présence Africaine*. Working in collaboration with a host of artists, intellectuals and scholars, the magazine attempted to capture and reflect the development of Pan-Africanism with artistic contributions from all corners of the Diaspora. A Senegalese migrant, Diop had come to Paris to continue his studies at the Sorbonne and, upon completion, became a professor of classical literature. Through his academic work, he cultivated a network of artists and intellectuals that would facilitate the publication of the first edition of the magazine in 1947.[14] During his studies, he formed bonds with students from other Francophone colonies in Africa and the Caribbean. This small intellectual community comprising mostly college-aged students founded the Négritude movement. Led by Aimé Césaire, a student from Martinique, and Léopold Senghor, a student from Senegal, Négritude asserted "a common cultural identity among all peoples of African descent."[15] As the Harlem Renaissance in the United States had done in the 1920s, Négritude centered Blackness as a component of cultural, political, and social contributions to the world and inspired Francophone students to embrace their racial identity. Senghor was particularly affected by the work of Black writer Claude McKay, himself a Jamaican immigrant.[16] Published in 1926, McKay's novel *Banjo* blends the personal with the political in his portrayal of characters grappling with the themes of Black internationalism—experiences with racism in the United States as well as in France, assimilation, Black nationalism, and Black separatism. Senghor considered McKay "the true inventor of [the values of] Négritude."[17]

Building on these twin pedestals of diasporic identity and political protest as expressed through art, *Présence Africaine* welcomed literary contributions for its inaugural edition.[18] While the Harlem Renaissance had amplified the Black experience in the United States, Négritude and *Présence Africaine* gave birth to "the voice of the *monde noir* (Black world), first in France and the French-speaking colonies, and later throughout the entire African continent, including English and Portuguese-speaking areas."[19] In the journal's consideration of diasporic voices, four figures provided worldwide recognition and credibility to the publication: Aimé Césaire, Léopold Senghor, Richard Wright, and Jean Price-Mars.

In its first edition, the magazine "established a great dialogue" between the Western world and Black populations globally.[20] This dialogue sought to decenter white voices in global discourse by promoting the experiences and voices of Black people. It demanded that Black voices mattered. French language contributors examined questions of diasporic unity, the impact of racism upon masculinity, and definitions of justice. Although French contributions dominated the first edition of *Présence Africaine*, the editors engaged pan-African perspectives with the inclusion of two pieces by African American authors that not only addressed racial injustice and police brutality but also grappled with questions of class and gender. Richard Wright's short story "Bright and Morning Star" and the poem "Ballad of Pearl May Lee" by Gwendolyn Brooks focus on African Americans and serve as points of connection and departure from their Francophone cousins. Originally published in 1938 in the Communist journal *The Masses*, "Bright and Morning Star" was reprinted in *Présence Africaine* the same year that Richard Wright emigrated to France. The protagonist, Sue, is a descendent of slaves whose two sons turn to Communism as a means to combat racism in the Jim Crow South and gain political power. As Sue learns more about Communism, she struggles to reconcile her Christian faith with socialist ideas. In the end, both she and one of her sons die at the hands of the police.[21] In this way, the story introduced to French audiences the concerns of Black people grappling with the political, religious, carceral, and gendered implications of white supremacy in America.

Gwendolyn Brooks was one of the few women published in *Présence Africaine* during its early years and the only woman to appear in the first edition. "The Ballad of Pearl May Lee" centers on the pain of a Black woman who witnesses the lynching of her lover after he engages in a consensual encounter with a white woman. Sammy's cheating leaves Pearl feeling betrayed; his subsequent murder, though, complicates and fuels her pain, and she concludes that his death was inevitable. Both pieces depict the pervasive power of American racism as trapping Black Americans in an endgame of legal and extralegal violence. Black bodies that protested discrimination and injustice put their lives at risk—a grim but plausible reality that Black people engaged in liberation movements historically have had to bear throughout the Diaspora.

Congress of Black Writers and Artists: A Meeting of the Minds?

In 1955, less than ten years after *Présence Africaine* issued its rallying cry to the people of the African Diaspora to take a larger role in the expression of their own culture, identity, and political futures, leaders from twenty-nine African, Middle Eastern, and Asian nations declared their independence from colonial powers at the Bandung Conference. Not only did this conference herald a bold step in the multiple processes of decolonization, but it also signaled a break from assimilation efforts. On the heels of this event, the First International Congress of Black Writers and Artists took place in Paris in September 1956. Delivering the opening address to the Congress, Alioune Diop framed the conference as a cultural counterpart to the more diplomatically oriented Bandung Conference. Diop and Léopold Senghor were central French-speaking delegates. In their remarks, they proposed a singular Black diasporic identity, which left American delegates feeling isolated from the unique experiences of cultural and political hybridity. Participants from the US delegation included Richard Wright, John Davis, Mercer Cook, William Fontaine, Horace Bond, James Ivy, and James Baldwin, the last of whom chronicled his observations in the essay, "Princes and Powers."[22]

Not only did Baldwin's essay disseminate the conference proceedings to an English-speaking audience, but his work also underscored a deep-rooted discontinuity between how the American delegation chose to frame their hybrid racial and cultural identity in comparison to the singular Black identity and culture posited in the speeches of Aimé Césaire and Léopold Senghor.[23] Baldwin acknowledged the tension and separation between the American delegation and the francophone participants. During the conference proceedings, Richard Wright echoed this sentiment with the question, "This is not hostility; this is not criticism. I am asking a questions of brothers ... where do I, an American Negro ... stand in relation to that culture?"[24] Scholar Brent Hayes Edwards best explains this tension in the expression of Black identity: "The difference between Negro-Americans and Negro-Africans is more slight. In reality it involves a simple *decalage* [gap]—in time and space."[25] In fact, this gap that separates the US delegation from his African brothers is actually the link that Baldwin proclaims to be the connective tissue between Africa and the West.[26]

Baldwin notes that in one of the final addresses at the conference, Richard Wright shared the disturbing realization that not a single woman had addressed the audience of great "race men."[27] In CRM efforts that would unfold over the next decade in the United States, women would play a significant role in organizing race-based activism; here, too, American expatriate and entertainer Josephine Baker-Bouillon had served on the conference's planning committee, although she expressed her regret that she could not attend the meeting in person.[28] For the most part, however, women were featured only in photographs of the Congress afterward and in an anonymous note published in *Présence Africaine* by a "Group of Black Women," which affirmed that, "in an event as important for the Black World as this Congress, we could not remain simple observers, because we believe that the Black Woman has had and will have an important and weighty role to play alongside men in the building of his country."[29] Women were "seen, but not heard": even as the Congress challenged global systems of racial hierarchy, they replicated the patriarchal gender norms of the day.

Josephine Baker: The American (ex)Patriot

Although Josephine Baker did not attend the 1956 Congress of Black Writers and Artists, she had established herself in France as a resistance spy during World War II and an entertainer with an international audience. More importantly, she surrendered her American passport in 1937 for French citizenship, which, in many ways, required the US government to provide protection for her as a foreign national as she traveled around the United States working in support of civil rights. Her combination of global stardom and local activism made her a critical link between French support of the US CRM and domestic organizing on American soil. By the early 1950s, Baker spent considerable time in the United States working with the National Association for the Advancement of Colored People (NAACP) to desegregate performance spaces in cities across the country, including Las Vegas, Miami, Atlanta, St. Louis, and New York City. Honoring her refusal to perform in front of segregated audiences, as well as her efforts to halt the execution of Willie McGee (a man accused of rape in 1945 on the basis of paper-thin evidence), the NAACP declared May 20, 1951, "Josephine Baker Day."[30] That same year, the legendary Stork Club in New York City refused her service, and much to the chagrin of the club owner, Baker protested in front of the establishment not only with representatives from the NAACP but also with the Hollywood actress and soon-to-be Princess of Monaco, Grace Kelly. This act of public protest, which shone the brightest lights on the racism tolerated in American democracy, and which occurred just as the United States navigated the geopolitical exigencies of the Cold War, resulted in the US government's denying Baker's visa applications for over a decade.[31]

After this protracted period of visa rejections, Josephine Baker triumphantly returned to the United States in 1963 for the March on Washington. Ascending to the dais in her World War II Resistance uniform and proudly displaying her *Légion d'honneur* medal, she was recognized in A. Philip Randolph's "Tribute to Negro Women Fighters for Freedom." While the crowd acknowledged Rosa Parks, and Daisy Bates offered a brief speech, Josephine Baker was the only woman to provide an extended public address to the audience of more than 250,000 people assembled on the Mall that day.[32] In the days leading up to the march, organizers had contested her participation on two grounds—first, her supposed lack of respectability due to her former employment as a vaudeville and cabaret dancer, and second, her French citizenship, which some believed invalidated her qualifications as an American Civil Rights leader.[33] Nonetheless, Baker delivered an honest and moving speech that addressed the tension between her citizenship, her experiences as a Black woman, and her embrace of France as a result of racism in the United States. On the steps of the Lincoln Memorial, Baker declared:

> When I was a child and they burned me out of my home [in St. Louis], I was frightened and I ran away.... It was to a place called France.... I do not lie to you when I tell you I have walked into the palaces of kings and queens and into the houses of presidents.... But I could not walk into a hotel in America and get a cup of coffee, and that made me mad. And when I get mad, you know that I open my big mouth.... And when I screamed loud enough, they started to open that door just a little bit, and we all started to be able to squeeze through it.... Now I am not going to stand in front of all of you today and take credit for what is happening now.... I cannot do that.... But I want to take credit for telling you how to do the same thing, and when you scream, friends, I know you will be heard.... And you will be heard now.[34]

These screams for freedom, equality, and justice by Black men and women would grow louder and more frenzied in the following years. They would reach a critical pitch in 1968.

1968: When All Hell Broke Loose

The events of 1968 prompted an unprecedented number of demonstrations around the world. On April 4, the assassination of Martin

Luther King Jr. precipitated protests in more than one hundred cities in the United States.[35] The violent nature of these demonstrations spoke to Black people's rage that—after generations of Civil Rights struggles—the country still did not live up to its tenets of equality and justice for all. As the embers cooled, Coretta Scott King traveled to the Netherlands to ask if Josephine Baker would return to the United States to take up the mantle as a leader in the CRM. After careful reflection, Baker declined, observing that her children were "too young to lose their mother."[36] Baker's rejection of the leadership role acknowledged the reality of death for activists: fallen leaders of the sixties already included Herbert Lee (1961), Medgar Evers (1963), Malcolm X (1965), and many others.

In 1968, US college campuses erupted in protests. For example, students at Harvard and Boston University held an anti-Vietnam War hunger strike.[37] More than five hundred students at New York University led campus-wide demonstrations against the Dow Chemical Company.[38] Students at Columbia University protested the institution's racist policies in April.[39] These youth-driven protests also occurred in France the following month. Inspired by the success of Black activists in the United States, Sub-Saharan migrants in France escalated demands and tactics to garner attention for their dilapidated housing conditions and racist interactions with the police.[40] Four years later, African students protested at Cité Universitaire (the main Parisian housing center for foreign students) on May 16, 1968.[41] Their efforts coincided with an avalanche of activism that overtook France during the month of May. In addition to interracial demonstrations and labor coalitions, a number of Black migrants collectively laid claim against the French state. Organized under the banner Fédération des Étudiants D'Afrique Noire en France (FEANF), Black students from various countries in Francophone Africa campaigned to protest racism and the establishment of French neo-colonial power in their native nation-states.[42]

In addition to student-led protests, African migrant workers led strikes in factories and public housing buildings.[43] Protesting inequitable wages and lack of access to clean running water, they were joined in public displays of solidarity by Black student and labor organizations, who saw their grievances as interconnected. Their activism met significant reproach by the government in the form of deportations, arrests, and new restrictions on work and student visas.[44] In the wake of the 1968 protests, the French government expanded its policing powers over African migrants living and working in Paris. The police department warned, "African migration poses serious problems, specifically in the African [working neighborhoods] that are becoming increasingly disturbed by a climate of demands and violence in the face of which the management organizations appear powerless."[45] They accordingly ramped up aggressive surveillance of Black communities, which in turn engendered a growing distrust of the French police among Black populations in Paris.

These claims against the state also reverberated in the United States. As nonviolent direct action protests met with massive resistance, younger activists shifted their tactics and priorities. The emergence of the Black Power Movement sought to foreground the economic inequality that Jim Crow had reinforced. Emboldened by the anticolonial rhetoric of African nations in their bids for independence, Black Power activists in the United States stressed the need to foster economic, social, and political power within Black communities, rather than focusing on the goal of integrating into a society that would never willingly grant Black people equality and full citizenship. These vocal demands for power, and the embrace of Black beauty, culture, and ties to Africa, elicited brutal repression by the United States government.[46] Various chapters of the Black Panther Party throughout the United States became police targets. Both the established Black Panther Party and Afro-French activists met significant resistance from the government. African students that engaged in sit-ins were denied re-entry visas or were deported. At the same time, COINTELPRO targeted Black Panther Party leaders, which facilitated the organization's rapid decline.[47] These repressive policies continued for years.

If Black activists in both France and the United States saw their protests met by the expanding force of the carceral state, the governmental repression of Black protest in France took on an additional international dimension. In the 1970s, the French government sought to suppress urban dissent by further constraining the arrival of Black immigrants; changing immigration laws to curtail family reunification and complicating the process to naturalization and citizenship. French authorities hoped that "whitening" the metropole would curtail the protests.[48] They were wrong: public demonstrations and uprisings led by Black French migrants enveloped large swaths of the country.[49]

By the 1980s, French police were conducting mass deportation raids and killing protesters.[50] For instance, the 1981 uprisings in Lyon brought intense attention to the inequitable treatment of African populations. Later that year, the government drafted new legislation that complicated the process of regularizing work and residency permits, resulting in approximately one-hundred thousand immigrants becoming *sans-papiers*, meaning "without papers [legal documentation]." This shift in legislation forced many migrants from the category of "legal" to "illegal," which not only facilitated their further marginalization and vulnerability to exploitation but also justified an increase in the police surveillance of Black communities to monitor and check for paperwork. A byproduct of the massive presence of policing forces was an increase in violent interactions between citizens and officials.[51]

The legislative debates over immigration that have dominated French political discourse since the 1980s came to a head in 1996 with the occupation by "illegal" African immigrants of the Saint-Bernard parish, hunger strikes, and public protests in the city square. On March 18 of that year, three hundred undocumented immigrants, primarily from Mali and Senegal, sought sanctuary from deportation in a church. The Archbishop of Paris, Cardinal Lustiger, requested that police forcibly remove them.[52] Dressed in riot gear, officers carrying batons entered the Saint Ambroise church on March 22, 1996, and beat several of the men participating in a hunger strike. Chronicling the protest in his diary, one of the participants, Mamady Sané, detailed the chaos: "Sixty-two adults were arrested, and the others who had escaped were surrounded by policemen. They told them that they should know Blacks had no place here in France."[53]

Black Lives Matter: A Global Network

> "The death of George Floyd has a strong echo in the death in France of my little brother. . . . What's happening in the United States is happening in France. Our brothers are dying."[54]

On February 26, 2012, George Zimmerman, a neighborhood watch coordinator in Sanford, Florida, shot seventeen-year-old Trayvon Martin as he walked home from a convenience store. The story of Martin's death reached national attention approximately two weeks later on March 7, whereupon a broad cross section of society weighed in on these events.[55] Covered by the mainstream press, news of Martin's murder was also shared via an emerging Twitter campaign that would birth an international movement. This use of a digital platform marks a new phase of the Black Freedom Struggle and underscores the role social media has played as a critical tool for activists in the twenty-first century. #BlackLivesMatter became more than a Twitter hashtag when Alicia Garza, Patrisse Cullors, and Opal Tometi used social media platforms to raise awareness about the deaths of unarmed Black men and women across the nation.[56] They rallied a host of local activists across the nation to organize peaceful protests, stage demonstrations, and raise money to expose the alarming number of Black men, women, and children killed every year by the police and by civilian vigilantes with impunity.[57] As the hashtag blossomed into a movement, cities and towns established BLM local chapters, laying the foundation for the BLM Global Network. This network of national and international chapters leverages grassroots leadership and a flexible programmatic agenda to support organizers fighting for justice in transnational contexts.[58]

In 2016, French activists organized a BLM chapter in response to intrusive identity checks by the police, which had contributed to the death of African immigrant Adama Traoré. On the evening of July 19, 2016, police confronted Traoré and his brother, Bagui Traoré, demanding to see their immigration papers. Adama fled the scene in an attempt to avoid an identity check, because he had forgotten to carry his ID.⁵⁹ Three officers pursued and forced him to the ground, despite his cries that he could not breathe. They handcuffed and transported him to the precinct, where he lost consciousness and later died in police custody. In part because his death at the hands of police so resembled the deaths of Eric Garner (who pleaded, "I can't breathe"), Freddie Gray (who died while being transported to the police precinct), and George Floyd (who was forced to the ground and asphyxiated), Adama Traoré's death and its impact on his family became a touchstone for activism around the question of police brutality in France.

In the wake of Adama Traoré's death, activists focused their efforts on exposing the brutal tactics of the French police. Protected by law, police can stop anyone they deem to be disorderly.⁶⁰ Deliberately vague and therefore ripe for abuse, officers most often apply the label "disorderly" to those they stereotype as suspicious, which means that Black youth bear the brunt of police harassment and violence. Police in France overwhelmingly target males of North and Sub-Saharan African descent: a national study conducted in 2017 found that Black and Arab young men were "twenty times more likely than others to be stopped."⁶¹ Black youths and adults describe these police actions as often going well beyond a routine identification check, ranging from orders to empty their pockets and bags to full body searches.⁶² On July 19, 2016, over one thousand people marched to protest Adama Traoré's death and the excessive brutality of French policing in the Parisian suburb of Beaumont-sur-Oise. In response to this display of solidarity, the BLM branch in Cincinnati, Ohio, posted the following message to their Facebook site: "In the streets of Paris people are screaming Black Lives Matter. Last Tuesday, the French Police [took] away the young life of Adama Traoré on his 24th birthday. But our French brothers and sisters have said enough is enough and have flooded the streets again over the weekend. Our movement has long crossed our country's borders and it is becoming a global phenomenon . . . until we get justice we will have no peace."⁶³ The American rallying cry, "no justice, no peace," echoed throughout France (in English and French) as protesters took to the streets to demonstrate against police brutality.

The Traoré family became targets for retribution after raising their concerns and organizing protests. When they and local supporters arrived at a local council meeting to request more information about the death, police barred them from entry and used tear gas to disperse the crowd. On the day of the second council meeting, police arrested Traoré's brothers, Bagui and Youssouf Traoré, in their own homes. Charged with verbal and physical abuse toward the police, the brothers were denied bail by the local judge and were eventually sentenced to several months in jail, fined 7,000 euros in damages, and banned from living in Beaumont-sur-Oise for two years, despite the fact that local authorities could only offer contradictory testimonies.[64] To justify banning the Traorés from residency in Beaumont-sur-Oise, the court cited a "need for serenity" and framed the Traorés' presence in the city as a threat to public order. Residency bans are commonly leveraged in French law in response to domestic violence and drug trafficking cases.[65] They protect civilian victims from further harassment or contact with an assailant and attempt to remove threats to a community's health and wellness. The application of the law to a resident protesting police violence, however, represented a new interpretation and underscored the claims made by Black French protestors about the judicial bias they face in their interactions with the French justice system. A tool of repression, the residency bans bar individuals from living in communities where they carry political influence. Traoré's sister Assa went further, framing the punishment as a weapon of family destruction: it killed one brother and imprisoned two others while banning them from their neighborhood. After an appeal, the court reduced Bagui Traoré's sentence to six months in prison, but it still took several public protests for the courts to lift the residency ban.[66]

Emerging as the family's spokesperson, Assa Traoré maintained the ability to speak out without suffering the same criminal sanctions as her brothers due to her gender. Her capacity to enter into politically charged spaces and critically engage individuals wielding political, cultural, and social power was a strategic tactic. She called upon local organizers, politicians, and cultural icons to help deliver the message: "Justice and truth for Adama."[67] Her message galvanized a collective of high-profile artists, athletes, actors, writers, and academics who drafted an open letter to local and national authorities outlining the inconsistencies of the official police report and violations in police conduct:

> The Adama Traoré affair is everybody's business: to affirm and defend equal rights . . . we, artists, athletes, actors, [and] writers . . . relay . . . [that] the inhabitants of working-class neighborhoods are hit daily by economic and racial violence. . . . That is why we . . . support the demand of truth and justice for Adama . . . [and] all the victims of violence by forces of law and order. It is our common cause: together against police violence and their impunity.[68]

Mobilizing their efforts to increase the visibility of the cause, several of the signatories volunteered to perform at La Cigale in Paris on February 2, 2017. Performing under the banner "Vérité pour Adama" (Truth for Adama), some of French rap's biggest stars, including Kery James, Mac Tyer, Medina, Sofiane, Ärsenik, and Youssoupha, organized to raise funds for the family's legal fees. This use of Afro-French performers deploying their social and cultural capital for political movements echoes the longer history of activism by Black artists, writers, and athletes from the United States and abroad, including James Baldwin, Josephine Baker, Fela Kuti, and Paul Robeson, some of whom I have outlined here. And the "Vérité pour Adama" concert in 2017 found its transatlantic counterpart in the efforts of contemporary American athletes and entertainers like Colin Kaepernick, Janelle Monáe, and Kendrick Lamar, who celebrated the #BLM protests through athletic contests, musical performances, branding, and donations. Unifying earlier generations of performers with millennial artists, these transnational efforts to raise awareness of a long history of police brutality fits within a continuum of Black celebrities as political figures and protest artists.

The 2020 death of George Floyd in Minneapolis revived the salience of Traoré's murder, and once again, Assa Traoré helmed the movement against police brutality in France.[69] Leading thousands of protesters in the Parisian city center, Assa declared, "The death of George Floyd has a strong echo in the death in France of my little brother. What's happening in the United States is happening in France. Our brothers are dying."[70] Marching in the streets, people carried signs and chanted, "Je n'arrive plus à respirer," or "I Can't Breathe."[71] Repeating the refrain "I can't breathe," Assa Traoré reminded protesters that police in both the United States and France frequently use excessive force, especially in their interactions with people of color, and these interactions all too often end in death. In the wake of these protests, public campaigns around racial identity and "Frenchness" received increased exposure under the banner "Je suis noire, pas Black." This slogan, codified in film, merchandise, marches, and music, empowers Afro-French populations to reclaim the word "noire" to describe their racial identity instead of the English term "Black."[72] More than a repudiation of transatlantic alliances with #BLM, "Je suis noire, pas Black" demands French ownership of its own brand of antiracism despite the French state's resistance to contending with race, national identity, and belonging.

The interconnected relationship between race, history, and French national identity has evolved, shifted, and transformed over the years. Nevertheless, Black people's demands for greater visibility and their wrestling with society's institutional inequality remain permanent features of their experiences in France. Three generations of Black migrants have added complexity and nuance to previously unilateral positions on these questions of citizenship, rights, and belonging. Yet long after the hopeful moment of decolonization—which gave rise not only to *Présence Africaine* but also to the Congress of Black Writers and Artists—fizzled, police brutality and the frustration of Black communities embodied in the suburban uprisings from the 1980s to the new millennium persist. Struck from the French Constitution in 2018, "race" is no longer a component of identity recognized as a legal category.[73] Former French president François Hollande celebrated this change, declaring, "There are no different races ... [race] has no place in the Republic."[74] In reality, this Constitutional transformation merely means that activists, lawyers, and citizens lack the legal lexicon to call attention to racial discrimination. The French government's resistance to acknowledging race in the face of overwhelming evidence that police view Black people as criminals is an attempt to silence the deafening cries of Black French people, proving that race still very much matters.

The search for truth and justice is an uneven and ever-evolving process. This chapter set out to chronicle the synergic activist connection between the United States and France over the past seventy years. Tracing the paths of writers, entertainers, and activists as they contested inequality and injustice on both continents, the CRM revealed how participants were impacted by white supremacy, classism, homophobia, patriarchy, respectability politics, and misogyny. These forces constrained the movement's redemptive goals. In the new millennium, the quest for Black liberation continues.

NOTES

1. James Baldwin details his experiences and rationale for leaving the United States in a 1984 interview with the *Paris Review*. See Jordan Elgrably, "James Baldwin, The Art of Fiction," *Paris Review* 91 (Spring 1984), https://www.theparisreview.org/interviews/2994/the-art-of-fiction-no-78-james-baldwin.
2. Pauline Guedj, "Perspective through Exile: James Baldwin in France - France-Amérique," January 22, 2021, https://france-amerique.com/perspective-through-exile-james-baldwin-in-france.
3. Two years after moving to France, Baldwin wrote, "The African . . . has endured privation, injustice, [and] medieval cruelty" in "Encounter on the Seine: Black Meets Brown," first published in *The Reporter* on June 6, 1950, as "The Negro in Paris." This article cites the republished essay from James Baldwin, "Encounter on the Seine," in *Notes of a Native Son* (London: Penguin Books, 1995), 88–89.
4. This number is an estimate because it is illegal for the French state to collect data on ethnicity and race. For more information, see Erik Bleich, "Race Policy in France," Brookings Institution, May 1, 2001, www.brookings.edu/articles/race-policy-in-france.
5. Annette Gordon-Reed, *The Hemingses of Monticello: An American Family* (New York: Norton, 2009), 169–77.
6. Guy Sorman, "Black Lives Matter in Paris: An American Movement in France," *France-Amerique*, September 14, 2020, https://france-amerique.com/en/black-lives-matter-in-paris-an-american-movement-in-france.
7. This section was published first in my dissertation, Kishauna Elaine Soljour, "Beyond the Banlieue: French Postcolonial Migration and the Politics of

Sub-Saharan Identity" (PhD diss. Syracuse University, 2019), https://surface.syr.edu/etd/1002. For a list of monographs discussing white French activism in May 1968, see Julian Bourg, *From Revolution to Ethics: May 1968 and Contemporary French Thought* (Montreal: McGill-Queens University Press, 2017); Ronald Fraser, *1968: A Student Generation in Revolt* (New York: Pantheon Books, 1988); Kristin Ross, *May '68 and Its Afterlives* (Chicago: University of Chicago Press, 2008); Daniel Singer, *Prelude to Revolution: France in May 1968* (Chicago: Haymarket Books, 2013).

8. Jadine Labbé Pacheco, "Je suis noire, pas 'black,'" *L'Obs*, August 29, 2017, https://www.nouvelobs.com/rue89/nos-vies-intimes/20170828.OBS3873/je-suis-noire-pas-black.html.
9. Gérard Noiriel, *The French Melting Pot: Immigration, Citizenship, and National Identity (Contradictions of Modernity)*, trans. Geoffroy De Laforcad (Minneapolis: University of Minnesota Press, 1996).
10. Noiriel, *French Melting Pot*, 87–90.
11. For works discussing the categorization of immigrants after 1975, see Martin Baldwin-Edwards and Martin Schain, *The Politics of Immigration in Western Europe* (New York: Routledge, 1994) and Rayna Bailey, *Immigration and Migration* (New York: Facts On File, 2008).
12. Abdoulaye Gueye estimates that by 1952 to 1953 there were about four thousand African students residing in France. See Abdoulaye Gueye, *Les intellectuels africains en France* (Paris: L'Harmattan, 2002), 72. For more about Black migrant workers, see Jean-Philippe Dedieu and Aissatou Mbodj-Pouye, "The First Collective Protest of Black African Migrants in Postcolonial France (1960–1975): A Struggle for Housing and Rights," *Ethnic and Racial Studies* 39, no. 6 (2016): 958–75.
13. See Pierre Bideberry, Director de l'Office National d'Immigration, "Bilan de Vingt Années d' Immigration—1946-1966," *Revue Française des Affaires Sociales*, no.2 (April-June 1967); Patrick R. Ireland, *The Policy Challenge of Ethnic Diversity: Immigrant Politics in France and Switzerland* (Boston: Harvard University Press, 1994); Baldwin-Edwards and Schain, *Politics of Immigration*; Dominic Thomas, *Black France: Colonialism, Immigration, and Transnationalism* (Bloomington: Indiana University Press, 2006); Paul A. Silverstein, *Algeria in France: Transpolitics, Race, and Nation* (Bloomington: Indiana University Press, 2004); and Bailey, *Immigration and Migration*.
14. Jacques Howlett, "Presence Africaine 1947-1958," *Journal of Negro History* 43, no. 2 (1958): 140–50. doi:10.2307/2715595.
15. Davidson Nicol, "Alioune Diop and the African Renaissance," *African Affairs* 78, no. 310 (January 1979): 3, doi:10.1093/oxfordjournals.afraf.a097079.
16. Claude McKay spent a considerable amount of time in France. A consistent participant in salon culture, McKay published work in the *Revue du Monde Noir*, founded in 1931. In addition to publishing poetry in this periodical,

McKay's novel *Banjo* takes place in Marseilles, France, focusing on the experiences of Black dockworkers and their treatment by white French populations.
17. Kwame Anthony Appiah and Henry Louis Gates Jr., *Africana: The Encyclopedia of the African and African American Experience* (New York: Basic Civitas Books, 1999), 193.
18. Alioune Diop, "Niam N'goura: Ou les raisons d'être de présence africaine," *Présence Africaine*, no. 1 (November–December 1947): 7–14, https://www.jstor.org/stable/24346671.
19. Marga Graf, "Roots of Identity: The National and Cultural Self in *Présence Africaine*," *CLCWeb: Comparative Literature and Culture* 3, no. 2 (January 2001), https://doi.org/10.7771/1481-4374.1121. While French was the primary language of the publication at its inception, the periodical published an English edition along with the French version from 1955 to 1961.
20. Mukala Kadima-Nzuji, Gbanou Sélom Komlan, and Mudimbé Vumbi Yoka, *L'Afrique au miroir des littératures, des sciences de l'homme et de la société mélanges offerts à V.Y. Mudimbe* (Paris, France: L'Harmattan, 2003), 5.
21. Richard Wright, *Uncle Tom's Children* (New York: Harper and Row, 1965), 184–85.
22. Baldwin's essay was originally published in the literary journal *Preuves/Encounter*, which was a CIA-fronted press. Baldwin, however, was unaware of this fact at the time. It was later reprinted in *Notes of a Native Son*. James Baldwin, *The Price of the Ticket: Collected Nonfiction, 1948–1985* (New York: St. Martin's, 1999), 43–45.
23. A central tension during the Congress was the limited role of the American delegation, as seen in M. Price Mars, "Débats: 19 SEPTEMBRE, à 21 H," *Présence Africaine*, Nouvelle Série, no. 8/10 (1956): 66–83, https://www.jstor.org/stable/24346890.
24. "Discussion," *Présence Africaine*, Nouvelle Série, no. 8/10 (1956): 67, http://www.jstor.org/stable/24346890.
25. Brent Hayes Edwards, *The Practice of Diaspora: Literature, Translation, and the Rise of Black Internationalism* (Cambridge, MA: Harvard University Press, 2003), 13. Senghor quote extrapolated from Léopold Sédar Senghor, *Négritude et civilisation de l'universel* (Paris, France: Seuil, 1977), 274.
26. Baldwin, *Price of the Ticket*, 45.
27. Baldwin, *Price of the Ticket*, 57.
28. While Fejzula notes that her presence on the nineteen-person organizing committee may have been honorary, it is important to note that she later supported the Second Congress of Black Writers and Artists (1959) and the First World Festival of Black Artists (1966). Merve Fejzula, "Women and the 1956 Congress of Black Writers and Artists in Paris," *Black Perspectives*, April 2, 2017, https://www.aaihs.org/women-and-the-1956-congress-of-black-writers-and-artists-in-paris.

29. "Messages," *Présence Africaine*, Nouvelle Série, no. 8/10 (1956): 398–99, https://www.jstor.org/stable/24346916. Other materials used to suggest the presence of Black women during the events include photos and letters. See Fejzula, "Women and the 1956 Congress," for further description of these artifacts.
30. Baker's actions mirror generations of Black performers (others in her generation include Harry Belafonte, Billie Holiday, and Nina Simone) who also used their artistry and cultural influence to protest the evils of segregation.
31. Mary L. Dudziak discusses Baker's legacy both in the United States and in France, as well as her activism and French citizenship, in "Josephine Baker, Racial Protest, and the Cold War," *Journal of American History* 81, no. 2 (1994): 543–70, doi:10.2307/2081171.
32. Josephine Baker's speech was a prelude to the official program, and neither her name nor mention of the speech is represented in official documents. See Photograph, "Civil Rights March on Washington, DC," Aug. 28, 1963; NWDNS-306-SSM-4D(86)3, Records of the United States Information Agency, Record Group 306, National Archives. Two separate parades were held for the Civil Rights leaders, divided by gender. The men marched down Pennsylvania Avenue. The women, including Daisy Bates, Josephine Baker, and Rosa Parks, marched down Independence Avenue.
33. Jessica Goldstein, "March on Washington Had One Female Speaker: Josephine Baker," *Washington Post*, August 23, 2011, https://www.washingtonpost.com/lifestyle/style/march-on-washington-had-one-female-speaker-josephine-baker/2011/08/08/gIQAHqhBaJ_story.html.
34. Josephine Baker, "Speech at the March on Washington," 1963, *Blackpast*, September 22, 2019, https://www.blackpast.org/african-american-history/1963-josephine-baker-speech-march-washington.
35. Jean Marbella, "The Fire Both Times: Baltimore Riots after Martin Luther King's Death 50 Years Ago Left Scars That Remain," *Baltimore Sun*, June 30, 2019, https://www.baltimoresun.com/maryland/baltimore-city/bs-md-mlk-anniversary-riots-20180315-htmlstory.html.
36. Josephine Baker and Jo Bouillon, *Josephine* (Buenos Aires, Argentina: ANESA, 1977), 263–64.
37. Thai Jones, "Two, Three, Many Columbias." *New York Times*, January 4, 2008, https://www.nytimes.com/2008/01/06/education/edlife/hunger.html.
38. "Dow Chemical Attempts Recruiting at N.Y.U., and a Protest Results," *New York Times*, March 7, 1968, https://www.nytimes.com/1968/03/07/archives/dow-chemical-attempts-recruiting-at-nyu-and-a-protest-results.html.
39. Jennifer Schuessler, "At Columbia, Revisiting the Revolutionary Students of 1968," *New York Times*, March 21, 2018, https://www.nytimes.com/2018/03/21/arts/columbia-university-1968-protest.html.
40. As young people represented the forefront of Civil Rights activism in the United States, African students in France similarly led direct action protests throughout the decade of the 1960s. For example, Senegalese students

first occupied the embassy of Senegal in Paris on May 24, 1964. This moment of collective action is examined in both Félix F. Germain, *Decolonizing the Republic: African and Caribbean Migrants in Postwar Paris, 1946–1974* (East Lansing, MI: Michigan State University Press, 2016) and Wendy Pojmann, *Migration and Activism in Europe since 1945* (United Kingdom: Palgrave Macmillan, 2008), 25.

41. Françoise Blum, "Cité Universitaire (Afrique)," CHS, accessed May 18, 2022, https://chs-maijuin68.huma-num.fr/parcours/cite-universitaire-afrique.

42. This incident is referenced in Daniel A. Gordon, *Immigrants and Intellectuals: May '68 and the Rise of Anti-Racism in France* (Pontypool: Merlin Press, 2012). The Ministry of the Interior filed a report marked "secret and confidential" on the activities of "Les Etudiants D'Afrique Noire et Madagascar en France," and agents infiltrated meetings organized by Federation des Etudiants D'Afrique Noire en France (FEANF) and monitored their planning of protests throughout Paris (AN, 19960134/18).

43. Dedieu and Mbodj-Pouye, "The First Collective Protest of Black African Migrants in Postcolonial France," 964–65; Préfecture de Paris, Logement collectif à caractère non lucratif des travailleurs à Paris et dans les trois départements limitrophes, 1968 (AN, 20050150/61) and Fonds d'Action Sociale (AN, 19870056/1).

44. In a report by the Ministry of Interior, it states, "the number of foreigners actually blamed for public disturbances by political demonstrations has been significant. It was 270 in 1968, and 53 in 1969. It was 18 in 1970, 13 in 1971 and 7 in 1972." This significant decrease in number is reflective of the government crackdown on students (AN, 19960134/18).

45. Dedieu and Mbodj-Pouye, "First Collective Protest," 966. This led to proposals to relocate African migrants through the public housing system to prevent their continued political agitation (AN, 19870056/1).

46. Director of the FBI J. Edgar Hoover created COINTELPRO (an acronym for "Counterintelligence Program") in August 1956 to combat the advances made by Black activists. See "COINTELPRO and the History of Domestic Spying," National Public Radio, January 18, 2006, https://www.npr.org/templates/story/story.php?storyId=5161811.

47. Ward Churchill and Jim Vander Wall, *Agents of Repression: The FBI's Secret Wars against the Black Panther Party and the American Indian Movement* (Boston, MA: South End Press, 1990) and Robyn C. Spencer, *The Revolution Has Come: Black Power, Gender, and the Black Panther Party in Oakland* (Durham, NC: Duke University Press, 2016).

48. See Paul A. Silverstein, *Algeria in France: Transpolitics, Race, and Nation* (Bloomington: Indiana University Press, 2004); and Bailey, *Immigration and Migration*.

49. Andre Gorz and Philippe Gavi, "La Bataille d'Ivry," *Les Temps Modernes*, March 1970, 1388–416; Adrian Adams, "Prisoners in Exile: Senegalese

Workers in France," Institute of Race Relations, *Race and Class* 16, no. 2 (1974), https://rac.sagepub.com/content/16/2/157.full.pdf; and Ireland, *Policy Challenge of Ethnic Diversity*, 128–30.

50. See Anne Chemin, "Since the 19th Century, Immigrants Have Been the Scapegoats in France's Crises," *Le Monde*, February 19, 2023, https://www.lemonde.fr/en/france/article/2023/02/19/since-the-19th-century-immigrants-have-been-the-scapegoats-in-france-s-crises_6016449_7.html; Didier Fassin, "Compassion and Repression: The Moral Economy of Immigration Policies in France," *Cultural Anthropology* 20, no. 3 (2005): 362–87, https://www.jstor.org/stable/3651596; and Martin A. Schain, "Ordinary Politics: Immigrants, Direct Action, and the Political Process in France," *French Politics and Society* 12, no. 2/3 (1994): 65–83, https://www.jstor.org/stable/42844410.

51. Bailey, *Immigration and Migration*, 69–70.

52. See Kay Chadwick, *Catholicism, Politics, and Society in Twentieth-Century France* (Liverpool: Liverpool University Press, 2000), 187–90; Walter Nicholls and Justus Uitermark, *Cities and Social Movements: Immigrant Rights Activism in the US, France, and the Netherlands, 1970–2015* (Chichester, West Sussex, UK: John Wiley, 2017), 194–97; Dominique Simonnot, "Des curés au côté des sans-papiers: Les Occupations à Paris et en banlieue accentuent les dissensions au sein de l'église," *Libération*, July 1, 1996, https://www.liberation.fr/libe-3-metro/1996/07/01/des-cures-au-cote-des-sans-papiers-les-occupations-a-paris-et-en-banlieue-accentuent-les-dissensions_177176/; and Craig R. Whitney, "African Immigrants Refusing to Leave France," *New York Times*, April 04, 1996, https://www.nytimes.com/1996/04/04/world/african-immigrants-refusing-to-leave-france.html.

53. Mamady Sané, *Sorti de l'ombre: Journal d'un sans-papier* (Paris: Le Temps des Cerises, 1996), 45. Excerpt translated by Jane Freedman.

54. A quote from Assa Traore's address to protestors on June 13, 2020. See, "'Our Brothers Are Dying': Black Lives Matter Protestors Clash with Police in Paris," *CNBC*, June 13, 2020, https://www.cnbc.com/2020/06/13/our-brothers-are-dying-black-lives-matter-protestors-clash-with-police-in-paris.html.

55. Daniel Trotta, "Trayvon Martin: Before the World Heard the Cries," Reuters, April 3, 2012, https://www.reuters.com/article/us-usa-florida-shooting-trayvon/trayvon-martin-before-the-world-heard-the-cries-idUSBRE8320UK20120403; "Events Leading to the Shooting of Trayvon Martin," *New York Times*, April 1, 2012, https://archive.nytimes.com/www.nytimes.com/interactive/2012/04/02/us/the-events-leading-to-the-shooting-of-trayvon-martin.html; Erhardt Graeff, Matt Stempeck, and Ethan Zuckerman, "The Battle for 'Trayvon Martin': Mapping a Media Controversy Online and Off-Line," *First Monday* 19, no. 2–3 (February 2014): n.p., doi:10.5210/fm.v19i2.4947.

56. For more on Black Lives Matter, see Patrisse Khan-Cullors and asha bandele, *When They Call You A Terrorist: A Black Lives Matter Memoir* (New York: St. Martin's Press, 2019).
57. Jonathan Capehart, "From Trayvon Martin to 'Black Lives Matter,'" *Washington Post*, February 27, 2015, https://www.washingtonpost.com/blogs/post-partisan/wp/2015/02/27/from-trayvon-martin-to-black-lives-matter; Darran Simon, "Five Years after Trayvon Martin's Death, a Movement Lives On," CNN, February 27, 2017, https://www.cnn.com/2017/02/26/us/trayvon-martin-death-anniversary/index.html.
58. Barbara Ransby argues that Black Lives Matter is distinctive in its approach due to its shift from hierarchical leadership platforms that dominate national activist organizations to an emphasis on grassroots organization. For more information, see Barbara Ransby, "Black Lives Matter Is Democracy in Action," *New York Times*, October 21, 2017, https://www.nytimes.com/2017/10/21/opinion/sunday/black-lives-matter-leadership.html. Ransby further details her argument in the book *Making All Black Lives Matter: Reimagining Freedom in the Twenty-First Century* (Oakland: University of California Press, 2018).
59. There are multiple and conflicting accounts of what occurred after this arrest. For a more detailed account of the events leading to Adama Traoré's death, see Timothée Boutry, "Les dernières minutes d'Adama Traoré," *Le Parisien*, August 2, 2016, https://www.leparisien.fr/faits-divers/les-dernieres-minutes-d-adama-traore-02-08-2016-6010063.php; Sarah Paillou, "En images: Mort d'Adama Traoré: La marche bloquée par les CRS," *Le Parisien*, July 30, 2016, https://www.leparisien.fr/beaumont-sur-oise-95260/en-images-mort-d-adama-traore-la-marche-bloquee-par-les-crs-30-07-2016-6005987.php.
60. Plausible reasons for an identity check include committed or attempting to commit an offense; preparing to commit a crime or offense or can provide information about a crime or offense; is the subject of research ordered by a judicial authority or has violated the obligations or prohibitions to which it is subject in the context of a judicial review; a house arrest with electronic surveillance; and a sentence or a measure followed by the judge of the penalties applications. See "Contrôle d'identité: Quelles sont les règles?," Service-Public-Fr, https://www.service-public.fr/particuliers/vosdroits/F1036.
61. Much like the "stop and frisk" policy in New York City, this approach fits within a paradigm of global policing tactics. See "Discrimination, contrôle au faciès... quelles sont les règles du contrôle d'identité?," *France 3*, October 22, 2018, https://france3-regions.francetvinfo.fr/paris-ile-de-france/seine-saint-denis/discrimination-controle-au-facies-quelles-sont-regles-du-controle-identite-1562604.html.

62. "'The Root of Humiliation': Abusive Identity Checks in France," *Human Rights Watch*, January 26, 2012, https://www.hrw.org/report/2012/01/26/root-humiliation/abusive-identity-checks-france.
63. This excerpt was extracted from a larger article about Black Lives Matter France: "After Police Killings, Black Lives Matter Comes to France," *TeleSUR*, July 27, 2016, https://www.telesurenglish.net/news/After-Police-Killings-Black-Lives-Matter-Comes-to-France-20160726-0048.html.
64. Julia Pascual, "Bagui Traoré condamné à huit mois ferme pour violences," *Le Monde*, December 15, 2016, https://www.lemonde.fr/police-justice/article/2016/12/15/un-des-freres-d-adama-traore-condamne-a-huit-mois-ferme-pour-violences_5049076_1653578.html.
65. The text of the law reads, "The prohibition of residence prohibits the defendant from appearing in certain places determined by the jurisdiction. It also includes surveillance and assistance measures. The list of prohibited places and the measures of supervision and assistance may be modified by the judge of the enforcement of sentences, under the conditions set by the Code of Criminal Procedure. The prohibition of residence may not exceed ten years in the case of a conviction for a crime and five years in the case of conviction for an offense." See "Article 131-31, Created by Law 92-683 1992-07-22 JORF 23 July 1992 Corrigendum JORF 23 December 1992 in Force on 1 March 1994," Légifrance, Le Service Public de l'Accès au Droit – Accueil, https://www.legifrance.gouv.fr/codes/article_lc/LEGIARTI000006417303.
66. For more detail on the residence ban and press coverage of Bagui Traoré's arrest, see Claire Hache, "Affaire Traoré: Comment expliquer l'interdiction de séjour à Beaumont-sur-Oise?," *L'Express*, December 15, 2016, https://www.lexpress.fr/actualite/societe/justice/affaire-traore-comment-expliquer-l-interdiction-de-sejour-a-beaumont-sur-oise_1860749.html; "Affaire Adama Traoré: Le point sur la situation," *Clique*, July 19, 2018, https://www.clique.tv/affaire-adama-traore-depots-de-plainte-et-financement-de-frais-de-justice-pour-la-maire-de-beaumont-sur-oise; Pascual, "Bagui Traoré condamné"; Romain Chiron, "Beaumont-sur-Oise: Les frères d'Adama Traoré condamnés, le plus jeune remis en liberté," *Le Parisien*, December 14, 2016, https://www.leparisien.fr/beaumont-sur-oise-95260/beaumont-sur-oise-prison-ferme-requise-contre-les-freres-traore-14-12-2016-6456504.php; Antoine Hasday, "La mort d'Adama Traoré, une affaire d'état," *Slate*, July 26, 2017, https://www.slate.fr/story/149028/mort-adama-traore.
67. Louise Couvelaire, "Assa Traoré, la sœur d'Adama, porte-voix des quartiers malgré elle," *Le Monde*, December 14, 2016, https://www.lemonde.fr/societe/article/2016/12/14/assa-traore-porte-voix-des-quartiers-malgre-elle_5048631_3224.html.
68. Signatories included the French rapper Fik's Niavo, rapper Casey, filmmaker Alice Diop, journalist Rokhaya Diallo, actor Omar Sy, Joan W. Scott

(historian and Professor Emerita at Princeton University), and Sylvie Tissot (French sociologist, activist, and documentary filmmaker). For the full manifesto, see "Mort d'Adama Traoré: "Si on se tait, c'est toute notre société qui se salit," *Libération*, February 14, 2017, https://www.liberation.fr/france/2017/02/14/mort-d-adama-traore-si-on-se-tait-c-est-toute-notre-societe-qui-se-salit_1548531.

69. George Floyd died on May 25, 2020, in 9 minutes and 29 seconds after a Minneapolis officer pinned him to the group and kept a knee on his neck. For further detail on these events, see Evan Hill, Ainara Tiefenthäler, Christiaan Triebert, Drew Jordan, Haley Willis, and Robin Stein, "How George Floyd Was Killed in Police Custody," *New York Times*, May 31, 2020, https://www.nytimes.com/2020/05/31/us/george-floyd-investigation.html.

70. "'Our Brothers Are Dying': Black Lives Matter Protestors Clash with Police in Paris," CNBC, June 13, 2020, https://www.cnbc.com/2020/06/13/our-brothers-are-dying-black-lives-matter-protestors-clsh-with-police-in-paris.html.

71. For more context on these events, see "#Blacklivesmatter / Adama Traoré, George Floyd et la police," June 3, 2020, *La Meute*, https://www.lameute.info/posts/blacklivesmatter-adama-traor-george-floyd-et-la-police.

72. Amadine Gay's 2017 film *Ouvrir la voix* (Speak up) contends with these sentiments through a series of interviews with Black French women. See *Ouvrir la voix*, written and directed by Amadine Gay, 2017, accessed February 10, 2019, https://ouvrirlavoixlefilm.fr.

73. "Race" was added to the 1946 iteration of the French Constitution in the wake of World War II. In response to the racially charged crimes of German Nazis and the Vichy regime, France used the term "race" to position itself against racism. The first article of the 1946 constitution read, "All citizens are equal before the law *regardless of origin, race or religion*" (emphasis added). Lawmakers agreed to remove the term "race" and replace it with "gender." The current first article of the constitution reads, "All citizens are equal before the law *regardless of gender, origin or religion*" (emphasis added). For more information on the removal of race from the French Constitution, see Etienne Balibar, "Le mot 'race' n'est pas 'de trop' dans la constitution française," *Mediapart*, October 5, 2015, blogs.mediapart.fr/etienne-balibar/blog/051015/le-mot-race-nest-pas-de-trop-dans-la-constitution-francaise; Rokhaya Diallo, "France's Dangerous Move to Remove 'Race' from Its Constitution," *Washington Post*, July 13, 2018, https://www.washingtonpost.com/news/global-opinions/wp/2018/07/13/frances-dangerous-move-to-remove-race-from-its-constitution; "'Race' Out, Gender Equality In as France Updates Constitution," *France 24*, June 28, 2018, https://www.france24.com/en/20180628-race-out-gender-equality-france-updates-constitution.

74. "'Race' Out, Gender Equality In."

CHAPTER 7

The Ambivalence of Activist Photography

July 10, 2016

David V. Mason

Around 6:30 p.m. on July 10, 2016, social media alerted me to the fact that people had stopped traffic on the Hernando de Soto Bridge. Interstate 40 crosses the Mississippi River atop this two-mile bridge, linking the city of Memphis and much of the eastern USA to the west. Any obstruction of traffic across this bridge constitutes a significant disruption of things far beyond Memphis's own day-to-day operations. The gathering apparently began less than two miles away at the FedEx Forum, Memphis's eighteen-thousand-seat indoor arena. Police in Baton Rouge, Louisiana, had killed Alton Sterling on July 5. The following day, a police officer in Minnesota killed Philando Castile.[1] What people in Memphis heard from the various police departments, from the news, and through the media maelstrom did not say anything that denied the brutality—the senseless device—of the killings. In response, a few hundred Memphians assembled outside the Forum in the waning afternoon.[2] This first crowd gathered across from Clayborn Temple, on the other side of Dr. Martin Luther

King Jr. Boulevard, where, in the spring of 1968, African American sanitation workers organized a strike and staged public protests against the city's barbaric policies that financially exploited Black sanitation workers and placed them in physical danger.[3]

A forum—the FedEx Forum—it seems, was not enough. Chants bellowed through bullhorns for awhile, but the people wanted to speak louder and not only to each other. They walked away from the Forum's concrete plaza, set so comfortably out of the way of the city's important business, past the pockets of police officers staked out here and there, anticipating that the crowd would go southward, toward the National Civil Rights Museum, the transformed Lorraine Motel, where the city's protest marches typically conclude. Instead, the people pressed northward, into the city's downtown and its concentration of people and buildings. They moved past the police headquarters and city hall. About a mile from where they had first gathered, the marchers turned toward the Mississippi River, and the police regrouped to prevent the crowd from moving up Interstate 40's Front Street off-ramp. A brief standoff occurred there, where traffic descends from the bridge. When they discovered that a second group had gone up to the bridge on the Riverside Drive ramp, the police at Front Street relented. Men, women, and children then marched up Interstate 40's Front Street off-ramp onto the bridge. By 6:30 p.m., and only with their bodies, some hundreds—perhaps a thousand by this time—stopped the bridge's heedless flow of traffic.[4] The city's police force mobilized at all points. Helicopters churned overhead. Drivers stepped out of cars, now packed together, bumper to bumper, as tightly as though parked on a ferry. As the sun began to set, I was in my home, three or four miles away, catching bits of personal internet broadcasts sent out from the site. I made a short drive to downtown and approached the bridge on foot shortly before seven o'clock. The lights on the bridge were not yet on.

I remain ambivalent about going there with a camera. I could not stay away, yet that bridge at that moment was not my place. Stephen Shames—a white man who photographed the Black Panther Party in a more-or-less official capacity in the late 1960s—asserted to scholar Leigh Raiford that a photographer's fundamental impetus is "wanting to be there."⁵ I felt similarly. I certainly wanted to be there, but I left the house knowing that the camera lens always stands in the way of a photographer being anywhere but in some unarrived moment of the future. The photographer expects to create that future moment by staying behind the lens, distinctly apart from wherever, from whenever, they are.⁶ I expect that I wanted to be able to say later that I was there, to show through photographs that I was there, but that aim certainly entailed being not altogether in that space that Black lives made matter.

I went to the bridge hoping that I could make something worthwhile, something that could amplify the bodies and their voices that were there on the bridge, something through which that moment might assert itself into the future, but I went also knowing that my act of making could distort and deform what was. In my reflection on going to the bridge that is this chapter, I hope to do three things, beginning with an acknowledgment of the conventional rationale by which documentary photographers—particularly white photographers—have justified what they have made of Black experience in the time of the Civil Rights Movement (CRM) and since. As the biases built into whiteness shape how white photographers see through a camera lens, that conventional rationale has distinct weaknesses, so the best of photographic intentions can yet pose a threat. My second aim is to articulate how the threats that we sometimes call *implicit bias* manifest themselves aesthetically, particularly in photographs and in the photograph-making process. *Seeing* might be a straightforwardly biological-neurological operation, but it is modulated, if not determined, by centuries of racially biased habit, so that photographs are the products of already habituated faculties. Certainly, CRM photos reveal the biases of their white makers and their white editors. Recognizing the threat of white photography as a function of racial habit, I offer, as my third aim, a reconsideration of the conventional justification for white photography of Black moments. I went to the bridge to make photographs, and if there is any justification for that endeavor, it could be that the photographic activity might have the power to make me. A well-considered practice, sustained over time, might reshape a person's racially biased habits and might make new *seeing*. Here in 2024, we might understand how making photos can contribute to a reformation of the biases that make photography dangerous. Maybe there is a fourth thing in this essay. As a model of the theory I attempt here, and as an illustration of the paradox that photos present, I offer some of my own photos from July 10, 2016.

The several terrible things that occurred in May 2020 lead to the customary justification for documentary photography. Around May 6, 2020, video emerged of white men killing Ahmaud Arbery while he was jogging in Brunswick, Georgia. News that the FBI had opened an investigation of the death-by-police-gunfire of Breonna Taylor in Louisville, Kentucky, began to circulate around May 21. A video of Amy Cooper, a white woman calling 911 to falsely report that Christian Cooper (no relation), a Black man bird-watching in Central Park, was threatening her life went viral on May 25. On the same day that the Amy Cooper clip made its rounds, another video circulated that showed a police officer in Minneapolis, Minnesota, pressing his weight on George Floyd's neck until Floyd died. This was the avalanche of rottenness in that one month.

In that terrible month, some in Memphis, as elsewhere around the world, could not do nothing, even under the added threat of the COVID pandemic that mitigated against gatherings. Memphians planned a silent affirmation that Black Lives Matter for the evening of May 27, to proceed in a manner that would give necessary, carefully spread-out deference to the risk of COVID infection. Around 7:00 p.m., I went to Union Avenue with my camera and a homemade mask on my face, anxious about the health risk that a gathering of people posed yet still wanting to be there.

Perhaps in a manner that emblematized everything that summer, what would/should have been a silent and reasonably safe sixty-minute, sidewalk-bound demonstration became a six-hour ordeal. The turn came with the appearance of two white men with signs reading "Stop Black on Black Crime" and "Police Lives Matter Comply Confederate 901." It ended, finally, in the deep night, long after the neo-confederates had gone home, with a couple score of police in armor and shields, violently imposing themselves on the space and the people in it.⁷ That night, late May 2020, was the first of more than two weeks of daily protests in Memphis. The National Guard showed up downtown. Tear gas, too, was used on Front Street, when a solid group of citizens again approached the Hernando de Soto Bridge, below the short monorail and walking bridge that links downtown to a bit of island in the river.

Meanwhile, elsewhere in the world, the terribleness similarly worsened. A police station in Minneapolis burned, and police in Los Angeles, New York, and Buffalo beat people indiscriminately.⁸ Then president Trump dropped militarized violence on citizens for the sake of an obscene photo op.⁹ Something resembling a force of secret police thrust itself into the nation's capital city.¹⁰ By June 6, protests had occurred in all fifty states.¹¹ The demonstrations, protests, and civil disobedience went global—to Paris, to the occupied West Bank, to Tokyo.¹² Summer 2020 saw weeks of global outrage and action, and, in the midst of it all, more murders of Black people.

Video imagery lit the world that month. We know the world demonstrated together that summer because the photos have told us. The steady documentary stream surely made people and actions in Minneapolis, Los Angeles, New York, and as far as Hong Kong appear as a unified and united body.¹³ The photos of pain, outrage, anger, civil disobedience, violence inflicted, and violence suffered, gave people in the world something that they needed, as much as it also wounded them.

This conclusion about the helpfulness of photography is the most ready means of accepting the photographs of awful things and in awful times. Darnella Frazier received a Pulitzer Prize for the video record she made of George Floyd's murder, and the award committee expressly noted, as part of the rationale for the award, that Frazier's video "spurred protests against police brutality around the world."¹⁴ Dangerous as they may be, photos can be characterized as necessary to preserve acts that might otherwise disappear. As the conventional defense of documentary photography argues, photographs can collate and amplify people and their actions and keep them present for everyone. Through the internet's ever-immediacy, photographs can bond together disparate efforts that in decades past could never add to each others' power. Photographs can cohere fragments into a whole that more strongly defies authoritarian erasure. As in the course of the CRM decades ago, the moment that was summer 2020 seemed to say that, indeed, the photographer must *be there*, must push the lens at people in their jeopardy so as to mark their suffering, to sustain their efforts, and to propel earnest people and what they earnestly do toward a common future.

Even so, this most ready of justifications cannot overcome all critique. Even as we intuit that the visual record is necessary, an objection is equally necessary. Scholar Clarissa T. Sligh poses the questions that photographs themselves make us think are unaskable: "[To] the average person, news photographs represent reality," Sligh says, confirming the value we all find undeniable in those difficult photographs that plot the continuum from Birmingham in 1963 to Minneapolis in 2020. Yet, Sligh asks, without a pause, "Whose reality?" Also: "Why?"[15] The photograph is never a pure report, and neither the camera nor the photographer is merely a conduit through which *what is* passes, untouched and unmanipulated. A picture "is at once neutral and partisan," says scholar Leigh Raiford. It is "authentic yet unreliable."[16] That is, as a partisan and unreliable object, a picture poses a threat to truth, to reality, to people—the activity of making a picture perhaps even more so.

The language of photo making indicates the threat that photography poses. On the scene, a person *aims* a camera and *shoots* and *captures* the moment (see fig. 1). A person *takes* a picture. The power *to take* a fraught moment is itself an affirmation, an assertion, of that power that keeps one person secure from the jeopardy that is for others clear and present.

Noble intent is too obviously too little mitigation of photography's danger. The power that a photographer has to keep the taken moment in their own archive, to select and to issue afterward, cannot be trusted. Ambivalently, even while cameras gave crucial visibility to the CRM in the 1950s and 1960s, they also unmistakably *captured* and *took* Black agency, particularly when the photographer was white. Scholar Martin A. Berger's considered opinion is that photos that imaged the Movement's events in the 1950s and 1960s,

FIGURE 1. A photographer aiming a camera lens. Photo by David V. Mason

however well-meaning, too often stood against the Movement's own aims. The images that white photographers made, writes Berger, "impeded efforts to enact—or even imagine—reforms that threatened white racial power."[17] White photographers and the white editors of newspapers and magazines made post-facto selections of CRM photographs that accorded with their own biases and rationales and senses of the market, delivering consistently—no matter their liberal aims—"a picture of black inactivity."[18] Amid the glut of images of fire hoses slamming Black people to the ground, of dogs lunging and biting, and of white people literally pouring abuse on Black people in restaurants, alternatives did exist—photographs that showed Black people as actors and not as objects. We know that images in which Black people *did* appear as active agents *did* exist, not only from archival research but also because such photos did appear in the Black press of the time. Nevertheless, such imagery "gained little traction with whites" and did not make its way into mass (white) print circulation.[19] Berger shows that the print media even went to some pains to alter photographs, through cropping and even airbrushing, in order to produce imagery of the CRM in which Black people were passive—either the victims of white rage or suing somehow for the favor of white beneficence.[20]

The transformation of what *is* through what a photograph *shows* is not only the consequence of editorial, post-facto selection. The problem may run even deeper. The photo makers and editors of Berger's concerns needed no reasoning, no expressly selective rationale, when they had already themselves embodied, in their very eyes, the ethos of whiteness's immutable supremacy.[21] Though the after-the-fact selection of photos to accord with and to affirm biases threatens movements and the people who move them, the confident superiority of whiteness imposes on the very making, the violent *taking*, of photos, in the instant of pointing and framing and clicking, and in the moments just preceding. Sligh contends that photographers "base the photographs they make on pictures they already have in their minds."[22] In the moment of being there, the photographer's seeing gives its function to the photographer's self, immediate and ineluctable. The photographer's self already embodies a history and culture and practice, so what the person with the camera feels is worth seeing—what the person with the camera might perceive as already conveniently arranged for viewing, what the person senses will be of value if preserved, and how the person figures such moments might be best captured for the sake of the posterity that might receive them—affirms a race privilege. Even before the shutter snaps open, the photographer's self rolls an avalanche over the real, twisting it, smashing it, flattening it into some form that the photographer brought along.

No doubt, Frederick Douglass intuited just this in the nineteenth century, when he asserted, "Negroes can never have impartial portraits at the hands of white artists."[23] To the extent that portraitists make images according to the pictures they already have in their minds, so also the presumptively objective record of the protest (de)forms what is, from and according to the archive that lives in the recorder. When I, a white photographer, went to that bridge that July in 2016, I surely carried my whiteness with me, and aimed it, and threatened to take what was done there, to (de)form it, and I could hardly do otherwise.

The threat in photography rises from habit. In *Democracy in Black*, Eddie S. Glaude Jr. speaks of *racial habits*, which Glaude maintains are not merely learned behaviors that we naturalize in repetition, but rather behaviors that in repetition we so naturalize that they become embodied dispositions, fibers of the very structure of our brains, embedded in our bodies so that they manifest to a person as a sense of what makes reality—as, say, a sense of the beauty in a photograph and as a sense of what photos a newspaper market will value. Glaude likens such racial habits to bike riding: "For example," he writes, "when I first learned how to ride a bicycle I found myself thinking about every detail. Balancing the bike. Holding on to the handlebars. Pedaling. Avoiding that damn mailbox. Now, even though I haven't ridden a bicycle in years, I could just get on one and the basal ganglia would take over."[24] So naturally embodied is a habit like bike-riding that it would probably be impossible, under ordinary circumstances, for anyone who has once learned to ride a bike to find again a condition of not knowing how it is done. Alluding to the kind of cognitive theory that recent neuroscience has made possible, but echoing a tradition of thought that precedes the fMRI machine, including theorists Marcel Mauss and Pierre Bourdieu and Judith Butler, Glaude characterizes racial bias as the consequence of such bike-riding habituation, the top layer of a lifetime, and lifetimes preceding, of cultural sedimentation laid down year upon year, century upon century, "through the details of daily life . . . not as rules, but as habits." These generationally embodied habits add up, in the present, to the way we "interact with people of different racial backgrounds" and also "how we think about and value groups collectively."[25] I would add that the outcome of the habituation that Glaude describes is not merely a manner of *thinking* and *valuing*, both of which have a hint of the conscious about them. The way that the habits of Glaude's concern become embedded in our bodies, in our sensory organs, means (among other things) that our racism is felt. It is *aesthetic*. Racism that can shape the making of photographs does not rest primarily *on* things we think; it resides *in* our senses, which work faster and more surreptitiously than thought.

Glaude's argument indicates why the simple sense mechanism that we call *seeing* is not itself neutral, with or without the camera. Bike-riding-esque habit operates our sense experience of the people around us, and the varied valuations that we attach to that sense experience reveal the racialized quality of this habit. What Frederick Douglass knew, in the dawn of photography itself, was that a white photographer could not step out from under the long-laid-down sediments of racial aesthetics and would inevitably produce the figuration of their racial bias, simply because the white gaze—the very manner in which a white person looks at another person—has already been built.

How we look at things, the way in which we point our eyes and give our retinas to light, is guided by racial habits that are historical and cultural, in addition to being personal. The mechanics of making pictures flows similarly from habituation, and those mechanics are, then, inescapably racialized. Camera in hand, the photographer approaches a moment already sensing albums of photos to make, and, raising the camera, the photographer's eye and elbows and fingers slip into what Glaude calls "furrowed pathways of behavior."[26] The image(s) that follow necessarily run in that ditch.

Setting Berger's argument beside Glaude's theories of the body, and also beside what Frederick Douglass and Clarissa T. Sligh suggest, we can see how white photographers and editors during the CRM brought their own images—already racially biased and privileged—of Black activists to their endeavor. The photographers' and editors' habits ran in an already-dug trench, and their sympathies for the Movement—as well-meaning as they might have been—flowed still the same, dredging the en-habited channel deeper, sharpening and smoothing it, carrying their biased images carefully ahead.

The call to white photographers in the present might be to change their habits—to know the ways of sensing, the ways of looking, that prevailed in photo-making of the past and to find modes of photo-making that can block and divert that flow, make it overspill its banks, and cut new furrows in their seeing and, thus, in *everyone's* seeing. Douglass, prophetically, knew what radical image-making practice could do: "For the *habit* we adopt, the master we obey in making our subjective nature *objective, giving it form, colour, space, action and utterance,* is the all important thing to ourselves *and to our surroundings.*"[27]

I went to the bridge in 2016, DSLR in hand, because I could not not go, although I knew that I was myself a threat. I went partly to find an un-en-habited practice. Should racial habits indeed be preconscious, at work pre-reflectively in our bodies' naturalized inclinations, no extent of thinking about them will divert them—not any more than reflecting on riding a bike will help a person acquire that ability. Only doing differently, deliberately, repeatedly, and over time can disrupt the racist attitudes that flow with racial identities.[28] As fire to fire, the image-making labor of making photos—even more so, perhaps, than the photos themselves—might be the mechanism by which to change the image(s) that I already have, those image(s) that I bring not only to bridges but also to colleges, to marketplaces, to sidewalks and parking lots, to Wendy's "drive-thrus," those images that make me and that must be changed if I am to operate in new, less threatening habit. I needed not only to be there, but also to fashion a "productive look," as Kaja Silverman would have it—a look that does not *take* the things on which it falls.[29] I wanted to bracket, phenomenologically, those habits that make how I see. Inasmuch as I incorporate, by doing, the racial habits that I inherit, I hoped that by doing differently, by pursuing a "conscious constant reworking of the terms under which [I] unconsciously look," that I could form different habits and improve on the photographic practice that has preceded me.[30] That hope was part of what called me to the bridge in July 2016. I hoped that by looking deliberately I might begin to look differently. That hope produced the selected photographs that follow.

A woman looks back at the camera, and I believe at *me* on the other side of it (see fig. 2). I went to the bridge to look, and I went fully confident that I could look without repercussions. When I arrived on the scene, the bridge was already taken. The protestors, in their audacity and courage, had taken it, by and for themselves. Arriving late, I had no worry that by stepping onto the bridge I might be stepping into some danger, and I went in with a presumption that I would go innocuously and invisibly. I would be merely a person among people,

FIGURE 2. The backs of a crowd; at center, a woman looks back over her shoulder; on the edge of the frame is a sign that reads, "I Am a Man." Photo by David V. Mason

I imagined, perfectly welcome and perfectly anonymous, perfectly free to enjoy my being there to look and to aim and to capture, and then to walk away at my leisure—away from the bridge and from those who had taken it, with my photos in hand, to my Honda Civic and back to my life that always never must assert its mattering. As it happened, I was not invisible, nor perfectly welcome. The lookback, aimed at me, did not let me walk away uncaptured. Observed suddenly, my surveillance suddenly surveilled, this look-back, this displacing gaze, caught the colonizing force that I imposed by being there.[31] "We are beings who are looked at," according to Jacques Lacan, who was not attending to the world's increasing capacity for surveillance but was trying to describe how we are made into selves.[32] Roland Barthes, similarly, though perhaps more superficially: "Now once I feel myself observed by the lens . . . I instantaneously make another body for myself."[33] No less, I am certain, do we make ourselves when we see that we are observed *through* the lens, no matter who holds the camera or whether the camera has long since given way to the print. The look-back, each time it appears, calls up that self-consciousness that foments self and re-directs it, each time, against what seems its necessary movement.

The image is not a sign. There is the sign, of course—literally, in Figure 2, *the sign* that Ernest Withers's photographs of the sanitation workers' strike in Memphis made sacred in 1968. The written sign seems to demand that we read the photo as a statement. "I Am a MAN" juxtaposed with a woman's searching face might read as a comment on oppressive patriarchy in the BLM Movement. Perhaps we would read the photo as a bit more complex. Perhaps we would read it as paradoxical. But maybe the written sign is a red herring. Should a written statement be called for, there's no need for a photograph, and words, superimposed on an image, can wreck it. "Adding words to a photograph can make it say almost anything," says Sligh.[34] Never mind how we might *read* this image. What does the photo *do*? That is the question. More than making some rhetorical statement, this photo *moves*. The crowd in it moves. In this moment, those who took the bridge are leaving, beginning a walk of some miles on the thoroughfares that ring downtown Memphis—Poplar Avenue, Danny Thomas Boulevard, and Beale Street—taking the city, too. The person in the midst of the composition is moving, but in looking back, she is also halting. She is fleeing, stopping, and approaching all at once so that she makes us move and halt at the same time.

Fred Moten calls the phenomenon *blackness as fugitivity*. Describing a woman who appears in a Thomas Eakins photo from 1882, Moten writes:

In the photograph, she quickens against being stilled, studied, buried, stolen, as she steals away, moving without moving.... She steals away from forced movement in stillness.... poses a problem, posing as a problem, as a kind of thrownness; thrown into a problem and a pose and that pose's history, she exposes the venal etiolation of publicness that imposes exposure upon her ... a form of life and the emergency it prompts is held and revealed.[35]

More important to me than the meaningless meaning of the words on a sign in Figure 2 is the frozen motion that seemingly pushes forward in the image and that pushes back against my own eye, posing a problem for my eye and interrogating the exposure that I have imposed on the photo's central subject. The bodies moving to the edge of the frame and the look-back from the photo's subject resist the photo's attempt to freeze the moment that I would so like to carry away.

Not everyone went up on the bridge. Some, it seems, were content to look from a vantage point prior to the police cordon (see fig. 3). In waiting, apart, the people in the photograph rather neatly organized themselves, as though for my benefit, according to the Rule of Thirds. In its clumsy obviousness, this image is a fine illustration of the fact that a photograph is not merely a document but also the affirmation of a history that a photographer carries. Photography 101: When you go to photograph, imagine straight lines in the view, two side-to-side and two up-and-down, that divide the frame into a tic-tac-toe grid. The view that many cameras give these days places these lines on what you see through the viewfinder. To make a photo of value, all that one must do is be sure that the important thing in the image does not fall in the center square. Simple.[36] A photo will be especially effective if its subject sits on one or another of the four points at which the horizontal and vertical lines cross. The technique that this image affirms goes back centuries, into the tradition of fine, patrician painting in Europe. Indeed, we might consider the extent to which the Rule of Thirds is one of those historical practices that constructs our racialized habits of seeing. Figure 3, then, may offer an illustration of the privileged and biased process by which

FIGURE 3. Several people looking at the Hernando de Soto Bridge from a distance. Photo by David V. Mason

photographers make photos, both in the 1960s and now. Approaching the occupation of the bridge on foot and coming upon this scene, I found a vantage point from which things appeared to my sense as well organized and ordered. That is, I brought the Rule with me, and I waited for the scene to conform to it.

This image (fig. 3) is also a classic example of obscuring Black agency. In the manner that Berger and Raiford identify in many CRM photos, the human figures here are in a posture of inactivity, and the direct action portion of the nonviolent direct action of July 10, 2016—the people actively blocking traffic on the bridge—does not clutter the scene. White photographers during the CRM composed their photos of "legible and comfortable formulations," depicting the disenfranchised as dignified and also as "in no position to take anything."[37] While the people I would capture in this photograph milled about, I waited for some time—because, of course, I *could* wait. Then when the people here finally moved into my favored positions, I could make my image.

Of course, a person must not present civil disobedience as happy (see figs. 4 and 5). The tradition of protest photography says so. Joyful

FIGURE 4. A crowd of people dancing on a freeway bridge. Photo by David V. Mason

FIGURE 5. A crowd of people carrying signs, one of which reads "I DON'T APOLOGIZE FOR MY BLACKNESS"; many of the people are smiling. Photo by David V. Mason

dancing before the interstate traffic that one has halted is awfully disrespectful, and the photographer who sympathizes with those who jeopardize themselves for justice—and who wants to ensure that the more things change, the more they stay the same—must certainly mute any disrespect to whiteness in the pictorial record. Very well known is Johnny Jenkins's photo of Elizabeth Eckford, stoically de-segregating Little Rock Central High School. Less visible in the record is Charles Moore's photo of a "Jeering Mob," its 1963 appearance in *Life* notwithstanding.[38] The photo, in which several Black protestors are shown smiling, appears in the magazine article alongside at least fifteen other photographs, in which all figures are somber, serious, angry, or in tears.

Sedimented sense tells us that joy, imaged, will display to white eyes that protestors are exactly the miscreants that white eyes expect to see—shiftless, frivolous, mere runaround hooligans whose only aim is causing trouble.[39] The best-known CRM photos by Charles Moore and other acclaimed white photographers, such as Bill Hudson and Bob Adelman, show the serious, solemn business of activism. Danny Lyon's work, too, curated by SNCC's own James Forman, shows oppression and suffering—rather than joy—in order to "rile up" more people to act.[40] Photographers and editors, then, presumed that long-term change surely depended on white approval, and to secure that approval, they expected photographs to image active resistance to the mechanisms of the state as a solemn, even fearful endeavor, conducted in a manner that would present disruptive protest only as a last resort. Sarcasm aside, documenting too much joy in protest does not do the political work that protest may mean to do. Yet being deliberate about a practice that might disrupt habit calls a photographer to not ignore protest joy.

Black and white: I was not shooting in black and white, obviously, only draining the images of color before releasing them. In this case there is a practical reason for it. The sun was setting directly behind the crowd and behind the features of the bridge that identifies Memphis (see figs. 6–8). The consequence was the whole visual field's inclination toward silhouette. In the days of digital photography, converting images made in color to black and white makes it possible

FIGURE 6. A crowd of people holding signs on a freeway offramp; the distinctive arches of the Hernando de Soto Bridge are visible in the background. Photo by David V. Mason

FIGURE 7. A crowd of people holding signs on a freeway offramp; the distinctive arches of the Hernando de Soto Bridge are visible in the background. Photo by David V. Mason

FIGURE 8. A crowd of people holding signs on a freeway offramp; the distinctive arches of the Hernando de Soto Bridge are visible in the background. Photo by David V. Mason

to bring out shadowed faces. With a computer, the ones and zeroes in an image file that say red and green and blue can be manipulated to raise luminance in the silhouettes and shadows of what appears to any human eye to be simply black and white.[41] If not changed to black and white, the people in these images are mostly silhouettes. So, perhaps these photos have to be in black and white.

Yet, black and white photos have a purpose that is not merely practical and not entirely free of self-serving. Methods for producing color photographs go back to photography's earliest days, and consumer-grade Kodachrome came on the market in the 1930s. Nevertheless, color film remained expensive through the 1950s and 1960s, which limited its use for journalism and documentary projects, and it did not lend itself to capturing quick instants of action under challenging and quickly changing light. Black and white, consequently, became the visual inflection of the CRM, and making activism images in black and white today insinuates continuity with a body of photographs that are already recognized as significant. The halftones of bodies framed on the De Soto Bridge signal that these bodies pursue

FIGURE 9. People walking down the Front Street offramp. Photo by David V. Mason

the ongoing work that we all know similarly from, say, the Edmund Pettus Bridge. Yet the halftones that disclose a crowd on the De Soto bridge also claim that the photographer has a foot in the storied past. In these days, when a cell phone can catch in a fractioned second a full-color image that automatically corrects for back-light, there's no escaping the Orientalism of black and white photo-making and the way that it claims for its photos a dignity that others earned. It pretends that the photographer works in noble continuity with a history with which, in fact, he had nothing to do. The practice reiterates, too, the manner in which photographers bring images with them and impose those images on reality.

The marchers eventually left the bridge and proceeded down the ramp to Front Street and into the channels of the surveillance state (see figs. 9–13). From before and behind, as they moved into Memphis, they passed by lenses that sought to capture them. Even high above, an eye to hold them all (fig. 12). Under surveillance and past columns of flashing police cars, it was not the ordered rows of forward-focused people, sometimes arm in arm, that the oft-printed photos from the

FIGURE 10. The backs of a crowd of people walking toward Front Street. Photo by David V. Mason

FIGURE 11. A crowd of people gathered around a police car; one man holds a sign reading "BLACK LIVES MATTER." Photo by David V. Mason

FIGURE 12. From behind, a crowd of people walking down Front Street; tall buildings of downtown Memphis; a helicopter high in the sky shines a spotlight downward. Photo; David V. Mason

1950s and 1960s show. The flow was forward, certainly, but with an air of denouement. The walking was post-accomplishment, then: not marching to an objective, which was the bridge behind them, but felicitating the feat that almost no one had anticipated that morning. The core of people who had figured out how to stop interstate traffic, and had dared to do it, had held the bridge for four hours, during which

FIGURE 13. From behind, a crowd of people walking on Front Street. Photo by David V. Mason

time the word had gone out and the crowd had swelled. Then, under some unknown signal, it was done and it was time for the evening's walk home, which on this warm July evening just happened to be on the city's main and most famous thoroughfares. People stepped in silence, some chatting. Phones came out to record and to broadcast. Periodically, someone would shout, especially in proximity to the packs of uniformed officers warding the intersections.

I walked along, a middle-aged white guy, down the middle of Danny Thomas Blvd's southbound lanes, earnestly allied but not genuinely sharing the jeopardy that created the event. In the moments in which I raised my camera, barrel of a lens pointing at this one and that, some near me regarded me suspiciously—perhaps as more of a feature of the oppressive surveillance all around than as an ally. The gaze, *my* gaze, pointed and launched, strikes at the notion that the camera is only an instrument of truth, and on that evening it struck down any pretense to which I might have clung that I was walking in something other than my privilege.

On the 200 block of Memphis's Poplar Avenue (see figs. 14–16) sits the jail and the cluster of law offices and bail bondsmen, passed

FIGURE 14. A small crowd walking beneath a neon sign reading "LAW OFFICE"; one person holds a sign reading "BLACK LIVES MATTER." Photo by David V. Mason

FIGURE 15. A small crowd walking beneath a neon sign reading "A-1 BAIL BONDS"; one person holds a sign reading "BLACK LIVES MATTER"; another person holds a sign reading "1 Nation under God." Photo by David V. Mason

FIGURE 16. A few people walking beneath letters affixed to a brick wall reading "SHELBY COUNTY JUSTICE CENTER 201 POPLAR." Photo by David V. Mason

FIGURE 17. A crowd of people walking on Beale Street; a neon sign reads "Memphis Music HALL of FAME." Photo by David V. Mason

by the people least served by this system of selective discipline, the institutions that fomented the protest that had stopped the flow of usual business on the bridge no more than five hundred yards away.

Beale Street is where the Blues began, according to George Washington Lee's 1934 book (see fig. 17).[42] Under the guise of "renewal," the city and corporate caretakers largely wrecked Beale Street, this stretch of African American history, following the CRM. Photographer Ernest Withers' studio remains there (see fig. 18). The space is now a gallery and tribute to the man who, arguably, accelerated the Movement by capturing, surreptitiously and at real peril to himself, an image of Emmett Till's uncle, Mose Wright, when the sharecropper pointed an accusing finger at Till's murderers in a Mississippi courtroom in 1955. Notwithstanding Withers' role in passing his familiarity with Memphis activism and activists to the FBI, the CRM cannot be untied from his photos of Memphis's striking sanitation workers carrying "I Am a Man" signs in the spring of 1968.[43] As those who closed the bridge walked along Beale Street—many of them carrying these historic signs—they passed the Withers gallery. The "I Am a Man" slogan would not remain so poignant in the present were it not for Withers' photos from the past.

FIGURE 18. Three men standing in front of the Ernest Withers Gallery; one of the men holds a sign reading "I AM A MAN." Photo by David V. Mason

FIGURE 19. A man walking on Front Street; the distinctive arches of the Hernando de Soto Bridge and a portion of I-40 on which groups of people are standing and walking are visible in the background. Photo by David V. Mason

I remain ambivalent about going to the protest. At the very least, I worry, in a manner that might be called critical reflection. The visual record of the CRM makes clear that a visual record is necessary, but Sligh's question—*"Whose reality?"*—is also *"Whose visual record?"* I worry that my actions will follow in the same hazardous paths of the work of white photographers who have preceded me. Perhaps the best worry for the photographer—especially the white photographer approaching such things as the taking of a bridge—is over *the photographer's reality* and the visual record that the photographer might make for self and for self's sake. Worrying about one's own practice risks the possibility of producing self-centered work. The productive potential of that worrying is that the photo-making practice, done in frequency and in urgency, can un-habit a dangerous eye.

NOTES

1. Christopher Brennan, Nicole Hensley, and Denis Slattery, "Alton Sterling Shot, Killed by Louisiana Cops during Struggle after He Was Selling Music outside Baton Rouge Store," *New York Daily News*, July 6, 2016, https://www.nydailynews.com/news/national/la-cops-shoot-kill-man-selling-music-baton-rouge-store-article-1.2700548; Sara Pelissero, "Shooting in Falcon Heights, Minn.: What We Know," *USA Today*, July 7, 2016, https://www.usatoday.com/story/news/nation-now/2016/07/07/falcon-heights-police-shooting-philando-castile-what-we-know/86792886.
2. Jody Callahan, "Marchers Shut Down I-40 Bridge at Memphis During Black Lives Matter Rally," *Commercial Appeal*, July 10, 2016, https://archive.commercialappeal.com/news/tennessee-black-caucus-calls-for-calm-amid-racial-unrest—3714d93e-1078-6a7d-e053-0100007f134e-386214081.html.
3. The 1968 sanitation workers strike was sparked when the city's perennially defective equipment and dehumanizing policies killed Echol Cole and Robert Walker. For an account, see Michael K. Honey, *Going Down Jericho Road: The Memphis Strike, Martin Luther King's Last Campaign* (New York: Norton, 2007), 1.
4. Callahan, "Marchers Shut Down I-40 Bridge."
5. Leigh Raiford, *Imprisoned in a Luminous Glare: Photography and the African American Freedom Struggle* (Chapel Hill: University of North Carolina Press, 2011), 171. Jonathan Eubanks expressed much the same thing in his conversations with Raiford. Hearing that the Panthers were demonstrating in Oakland in 1969, Eubanks reported, "[I] put everything aside and said that was where I needed to be" (Raiford, 171).

6. Martin A. Berger, *Seeing through Race: A Reinterpretation of Civil Rights Photography* (Berkeley: University of California Press, 2011), 46. Susan Sontag identifies the same operation in looking at photographs, which, she writes, "suggests and strengthens the feeling that one is exempt." *On Photography* (New York: Penguin Books, 1977), 168.
7. My camera took moments from that night: the quiet individuals and their signs, six feet apart; the white supremacists, taunting and jeering from the lawn of the police station; the appearance of police barricades to mark a boundary for the original demonstrators but not for the white racists; the transformation of demonstration into protest as the demonstrators spilled over the boundary; the blocking and closure of the avenue; the advent of armored officers and the brutish kettling of the crowd that followed.
8. Adam Gabbatt, "Protests about Police Brutality Are Met with Wave of Police Brutality across US," *Guardian*, June 6, 2020, https://www.theguardian.com/us-news/2020/jun/06/police-violence-protests-us-george-floyd.
9. Tom Gjelten, "Peaceful Protesters Tear-Gassed to Clear Way for Trump Church Photo-Op," *NPR*, June 1, 2020, https://www.npr.org/2020/06/01/867532070/trumps-unannounced-church-visit-angers-church-officials.
10. Zolan Kanno-Youngs, "Unidentified Federal Police Prompt Fears amid Protests in Washington," *New York Times*, June 4, 2020, https://www.nytimes.com/2020/06/04/us/politics/unidentified-police-protests.html.
11. Larry Buchanan, Quoctrung Bui, and Jugal K. Patel, "Black Lives Matter May Be the Largest Movement in History," *New York Times*, July 3, 2020, https://www.nytimes.com/interactive/2020/07/03/us/george-floyd-protests-crowd-size.html. Also see "Cities on Edge as Fires Burn near White House," *New York Times*, May 31, 2020, https://www.nytimes.com/2020/05/31/us/george-floyd-protests-live-updates.html.
12. Nir Hasson and Noa Shpigel, "Hundreds March in Israel, West Bank for Palestinian, Black American Police Brutality Victims," *Haaretz*, June 3, 2020, https://www.haaretz.com/israel-news/2020-06-03/ty-article/hundreds-across-israel-and-west-bank-protest-for-police-brutality-victims/0000017f-e015-df7c-a5ff-e27fa6190000.
13. Consider the compact photo essay "Protests across the Globe after George Floyd's Death," CNN, June 13, 2020, https://www.cnn.com/2020/06/06/world/gallery/intl-george-floyd-protests/index.html.
14. "The 2021 Pulitzer Prize Winner in Special Citations and Awards: Darnella Frazier," *Pulitzer Prizes*, accessed August 12, 2022, https://www.pulitzer.org/winners/darnella-frazier.
15. Clarissa T. Sligh, "The Plaintiff Speaks," in *Picturing Us: African American Identity in Photography*, ed. Deborah Willis (New York: The New Press, 1994), 102.
16. Raiford, *Imprisoned in a Luminous Glare*, 212.
17. Berger, *Seeing through Race*, 7.

18. Berger, *Seeing through Race*, 18.
19. Berger, *Seeing through Race*, 23. Berger's argument rests on photographs by the principal white photographers of Civil Rights Movement action and reactive violence, including Bruce Davidson, who was on site in Birmingham in 1963. White photographer Fred Blackwell made the famous image of the abuse poured out on John Salter, Joan Trumpauer, and Anne Moody at the Woolworth's counter in Jackson in 1963. Danny Lyon, also a white photographer, photographed how the police dealt with sit-ins as early as 1963. Lyon's photo of Clifford Vaughs's arrest in in Maryland in 1964 lends itself to Berger's theory of the white preference for photos that show Black people as passive objects of white violence. Vaughs was himself a photographer, but history has not made Vaughs's photos famous in the way that it has Lyon's photo of Vaughs caught "helplessly" in the hands of white men.
20. In *Seeing through Race*, Berger provides a striking example of such deliberate alteration of a photograph. *Seeing through Race*, 22.
21. We can expect that some editors were motivated by an understanding of what would sell papers. Berger urges us to consider the parallel possibility that editorial choices arose from what editors *felt*—the inclinations they had for one picture over another, inclinations that manifested to the editors themselves as a perfectly natural sense for the quality and potential effectiveness of photographs. That natural sense is not natural at all, but rather the consequence of cultural history and habituation, as articulated by Eddie S. Glaude Jr., *Democracy in Black: How Race Still Enslaves the American Soul* (New York: Crown Publishers, 2016).
22. Sligh, The Plaintiff Speaks," 102. In conversation with Leigh Raiford about his authorized photographs of the early Black Panthers, photographer Stephen Shames confirms Sligh's point, referring to the famous civil rights imagery of the 1960s: "I wanted to take pictures like those other pictures." Raiford, *Imprisoned in a Luminous Glare*, 172.
23. Quoted in Laura Wexler, "'A More Perfect Likeness': Frederick Douglass and the Image of the Nation," in *Pictures and Progress: Early Photography and the Making of African American Identity*, ed. Maurice O. Wallace and Shawn Michelle Smith (Durham, NC: Duke University Press, 2012), 21.
24. Glaude, *Democracy in Black*, 56.
25. Glaude, *Democracy in Black*, 56–57.
26. Glaude, *Democracy in Black*, 58.
27. "'Rightly Viewed': Theorizations of Self in Frederick Douglass's Lectures on Pictures," in *Pictures and Progress: Early Photography and the Making of African American Identity*, ed. Maurice O. Wallace and Shawn Michelle Smith (Durham, NC: Duke University Press, 2012), 72.
28. Gail Weiss, "Phenomenology and Race (or Racializing Phenomenology)," in *The Routledge Companion to Philosophy of Race*, ed. Paul C. Taylor, Linda Martin Alcoff, and Luvell Anderson (New York: Routledge, 2018), 242–43.

In the essay, Weiss identifies in the concept of "critical race phenomenology" a power "to identify and thereby disrupt the racist natural attitudes that so often accompany [racial identities]." I am suggesting that an ongoing creative practice like photography can do the phenomenological bracketing and reduction that Weiss has in mind.

29. Kaja Silverman, *The Threshold of the Visible World* (New York: Routledge, 1996), 169.
30. Shawn Michelle Smith, "Looking at Oneself through the Eyes of Others: W. E. B. Du Bois's Photographs for the Paris Exposition of 1900," in *Pictures and Progress: Early Photography and the Making of African American Identity*, ed. Maurice O. Wallace and Shawn Michelle Smith (Durham, NC: Duke University Press, 2012), 293.
31. See Homi K. Bhabha, *The Location of Culture* (New York: Routledge, 1994), 127.
32. Silverman, *Threshold of the Visible*, 196.
33. Roland Barthes, "Extracts from *Camera Lucida*," in *The Photography Reader*, ed. Liz Wells (New York: Routledge, 2003), 22.
34. Sligh, "The Plaintiff Speaks," 102.
35. Fred Moten, "Taste Dissonance Flavor Escape: Preface for a Solo by Miles Davis," *Women and Performance: A Journal of Feminist History* 17, no. 2 (2007): 227–8.
36. Joel Sartore and Heather Perry, *National Geographic Photo Basics: The Ultimate Beginner's Guide to Great Photography* (Washington, DC: National Geographic, 2019), 42.
37. Berger, *Seeing through Race*, 8, 52.
38. "Ominous Spectacle of Birmingham: They Fight a Fire That Won't Go Out," *Life*, May 17, 1963, 36.
39. The *Life* editors captioned Charles Moore's "Jeering Mob" photograph thus: "Provocation like this, to most whites, is a wide-open invitation to full-scale racial warfare." "Ominous Spectacle," 36.
40. Raiford, *Imprisoned in a Luminous Glare*, 92.
41. When the color is restored to the adjusted images, the faces that we can see in the black and white versions show up sickly, glowing green.
42. George Washington Lee, *Beale Street: Where the Blues Began* (New York: R. O. Ballou, 1934).
43. At present, the most comprehensive account of Ernest Withers' role as an FBI informant in Memphis—from, perhaps, the mid-1960s to the early 1970s—is Marc Perrusquia's *A Spy in Canaan* (Brooklyn: Melville House, 2018).

CHAPTER 8

When the Cultural Revolution Comes

Anthem Making in the Era of BLM

Mickell Carter

Race-based vigilante violence was in the news in the United States in 2012. In February of that year, neighborhood-watch volunteer George Zimmerman fatally shot the unarmed seventeen-year-old Trayvon Martin as he walked home from a 7-Eleven in Sanford, Florida. Clad in a gray hoodie, Martin had been carrying a solitary bag of Skittles and a can of tea. Zimmerman's confrontation with Martin rested solely on the former's suspicion that the latter posed a threat, which made Martin a victim of not only gun violence but also racial profiling. According to philosopher Christopher Lebron, Martin's "only possible crime seemed to be walking while black."[1] Zimmerman's subsequent acquittal in court sparked the nationwide social and political protests that laid the groundwork for the launch of the Black Lives Matter Movement (BLMM). In 2013, Black women activists Patrisse Cullors, Alicia Garza, and Opal (Ayo) Tometi created the Twitter hashtag #BLACKLIVESMATTER. Transcending social media, however, #BLACKLIVESMATTER has become the banner under which a global twenty-first-century movement for Black liberation has united.

Massive protests and public outrage ensued in the years that followed Martin's death, after more victims of white vigilante and police violence made national news, including Tamir Rice, murdered at age 12, Michael Brown (aged 18), Freddie Gray (aged 25), Ahmaud Arbery (aged 25), Breonna Taylor (aged 26), Sandra Bland (aged 28), Alton Sterling (aged 37), Philando Castile (aged 32), Eric Garner (aged 43), and George Floyd (aged 46). These deaths forced a national reckoning with contemporary racism and birthed the largest social movement since the Civil Rights and Black Power Movements of the previous century.[2] While others have explored in greater depth the continuities and divergences between the leadership structures and protest strategies of these two activist moments, in this chapter I examine the influence of Black cultural producers.

Black cultural aesthetics, a liberating approach to upending anti-Blackness, inspired protests from athletes, artists, and musicians amid BLM. Continuities between Civil Rights, Black Power, and BLM are visible through the artistry of contemporary Black cultural producers. This chapter explores the influence of Black artists like the Last Poets, Childish Gambino, and Buddy to interrogate the ways in which audiences have developed and deployed art as movement-anthems in both the 1960s and 1970s and in the twenty-first century. Black artists have intentionally and unintentionally acted as both cultural producers and movement activists through the creation of their art and its re-creation by political and social revolutionaries, revealing how movement participants have recycled supposedly apolitical art into political vehicles based on the political and social climate of the time. Cultural productions of music and performance in both eras have transcended the initial intentions of artists to simultaneously promote movement ideologies. As artistic expression helps deepen political action, and the freedom struggle mobilizes, reinterprets, and repurposes Black art, this chapter illuminates the role of Black Power and BLM cultural producers, shows how they expanded the boundaries of resistance through Black expressive culture, and reveals the reciprocal relationship between culture, politics, and social movements.

Charting the Movement: Methods and Historiography

Over the past several years, activists and scholars have grappled with the intersections of Civil Rights, Black Power, and BLM, noting similarities and distinctions and drawing attention to the significant role of women and queer activists in these movements. Several works like BLM cofounder Patrisse Khan-Cullors' *When They Call You a Terrorist*, Keeanga-Yamahtta Taylor's *From Black Lives Matter to Black Liberation*, and Barbara Ransby's *Making All Black Lives Matter* have discussed the origins and development of BLM, a movement that draws attention to continued injustices while advocating for distinct approaches toward an equitable and just society.[3] Scholars have employed intellectual, social, and political lenses to highlight movement-activism and organizing, but they have offered few insights into how contemporary Black culture—in particular, music and performance—has shaped the Movement.

I am mindful of Taylor's advice to go beyond typical narratives to chart the history of Black political movements: as Taylor points out, Black liberation lies in an awareness of the legacies of anti-Blackness and a plan to move forward.[4] Consequently, in this chapter I demonstrate how Black artists articulated Black consciousness and liberation—deliberately and coincidentally—through anthems, revealing how audiences both individually and collectively refashioned artists' creations as vehicles for Black freedom movements. This social reconstruction situates BLM within a larger Black tradition of resistance, tracing its cultural roots to the Black Power era of the 1960s and 1970s.

When the Revolution Comes: Black Power and The Last Poets

Aspirations of revolution heightened during the turbulent political environment of the 1960s. Many Black cultural producers developed what Amiri Baraka—founder of the cultural and literary wing of Black Power known as the Black Arts Movement (BAM)—called "Revolutionary Art for Cultural Revolution." Black art functioned politically as it worked to spark change and uplift for Black people.[5] Throughout their quest for liberation, Black men and women employed their art to further Black revolution.[6] On May 19, 1968, at a birthday celebration for the deceased Black nationalist leader Malcolm X, a group of young Black poets came together to create a collective of what would become known as the Last Poets.[7] Baraka considered the group prototypes or godfathers of rap who uniquely merged rhymed poetry with African drumbeats.[8] The poetry collective's original members included David Nelson, Gylan Kain, Abiodun Oyewole, Felipe Luciano, Umar Bin Hassan, Jalal Nurridin, and Suliaman El Hadi, and they combined their distinctive rhythmic poetic delivery with the themes of militancy, Black pride, and the dismantling of white supremacy. Inspired by BAM, the collective spoke about the conditions that many Black people faced while simultaneously expressing Black Power ideologies. Through their poems about Black life and struggles, the Last Poets stirred their audiences' emotions to unify against white oppression.[9]

By 1970, the artists released their first album, *The Last Poets*, articulating the poets' revolutionary aspirations. The album fostered Black Power consciousness through its poems such as "Run, N*gger," "N*ggers Are Scared of a Revolution," and "When the Revolution Comes." The Last Poets captivated listeners by utilizing the "language of the streets" to depict Black struggles and critique the enemies of the impending revolution.[10] They captivated audiences with their performance style, consisting of Rhythm and Poetry (RAP), as they combined spoken words with Congo drumming, jazz, and/ or reggae beats as they pioneered the RAP genre.[11] The Last Poets' album revealed the intricate role of Black artists during the Black Power era: serving dual roles as both cultural producers and movement activists, the Last Poets used their intentionally revolutionary art to promote the cultural revolution through anthems.

Scholar Shana Redmond explains the significant role musical anthems played within the Black Freedom Struggle, defining Black anthems as "collectively imagined and practiced speech acts" that go beyond simply documenting world events or political issues.[12] Indeed, anthems function as vital actors within political struggles by communicating visions of liberation, fostering solidary, and encompassing the ideologies and beliefs of their participants.[13] This is visible through the songs produced and performed during the Civil Rights Movement (CRM) by artists such as Mahalia Jackson, Sam Cooke, Nina Simone, the Staple Singers, and numerous others who advocated for Black empowerment during the CRM. Similarly, artists during the Black Power Movement produced works that pushed the movement forward.

Anthems such as "N*ggers Are Scared of a Revolution" advocated for Black liberation by stating, "N*ggers tell you they're ready to be liberated! But when you say 'Let's go take our liberation,' N*ggers reply: 'I was just playin.'"[14] Although they encouraged liberation, the Last Poets criticized those who expressed revolution and freedom solely through their words, and they castigated persons who called for Black Power but whose inaction belied the strength of their beliefs. Instead, they expressed solidarity for movement participants who not only talked about revolution but also sought revolution through direct-action and protest.

The Last Poets further condemned activities that fostered cultural suppression—those activities such as gambling, prostitution, and drug use that undermined Black Power by demoralizing Black pride. Analyzing the lyrics of "N*ggers Are Scared of a Revolution" in 1970, Barbara Mahone McBain, writer for the historically Black magazine *Black World*, noted that the Last Poets extolled all the "traditional hustles and facades" of urban Black life that seemed trendy but in reality only complicated change and reform:[15]

> N*ggers shoot sharp glances at white women
> N*ggers shoot dope into their arm
> N*ggers shoot guns and rifles on New Year's Eve
> A new year that is coming in
> The white police will do more shooting at them
> Where are n*ggers when the revolution needs some shots?![16]

Although many of the Last Poets' anthems critiqued self-destructive problems plaguing many Black communities, the poets still articulated

Black pride and unity with refrains like, "I love n*ggers, . . . / Because n*ggers are me, / And I should only love that which is me."[17] These lines suggest that although some Black people did not seek to pursue revolution, there was, at the very least, a tacit acknowledgment of their connection to and pride in the Black community. The Last Poets celebrated both Black unity and difference. The poem, Umar bin Hassan argued, developed from his personal experiences as a Black resident in Harlem. To him, the poem acted as a spiritual call to action deeply rooted in his Black self-awareness and unity. Hassan states: "'N*ggers R Scared of Revolution' became a prayer, a call to arms, a spiritual pond to bathe and cleanse in. Because N*ggers are not just vile and disgusting and shiftless. N*ggers are human beings lost in someone else's system of values and morals. N*ggers are dreams and hopes, pleading for fairness and a true sense of justice."[18] The Last Poets were artists who saw themselves as linked to all Black people through a shared history of struggle and therefore expressed love for the Black community—both those who supported Black Power as well as those, unlike them, who disagreed with revolution. They understood that, to many, justice seemed unfathomable. Accordingly, The Last Poets used their anthems to uplift and motivate Black communities and to convey Black Power ideologies so that a broader audience might embrace the Movement.

While the Last Poets intended to uplift, they also sought to spark a Black Enlightenment among listeners. Abiodun Oyewole, in particular, acted self-consciously and intentionally as both a cultural producer and revolutionary. He explained, "we knew we could not build a movement on N*ggers or N*ggerisms," and this was why, he said, he wrote the poem "Run, N*gger."[19] He hoped the poem might serve as an educational tool, reminding audiences of the atrocities Black communities faced due to America's history of racism and discrimination and the powerful legacies these entailed:

> Screwing your woman (run n*ggers!)
> Whooping your ass (run n*ggers!)
> Stealing your culture (run n*ggers!)

Taking your life (run n*ggers!)
Killing your children (run n*ggers!)[20]

These lines describe the painful histories and realities of anti-Blackness in America, such as the rape or "screwing" of Black women, the brutalization or "whooping your ass" that might be meted out by law enforcement or vigilantes alike, and the indiscriminate murder of Black people—"Taking your life . . . Killing your children"—regardless of their age. Oyewole believed "N*gga" embodied the rage and pain Black Americans felt, as its meaning went "far beyond the negative connotations found in the dictionary."[21] The Last Poets performed these lines assertively and aggressively, thus displaying the rage that Black people collectively felt—or should feel—through their rhetoric and tone. The poets exclaimed each line loudly as they expressed not only anger but also fear. After each line, another voice screams, "Run, n*ggers!" as if danger is lurking nearby. Their cries underscore the fears of the Black community that if one hopes to survive the brutality and violence of life in America, one must run.

The poem "Run, N*gger" also considers complacent Black people who do not concern themselves in the matters of "N*ggers" and functions as a poetic call to action against white oppression. The poets attack anti-Blackness, express the urgency of liberation, and rally Black people to rebel by asserting the necessity of revolution through the repeated phrase "time is running out":

Time is running out of talks, marches, tunes, chants, and all kinds
  of prayers
Time is running out of time
Heard someone say, "Things were changing" (Changing - things are
  changing!)
Change, chan-chan-chan-changing
From brown to black
Time is running out on bullshit changes.[22]

Although the earlier phase of the CRM had brought about legislative changes like the *Brown v. Board of Education* decision, the 1964

Civil Rights Act, and the 1965 Voting Rights Act, many Black people believed in the necessity of dramatic societal change in order to fully realize justice and equality. In the face of massive resistance and the persistence of white supremacy, many in the younger generation refused to continue waiting patiently for societal transformation. Their frustration fueled their actions to dismantle white supremacy through dramatic political organizing and tactics of armed self-defense.[23] Like younger activists, the Last Poets expressed the urgent need for socio-political changes. Scholar Julius Fleming Jr. coined the term "Black patience" to describe Black people's fight for liberation, their history of waiting, and the rejection of waiting as a tactic. Fleming argues that calls for moderation equated to violence, as white supremacy weaponized Black people's patience as a way of encouraging Americans to tolerate and mask racism.[24] Like many Black Power activists and organizers, the Last Poets argued that the time for Black patience had passed as they called for Black people to take up arms and enact revolution now.

Black Is . . .

The institution of enslavement stripped Black people of their family, heritage, and culture, inserting racialized labels that played a significant role in constructing and (re)imagining Black America's identity.[25] During the nineteenth and twentieth centuries, the acceptance of Black racial labels changed from "Colored" to "Negro." To some, "Colored" seemed more inclusive, as the term included persons of mixed race with Black ancestry; however, after the Civil War and the passage of the Thirteenth Amendment, the term largely began to reference Black persons who had been free prior to emancipation. Prominent Black leaders like W. E. B. Du Bois and Booker T. Washington, too, led the charge for Black institutions and citizens to adopt the term "Negro," as they considered the term more grammatically flexible—usable as both a noun and an adjective.[26] Motivated by the call for Black Power in the late 1960s, another shift in racial labeling commenced as Black Americans questioned, "What's in a Name?"; some considered the word "Negro" a demeaning moniker that maintained Black subordination and advanced white superiority.[27] The topic became divisive as Black Americans wrestled between the terms "Negro," "Afro-American," and "Black." Many younger Black people embraced "Black" as an attempt to evoke racial pride and communicate self-determination; as a result, "Black" became the desired term by those who rallied behind Black Power.[28] The November 1967 issue of the widely-read magazine *Ebony* summarized their thinking: writer and senior editor Lerone Bennett Jr. explained that Black Power activists had adopted the term "Black" for "Black brothers and sisters who are emancipating themselves," while keeping "Negro" for those they dismiss as "still in Whitey's bag and who still think of themselves and speak of themselves as Negroes."[29] To Black Power advocates, reclaiming "Black" reflected freedom and articulated rebellion against Eurocentric standards; they proclaimed, "Black is Beautiful" through multiple forms of revolutionary cultural aesthetics like fashion, music, poetry, and art.[30] Black Power artists, advocates, and organizations, including Nikki Giovanni, Amiri Baraka, AfriCOBRA, and Maulana (Ron) Karenga's US organization, developed works and/or groups that embraced "Black" and portrayed a nonwestern aesthetic tradition and cultural practices for Black people that might serve as a counterweight to Eurocentrism. In the same vein, the Last Poets denounced Eurocentric standards through their articulations of "Black."

On their 1971 album *This Is Madness*, the Last Poets released an anthem that articulated and defined the term "Black." Associating "Black" with unity and liberation, they explain, "black is you, black is me, black is us, black is free." The poets suggest that not only does "Black" embody liberation, but it also exemplifies revolution. For example:

> Black is the old lady's grandchildren
> Yelling "Revolution" so that their grandmother will die free
> Black is misery, black is pain
> Black is marching in Alabama
> And getting nothing but rifle butts on the brain
> And not the freedom that you marched for.[31]

The poets acknowledge Black generational (and intergenerational) trauma through the line "Black is the old lady's grandchildren" and by associating "Black" with "pain" and "misery." Further, their lines express a continued quest for liberation, of which the current iteration of Black youth's efforts toward Black freedom through revolution was only the most recent chapter in a centuries-long freedom struggle. The poets address the violence white supremacists had levied against CRM demonstrators, referencing "Bloody Sunday," where, in 1965, Alabama state and local police violently attacked peaceful protestors as they crossed over the Edmund Pettus Bridge near Selma.

Although the poets associate "Black" with pain and misery, they also express Black beauty. The Last Poets demonstrate "Black is beautiful" through their lines:

> Black is such a shock, it's electrifying
> Black is a beautiful sister
> Walking past the Clairol sign
> And watching the sign literally ask itself,
> "I thought I knew for sure, I thought I knew for sure that I was beautiful."[32]

Emphasizing Black beauty and confidence, the poets revise midcentury American beauty standards, creating new associations that underscore Black women's attractiveness. To the poets, "Black" can be so electrifying and beautiful that it might even make an advertisement for Clairol—a white-owned hair-color and hair-care corporation—question its own definitions of beauty. Scholar Maulana Karenga explains that the value of Black art lies in its functionality, collectivity, and commitment to Black revolution.[33] In the era of Black Power, the Last Poets committed their art for Black people, as their anthems deliberately redefine "Black" and convey Black unity, beauty, and self- and community-empowerment.

As artists and Black Power activists, the Last Poets used their anthems to spread movement consciousness. The poets believed that to achieve Black liberation, Black people must obtain a sense of consciousness and unity. They used their artistry to bring awareness to societal issues and pointed to Black Power as the solution. The poets' revolutionary poems inspired other Black Power advocates and artists such as Gil Scott-Heron, who penned the poem "The Revolution Will Not Be Televised" as a response to the Last Poets' poem "When the Revolution Comes."[34] The Last Poets continued to inspire the artistry of late twentieth century rappers such as Common, Notorious B.I.G, and Chuck D and Public Enemy.[35]

Anthem Making in the Twentieth and Twenty-First Centuries

Black Power themes have resurfaced in works of Black artistic expression in the twenty-first century, such as Rap music. While many cultural producers during the late twentieth century were transparent about the connections between their artistry and the Civil Rights and Black Power Movements, artists in the twenty-first century have differed. Although their works embody the notions and themes of Black Power, some Black cultural producers of the BLM era do not publicly vocalize their connections to the Movement and are less invested in being the flag bearers of historical memory. Nevertheless, their work still plays a significant role in pushing the Movement for Black Lives forward. As the Movement for Black Lives took center stage, it reshaped Black art in the twenty-first century as it reflected a BLM consciousness.

This Is America: Childish Gambino and BLM

The current Movement for Black Lives has encompassed mass protests, uprisings, outrage, and awareness-raising efforts. Similar to Black cultural producers who participated, themselves, in the protests of the 1960s and 1970s, many Black artists today have not only taken to the streets in demonstrations but have also used their celebrity and cultural platforms to express solidarity and rage. In response to the murder of Black people at the hands of police, several artists like Plies, Janelle Monáe, and Wyclef Jean released songs of protests.[36] As the Movement for Black Lives gained momentum, more and more Black artists used their artistry to speak out. Scholar Tricia Rose has explained Rap's potential as a cultural response to the troubles of urban youth, as Rap music communicates, she says, "the joys and sorrows of urban Black life."[37] If artists can create anthems as forms of protest, Movement activists can also employ anthems regardless of the artists' initial intention. As much as activists of the Black Power era used the art of the time to forward their movement goals, BLM activists have used music as a vehicle to push the messages of the Movement forward, even when the artists have been unwilling to do so themselves. For example, the works of artists such as Childish Gambino and Buddy served as forms of protests, stirring Black audiences. The artists' lyrics and visual performances create a collective identity wherein audiences have interpreted their songs in ways that convey new (and old) visions of Black liberation. Through their interpretations, Movement participants have adopted the songs as anthems, underscoring the ways in which movements are multifaceted and demonstrating the unpredictability of a movement's evolution.

In May 2018, Childish Gambino stunned audiences with his controversial song and video "This Is America."[38] Like other songs produced during the BLMM, "This Is America" shines a spotlight on contemporary social and political issues of police brutality, gun violence, and the uprisings against them. Scholars Niyi Akingbe and Paul Ayodele Onanuga suggest Childish Gambino's "This Is America" recreates notions of resistance and "infuses protest counterculture" within its lyrics and visual performance.[39] For instance, one poignant scene depicts the fatal gunning of Black choir members singing and dancing. This violent scene demonstrates the power of art to reflect and refine reality: it refers to the 2015 slaying of nine Black churchgoers in Charleston, South Carolina, by a white supremacist they had invited in to worship with them.[40]

As the fight for Black Lives publicizes violence against Black people, "This Is America" aids in highlighting what journalist Mahita Gajanan explains as "the violent contradictions that come with being black in America."[41] In the middle of the violence and turmoil in the video, dancers perform popular African and Black American dance choreography. Sherrie Silver, a Rwandan-born creative who choreographed the video's dances, explains the important ways in which the choreography was designed to bring levity to the product: "there [were] a lot of dark themes in it, so they wanted us to be the light of the video.... We were there to smile and bring joy to everyone watching it, because the background is bringing so much darkness and reality."[42] Dance in "This Is America" is both a method of distraction and a source of Black pride. The choreographer and her dance moves suggest a connection with Africa and further exude Black Power by refuting Eurocentric perspectives. Furthermore, dance also links the video with the centuries-long Black Freedom Struggle and the roots of Black joy in artistic traditions.

Gambino's creative director, Ibra Ake, explains that the video seeks to "normalize blackness."[43] To Ake, normalizing Blackness means displaying both Black joy through dance and Black traumas through several depictions of violence—police brutality, mass incarceration, and mass shooting. Ake views the video as a window into how Black people are portrayed by others and how they see themselves. The piece embodies Blackness historically and unapologetically. Ake states, "This is how we would like to dance, but we have to be aware of the danger and the politics of how we're perceived and the implications of the history of how we were treated.... We're trying to not have to explain ourselves to others and just exist, and not censor what our existence looks like as people."[44] In other words, "This Is America" displays the duality of Blackness in America: anti-Black white supremacy, poverty, and police brutality, but also depictions of Black empowerment and Black joy.

Even linguistically, Childish Gambino echoes 1960s soul and Black Power anthems through repetitive phrases like "Black man" and "get down."[45] From the 1960s to the 1970s, "get down" was a common expression that suggested listeners let loose and throw abandon to the wind. However, as Black people continue to suffer from police brutality in the twenty-first century, the phrase "get down" now alludes to a critique of police brutality, as Childish Gambino couples the phrase with the ubiquitous "Black Man." Taken together, "Black Man, Get Down" references the police targeting of Black men, commanding them to "get down on the ground." In this contemporary moment, these echoes, therefore, underscore the connections between the Black Power Movement and the contemporary BLM Movement.

While "This Is America" does not flinch in its depiction of the violence facing Black communities in America today, critiques anti-Blackness, and echoes themes also popularized by the Black Power Movement, Childish Gambino has deliberately obscured these connections when interviewed about the message he intends for his audience. Asked about the meaning behind his video, Childish Gambino responded, "That's not for me to say."[46] Critics have castigated him for leaving interpretations of his video up to viewers, saying that unlike Black Power artists who intentionally and openly created purpose-driven work for their movement, his obfuscation suggests that he is opportunistically appealing to a broad audience, garnering mainstream appeal and revenues by maintaining a veneer of neutrality. An alternative reading of Childish Gambino's response, however, suggests that he may believe his work should have a life beyond his own understanding—that he intends for audiences, including BLM activists, to interpret it and make it their own.

"This Is America" received mixed reviews. Critics, fans, and activists took to social media with their thoughts and interpretations of the work; some reacted negatively. For instance, one cultural critic, Brittany Luse, condemned the video on Twitter for its vivid depictions of violence against Black people, arguing that its imagery was distasteful and not a form of art.[47] Others, like writer Israel Daramola, suggests that while "This Is America" functions as "political art about black plight," Childish Gambino might "simply [be] taking the opportunity to be a beneficiary" by capitalizing on societal issues for personal or financial gain.[48] While some people rejected Childish Gambino's music video, others applauded it, affirming it to be "art at its highest form."[49] The song became an anthem in America and even transcended US borders, resonating with Black artists throughout the diaspora. "This Is America" inspired songs such as "This Is the UK," "This Is Nigeria," and "This Is Jamaica," in which regional artists also depicted social and political problems in their locales.[50] In 2019, "This Is America" won a Grammy Award for Song of the Year and Best Music Video, and the song's popularity only grew when BLM protests reached their height in the summer of 2020.[51]

In February 2020, racist, white vigilantes stalked and murdered Black jogger Ahmaud Arbery in Glynn County, Georgia. Outraged Americans revisited Childish Gambino's record, stitching the tune to live footage and recordings of BLM protests for exhibition on social media platforms like Instagram, TikTok, and Twitter, where they gained viral attention.[52] Within eight days of George Floyd's murder by Minneapolis police officer Derek Chauvin, the song peaked at number two on the US Spotify chart.[53] Audiences continued to use the song in videos they created capturing footage of BLM rallies and police brutality against protestors, which then went viral on TikTok.[54] Additionally, by incorporating the hashtags #BLM and #BlackLivesMatter in their postings, protestors claimed the song specifically for BLM demonstrations.[55]

Through their use of the song and the hashtags, audiences repurposed "This Is America" for the Movement, making it a BLM viral anthem, despite Childish Gambino's own reluctance to link the two publicly. Scholar Kyle Booten explains that the employment of hashtags operates as a form of political activism, wherein the "hashtags themselves are not merely the tools of online politics but are also themselves objects of political discussion or protest in their own right," and BLM activists and supporters certainly utilized the BLM hashtags to communicate and spread movement consciousness nationally and internationally.[56] By using "This Is America" and #BLM and #BlackLivesMatter to accompany viral videos of BLM demonstrations, audiences embraced Childish Gambino's record as a tool for the Movement, demonstrating how audiences might remake art for their own political purposes, moving their message forward even when it runs counter to the original intentions of the artist.[57]

Buddy "Black": Unapologetically Black and Beautiful

The rise of BLM protests against white supremacy and anti-Blackness led to the creation and adoption of anthems. While commercially successful artists and songs like Childish Gambino's "This

Is America" grew in popularity, the works of lesser-known artists also resonated with Movement participants. For instance, the song "Black" by Compton-based rapper Buddy and A$AP Ferg presented a modern take on "Black is beautiful," adapting Black Power for the contemporary moment. With explicit themes of Black pride and self-determination, protestors and supporters used "Black" as a rallying anthem to organize and to communicate racial uplift and rebellion, much as the Black Power Movement had done earlier.

Buddy's "Black" threads messages of "Black is Beautiful," embracing Black pride, and celebrating Blackness in the song title and in the lyrics throughout. The opening lines read:

> Black
> Black, black, black
> Black on black, black
> Yeah, hey, okay Black, black, black
> Black on black
> Black my thoughts so black
> Black, black on black
> My skin is so black, I'm rocking that black on black
> It's black.[58]

Like the Black Power activists who came before him, who adopted a label initially intended to mark inferiority and oppression and turned it into a symbol of beauty and pride, Buddy embraced the word "Black" for its capacity to define an identity of which he and his community are justifiably proud.

Like Black cultural producers before him, Buddy also rejects Eurocentric standards of beauty: "rocking that black on black," Buddy manifests confidence and Black self-esteem. The BLMM has similarly embraced "Black is beautiful," adopting the mantra "Unapologetically Black" and incorporating it into speeches, emblazoning it on clothing, and using it in social media posts. Historian Barbara Ransby reveals the roots of "Unapologetically Black," pointing out that the term, devised by activist Fresco Steez (Angie Rollins) in 2016, became a popular phrase for BLM as the antithesis of white supremacy, as it acknowledges "the positive aspects of a shared connection to an African American past."[59] The "Black is Beautiful" ideas of the Black Power Movement and BLM's "Unapologetically Black" reverberate in both the lyrics and the music video of Buddy's "Black."

Buddy communicates his reverence for Black history through his incorporation of art and images. His music video depicts a mural of enslaved persons in shackles—acknowledging the Black Freedom Struggle's roots in enslavement and its protest of racial capitalism. His video also includes images of the notable Muslim boxer and advocate of Black Power, Muhammad Ali. Artwork of Black women with afros wielding guns and Black Power fists permeate the video.[60] These depictions trace a powerful lineage of protest before, throughout, and beyond emancipation and voting rights. Akin to earlier Black Power artists like the Last Poets, who infused their lyrics with impatience, Buddy's music-video imagery indicates that Black liberation is born from Black resistance and militancy.

These notions of Black Power and being "Unapologetically Black" that Buddy leverages in his song, "Black," resonated with listeners and movement participants. As a result, audiences took to social media platforms, such as the comments of YouTube, claiming the song as "the movement theme song."[61] Buddy explained to journalists how protestors adopted his song after the murder of George Floyd: "They [were] tagging me at the protest just playing the original 'Black' song."[62] Buddy had not intended for his work to become a BLM anthem: when asked about the origins of his song, Buddy explained that "Black" had come to him inadvertently. Buddy went on to say he did not center his art on "being Black in America, and trying to be a prolific 'woke' writer/musician." However, "it just kind of happened, especially with Trayvon [Martin] at the time, just shining the light on how we have been treated and oppressed over the years."[63] Unlike the Last Poets, whose cultural productions purposely reflected their politics and movement consciousness, but in much the same way as Childish Gambino, who disavowed connections between his art and the protest movements that adopted it as their own, Buddy revealed that the alignment of his work with BLM goals had not been purposeful. Nonetheless, Black audiences embraced Buddy's messages and themes of Black pride and self-determination by ending their comments on his video with hashtags such as #BlackPower, #BlackNProud, #BlackIsBeautiful, and #BlackExcellence. As with "This Is America," BLM advocates reconceptualized "Black" and adopted it as an anthem for their movement. In the aftermath of George Floyd's murder, for instance, Twitter user NubianQueen_Kilo stated on the platform: "So is #Black by #Buddy the #BLM protest anthem or nah? It's been giving me life every day. #BlackLivesMatter."[64] In her post, NubianQueen_Kilo underscored the song's viability as a "protest anthem" and suggested its interconnection with the movement for Black Lives through her use of hashtags.

Black protestors bridged generational divides by participating in the process of anthem-claiming through hashtags. For example, Daphane Norwood shared her insights into the salience of "Black" as a work of protest via YouTube, stating that the song "needs to be the movement theme song. I love it and I am 52 years old. #black #blackisbeautiful #justiceforgeorgefloyd."[65] Norwood intentionally mentioned her age to express solidary with young people leading the movement, demonstrating that the ideas of "Unapologetically Black" and Black pride in the protest tradition transcend generations. She implied further that the song resonated with her own ideas and beliefs that "Black is beautiful." As an emerging artist, Buddy neither had a large-scale platform like the more established artist and entertainer Childish Gambino, nor did his politics explicitly align with BLM. Buddy's song "Black" also did not garner national or international attention in the same way that "This Is America" had done, spawning replicas around the world. Nevertheless, the themes of Black Power and Black pride that audiences saw in "Black" drew them to the song, and, through social media comments and hashtags, BLM advocates claimed and elevated the work as a movement anthem. As had happened with "This Is America," the messages and implications of Black anthems can go beyond their creators' intentions and personal politics. The audience, engaged in the social and political protests around them, assigned to the art the elevated status of "anthem," thereby co-creating and re-creating those works of art anew.

In short, Black art has long played a significant role within the Black Freedom Struggle. During the 1960s and 1970s Black Power

Movement, Black creators (particularly those in the Black Arts Movement) intentionally developed movement anthems to communicate Black Power ideologies to a broader audience. The Last Poets, for instance, played dual roles as cultural producers and movement activists, as their works centered themes of militancy, Black pride, and self-determination. Producing anthems that spread movement ideologies, the poets believed Black people must obtain a sense of consciousness and unity to gain liberation. The Last Poets employed rhythmic poetry to bring awareness to societal issues, call out white supremacy, express impatience with the pace of social change, and demand community and self respect for Black people. Their art pointed to Black Power as the solution and self-consciously forwarded Black Power ideas through art all while inspiring other Black Power advocates and artists.

These same ideas would inadvertently make their way into the artistic creations of Childish Gambino and Buddy over fifty years later, making these concepts salient for new audiences in the twenty-first century. In the wake of highly publicized racial murders, with pervasive widespread protests, BLM advocates took to social media platforms such as TikTok, Twitter, Instagram, and YouTube to engage in anthem-claiming. Taking ownership of Childish Gambino's "This Is America" and Buddy's "Black," they repurposed these songs for the contemporary moment. These artists had not *intentionally* created their art for the movement, yet the themes of pride, protest, and rebellion against white supremacy embedded within them allowed Black audiences to integrate the works within social media videos protesting police brutality and to assign them popular BLM hashtags. The significance of these works, then, lies beyond the artists' intentions, relying largely on movement activists and music enthusiasts who repost or retweet this music as anthems. Artistic expression has played an influential role in fostering movement consciousness and collective identity for both the Black Power and BLM Movements, and the movements themselves have, in turn, shaped and reshaped the Black art created in their eras. To obtain Black liberation, it will take more than the creation of cultural productions; nevertheless, we must acknowledge the reciprocal relationship between culture and politics in order to embrace all the elements in the quest for freedom.

NOTES

1. Christopher J. Lebron, *Making of Black Lives Matter: A Brief History of an Idea*, updated ed. (New York, NY: Oxford University Press, 2021), 8.
2. There were many more deaths, especially those of Black transgender people, whose victimization was revealed by the Black Lives Matter spotlight. While this chapter explores BLM as a continuation of the freedom struggle most recently expressed in the Civil Rights and Black Power Movements, Black resistance to white supremacy and oppression is a tradition that goes back centuries. See, for example, Cyril Lionel Robert James, *History of Pan-African Revolt* (Oakland, CA: PM Press, 2012); Cedric J. Robinson, *Black Marxism: The Making of the Black Radical Tradition* (London, UK: Penguin Books, 2021); Robin D. G. Kelley and Aja Monet, *Freedom Dreams: The Black Radical Imagination* (Boston, MA: Beacon Press, 2022).
3. Patrisse Cullors and asha bandele, *When They Call You a Terrorist: A Story of Black Lives Matter and the Power to Change the World* (Edinburgh, SCT: Canongate, 2021); Keeanga-Yamahtta Taylor, *From #BlackLivesMatter to Black Liberation* (Chicago, IL: Haymarket Books, 2021); and Barbara Ransby, *Making All Black Lives Matter: Reimagining Freedom in the Twenty-First Century* (Oakland, CA: University of California Press, 2018).
4. Taylor, *From #BlackLivesMatter*, 192.
5. Abiodun Oyewole, Umar Bin Hassan, and Kim Green, *The Last Poets on a Mission: Selected Poems and a History of the Last Poets* (New York: H. Holt, 1996), xv. See Ron Karenga, "Black Art: Muted Matter Given Force and Function," in *Black Poets and Prophets: The Theory, Practice, and Esthetics of the Pan-Africanist Revolution*, ed. Earl Anthony and Woodie King (New York, NY: Mentor, 1972), 174–77.
6. See Ashley D. Farmer, *Remaking Black Power: How Black Women Transformed an Era* (Chapel Hill: University of North Carolina Press, 2019); Kesha M. Morant, "Language in Action: Funk Music as the Critical Voice of a Post-Civil Rights Movement Counterculture," *Journal of Black Studies* 42, no. 1 (2010): 71–82, doi:10.1177/0021934709357026; Mark Anthony Neal, *What the Music Said: Black Popular Music and Black Popular Culture* (New York: Routledge, 1999); Rickey Vincent, *Party Music: The Inside Story of the Black Panthers' Band and How Black Power Transformed Soul Music* (Chicago, IL: Lawrence Hill Books, 2013).
7. Oyewole, Hassan, and Green, *Last Poets*, xxii.
8. Oyewole, Hassan, and Green, *Last Poets*, xiv.
9. "The Last Poets," *Lincolnian*, May 1, 1969, 1.
10. Barbara Mahone McBain, "The Last Poets," *Black World*, September 1970, 91.
11. Cynthia Davis and Verner D. Mitchell, *Encyclopedia of the Black Arts Movement* (Lanham, MD: Rowman and Littlefield, 2019), 176–85.

12. Shana L. Redmond, *Anthem: Social Movements and the Sound of Solidarity in the African Diaspora* (New York: New York University Press, 2013), 7, 13. Also see Kerran L. Sanger, *When the Spirit Says Sing!: The Role of Freedom Songs in the Civil Rights Movement* (New York: Routledge, 1995).
13. Redmond, *Anthem*, 6–15.
14. The Last Poets, "N*ggers Are Scared of a Revolution," *The Last Poets*, Douglas Records, 1970.
15. McBain, "The Last Poets," 91.
16. The Last Poets, "N*ggers Are Scared of a Revolution."
17. The Last Poets, "N*ggers Are Scared of a Revolution."
18. Oyewole, Hassan, and Green, *Last Poets*, 60.
19. Oyewole, Hassan, and Green, *Last Poets*, 49.
20. The Last Poets, "Run N*gger," *The Last Poets*, Douglas Records, 1970.
21. Oyewole, Hassan, and Green, *Last Poets*, 49.
22. The Last Poets, "Run N*gger."
23. See Hasan Kwame Jeffries, *Bloody Lowndes: Civil Rights and Black Power in Alabama's Black Belt* (New York: New York University Press, 2010); Charles E. Cobb, *This Nonviolent Stuff'll Get You Killed* (New York: Basic Books, 2014).
24. Julius B. Fleming, *Black Patience Performance, Civil Rights, and the Unfinished Project of Emancipation* (New York: New York University Press, 2022), 7.
25. See Orlando Patterson, *Slavery and Social Death: A Comparative Study* (Cambridge, MA: Harvard University Press, 1982); Sadiya Hartman, *Scenes of Subjection: Terror, Slavery, and Self-Making in Nineteenth-Century America* (New York: Oxford University Press, 1997).
26. Tom W. Smith, "Changing Racial Labels: From 'Colored' to 'Negro' to 'Black' to 'African American,'" *Public Opinion Quarterly* 56, no. 4 (1992): 496–514, https:// www.jstor.org/stable/2749204.
27. Lerone Bennett Jr., "What's in a Name?," *Ebony*, November 1967, 46–50.
28. Tom W. Smith, "Changing Racial Labels," 496–99.
29. Bennett, "What's in a Name?," 47.
30. Kobena Mercer, *Welcome to the Jungle: New Positions in Black Cultural Studies* (New York: Routledge, 2006), 101.
31. The Last Poets, "Black Is," *This Is Madness*, Douglas Records, 1971.
32. The Last Poets, "Black Is."
33. See Ron [Maulana] Karenga, "Black Art: Muted Matter Given Force and Function," in *Black Poets and Prophets: The Theory, Practice, and Esthetics of the Pan-Africanist Revolution*, ed. Earl Anthony and Woodie King (New York: Mentor, 1972), 175.
34. Marcus Baram, *Gil Scott-Heron: Pieces of a Man* (New York: St. Martin's, 2014), 64–66.
35. Common, "The Corner," *Be*, Sony Music Studios, 2005; Notorious B. I. G., "Party and Bullsh*t," *Who's the Man?*, Uptown Records, 1993; Antonino D'Ambrosio, "An Interview with Chuck D," *Progressive Magazine*, July 20,

2005, https://progressive.org/magazine/chuck-d-interview-antonino-d-ambrosio.

36. See Plies, "We Are Trayvon," Slip-N-Slide Records, 2012; Janelle Monáe, "Say Her Name (Hell You Talmbout)," Wondaland Arts Society, 2021; Wyclef Jean, "Justice," Heads Music, 2020.
37. Tricia Rose, *Black Noise: Rap Music and Black Culture in Contemporary America* (Middletown, CT: Wesleyan University Press, 1994), 2.
38. Donald Glover, "This Is America," performed by Childish Gambino, mcDJ RCA, 2018, https://www.youtube.com/watch?v=VYOjWnS4cMY.
39. Niyi Akingbe and Paul Ayodele Onanuga, "'Voicing Protest': Performing Cross-Cultural Revolt in Gambino's 'This Is America' and Falz's 'This Is Nigeria,'" *Contemporary Music Review* 39, no. 1 (February 2020): 7, doi:10.1080/07494467.2020.1753473.
40. Meg Kinnard, "Court Upholds Death Sentence for Church Shooter Dylann Roof," AP NEWS, August 25, 2021, https://apnews.com/article/religion-389bcc56019f268cb1056e37a517bd6c.
41. Mahita Gajanan, "Childish Gambino's 'This Is America': Breaking Down Symbols," *Time*, May 7, 2018, https://time.com/5267890/childish-gambino-this-is-america-meaning.
42. Eric Skelton, "The Story behind Childish Gambino's Symbolic 'This Is America' Dance Choreography," *Complex*, December 4, 2018, https://www.complex.com/pigeons-and-planes/2018/05/childish-gambino-this-is-america-dance-choreographer-sherrie-silver-interview.
43. Hayley Miller, "'This Is America' Producer Reveals New Details about Childish Gambino's Viral Video," *HuffPost*, May 15, 2018, https://www.huffpost.com/entry/ibra-ake-childish-gambino-this-is-america_n_5af326c0e4b0a0d601e94395.
44. Elijah C. Watson, "Childish Gambino's 'This Is America' Was Inspired by 'We Are the World,'" *Okayplayer*, May 10, 2018, https://www.okayplayer.com/music/childish-gambino-this-is-america-we-are-the-world.html.
45. Glover, "This Is America."
46. Israel Daramola, "Donald Glover Doesn't Want to Say What 'This Is America' Is About," *Billboard*, May 10, 2018, https://www.billboard.com/music/music-news/donald-glover-this-is-america-tmz-video-8455521.
47. Miller, "'This Is America' Producer Reveals New Details about Childish Gambino's Viral Video."
48. Israel Daramola, "The Cynicism of Childish Gambino's 'This Is America,'" *SPIN*, May 9, 2018, https://www.spin.com/2018/05/donald-glover-this-is-america-review.
49. Miller, "This Is America' Producer."
50. Don Andre, "This Is the UK," YouTube, May 25, 2018, https://www.youtube.com/watch?v=5QiBlsGL—E.; Falz, "This Is Nigeria," YouTube, May 25 2018, https://www.youtube.com/watch?v=UW_xEqCWrm0; J nel Comedy, "This

51. "Childish Gambino's 'This Is America' Makes Grammys History," February 11, 2019, BBC, https://www.bbc.com/news/entertainment-arts-47197236.
52. Paul McAuley, "Childish Gambino's 'This Is America' Is as Relevant as Ever," The Indiependent, June 5, 2020, https://www.indiependent.co.uk/childish-gambinos-this-is-america-is-as-relevant-as-ever.
53. Bryan Rolli, "Childish Gambino's 'This Is America' and Kendrick Lamar's 'Alright' See Massive Spotify Gains amid George Floyd Protests," *Forbes*, June 3, 2020, https://www.forbes.com/sites/bryanrolli/2020/06/03/childish-gambino-kendrick-lamar-spotify-george-floyd-protests.
54. See "This Is America – Tik Tok Compilation," YouTube, June 3, 2020, https://www.youtube.com/watch?v=jtJWFNDuEYg; and Raka Mukherjee, "'This Is America': TikTok Videos on #BlackLivesMatter Show Ground Reality of Police Brutality," News18, June 2, 2020, https://www.news18.com/news/buzz/this-is-america-tiktok-videos-on-blacklivesmatter-show-ground-reality-of-police-brutality-2648595.html.
55. Rolli, "Childish Gambino's 'This Is America.'"
56. Kyle Booten, "Hashtag Rhetoric: #AllLivesMatter and the Production of Post-Racial Affect," in *#Identity: Hashtagging Race, Gender, Sexuality, and Nation*, ed. Abigail De Kosnik and Keith P. Feldman (Ann Arbor: University of Michigan Press, 2019), 183.
57. One of the criticisms of Childish Gambino's reluctance to tie his video to the protest themes of BLM was that he hoped to maintain or augment the record's commercial success by remaining apolitical; ironically, in using the song as the soundtrack to their viral videos, BLM activists rejuvenated the record's commercial success.
58. Buddy, "Black," performed by Buddy, RCA Records, 2018, https://www.youtube.com/watch?v=tAOGX9AhoxI.
59. Ransby, *Making All Black Lives Matter*, 97–99.
60. Buddy, "Black."
61. Daphane Norwood (@daphenenorwood9762), "movement theme song," comment on Buddy, "Black," YouTube, 2020, https://www.youtube.com/watch?v=tAOGX9AhoxI.
62. Lea Winkler, "Meet Buddy, the Pharrell-Approved Rapper Bringing Janky Vibes to Hip Hop," *Document Journal*, August 7, 2020, https://www.documentjournal.com/2020/08/meet-buddy-the-pharrell-approved-rapper-bringing-janky-vibes-to-hip-hop.
63. Winkler, "Meet Buddy."
64. NubianQueen_Kilo, "So is #Black by #Buddy the #BLM protest anthem or nah?," Twitter, July 6, 2020, 8:22 p.m., https://twitter.com/KiLo_MinoLo/status/1269424354888220672.
65. Daphane Norwood, "movement theme song."

POSTSCRIPT

"Miraculous, Magnificent, and Messy"

Rights, Lives, and the Movement in Real Time

*Françoise N. Hamlin and
Charles W. McKinney Jr.*

As we were putting the finishing touches (so we thought) on our manuscript in January 2023, police officers in Memphis, Tennessee, brutally murdered Tyre Nichols.[1] The events that proceeded from this unnecessary and fatal encounter followed a similar pattern to previous moments: the bottomless rage and despair of a family and a community; activists convening to respond; city and law enforcement officials circling wagons, scrambling to create an "official" rendering of the incident, and asking for "calm"; political triangulation; the arrival of national media; mass-based protests. The Nichols murder became the latest real-time scenario that illuminated all of the perils and prospects of the movement work we hoped to chronicle in this book.

To paraphrase another scholar, the local is where the national is frequently situated.[2] The (local) tragedy of the Memphis murder uncovered and renewed many of the questions that rest at the heart of *From Rights To Lives*, and that many of the chapters reflect. Yet, what does movement-building look like now from the ground-up? How has *#BlackLivesMatter* shaped the terrain? What continuities and discontinuities regarding the struggle for Black Freedom can we glean from Memphis? Events there revealed more than simply the recurring themes of police brutality, Black death and rage, and mass-based movement. Memphis also reminded us—in a powerful way—of the *messy complexity* of movement making, another central theme the authors tackle in this book. The strategy, the wins, the losses, the coalition-building effort, the *stuff* of movement work is often lost in the breezy stories constructed about Black Freedom that reduce the calculus of social change to the simple arithmetic of marching, chants, and confrontation. The Black folks who sprung to action in the wake of Nichols' murder represent a powerful corrective to simplistic thinking about the construction of a new world. As such, we felt that the conclusion to this book had to contend—albeit briefly—with the events that unfolded in the Bluff City.[3]

We interviewed four activists on the ground in Memphis to ascertain how movement building happens in real time and how that movement is in a dynamic relationship with the past. Shahidah Jones heads the Official Black Lives Matter (BLM) Memphis chapter and is a central organizing figure in the city, having entered into formal organizing spaces following the murder of Trayvon Martin in 2012. Rev. Dr. Earle Fisher serves as the senior pastor of Abyssinian Missionary Baptist Church in Memphis and over the past decade has either organized or co-organized a number of grassroots organizations, most notably the Memphis Grassroots Organizations Coalition in 2015.[4] Joshua Adams is a self-proclaimed "paid troublemaker" with Memphis For All who also worked with BLM and Decarcerate Memphis. Amber Sherman is an organizer and activist who, in addition to engaging in independent protest actions, has worked with Decarcerate Memphis, the Official BLM chapter, and other local organizations.

Of course, all four activists were keenly aware that 2023 was not the first time local events in Memphis had national and international implications. Black union activists struggled for dignity, fair wages, and justice across the twentieth and into the twenty-first century.[5] The most famous and well-chronicled confrontation occurred during the 1968 sanitation strike following the grisly deaths of Echol Cole and Robert Walker, two Black sanitation workers crushed by a malfunctioning garbage truck. Sanitation workers began a boycott for better conditions and pay. Their actions laid the foundation of a movement that drew together support from multiple constituencies across the city. This coalition in turn generated enough momentum to warrant an invitation to Rev. Dr. Martin Luther King Jr. to join the protest, even as he was fully invested in his organization's Poor People's Campaign. Before his arrival, local people and strikers had taken to the streets in nonviolent protests, where police confronted them with tear gas and batons. Memphis's Black leaders formed a coalition to support the strike, for which King gave several speeches and sermons before a single bullet took his life in Memphis. The strikers persisted, now with enhanced media scrutiny, and ultimately got their demands met.[6]

Forty-four years later, George Zimmerman's murder of Trayvon Martin in 2012 marked the beginning of a series of deaths that sparked nonviolent direct action in Memphis (and elsewhere).[7] The abbreviated list of events that followed includes the 2014 police murder of Michael Brown in St. Louis, Missouri; the 2015 police murder of Darrius Stewart in Memphis (which, among other things, led Rev. Fisher and others to organize the Memphis Grassroots Organizations Coalition); the 2016 murders of Alton Sterling and Philando Castile at the hands of the police in Baton Rouge, Louisiana, and Falcon Heights, Minnesota, respectively; and the Hernando Desoto Bridge protests (known locally as the first bridge protest), which shut down I-40, the main artery into the city from across the Mississippi River, following the deaths of Sterling and Castile.[8] The national uprisings in 2020 following police murders of Breonna Taylor in Louisville, Kentucky, George Floyd in Minneapolis, Minnesota, and too many others saw its own expression in Memphis, where organized solidarity protests also focused on local issues.

These waves of public protests, whether in 1968 or today, rarely occur spontaneously. Rather, they are built with intention and direction. The four Memphis activists we interviewed reiterated that constantly, while also outlining the difficulties around coalition-building, organizing, and allyship, as well as how they have educated themselves to teach others. Each of the four arrived at this point from different paths. Joshua Adams joined the Progressive Student Alliance while studying at the University of Memphis. There he aired his frustrations about the poverty in which he grew up in Memphis and the deteriorating situation of the working class around him. Upon his 2016 graduation, Adams got more acquainted with the local BLM chapter, working with them on the Transformative Justice Campaign. He joined Decarcerate Memphis in 2021, one year after its founding in 2020, and worked at Memphis For All with the Brake Light Clinics (whose mission is to fix brake lights, a common cause for police stops, and to educate motorists about traffic stops), first as a volunteer before joining the paid staff.[9] Adams also organizes with the Justice and Safety Alliance (JSA), a broad multiracial coalition of nonprofit and faith-based organizations founded in 2021. With a progressive vision to reimagine safety and its relationship to current policing policies, this interracial and highly intersectional umbrella organization (akin to Mississippi's Council of Federated Organizations that sheltered the NAACP, SCLC, SNCC, and CORE from 1961 to 1964) pulls politics, resources, talents, constituencies, and voices to a huge table to demand justice and safety, particularly through participatory safety measures that provide alternatives to current police protocols.[10]

Like Adams, Amber Sherman also began her political organizing in college (University of Tennessee–Martin), but around the issues of health care and reproductive justice, when she joined Organizing for Action in December 2015 and organized campus protests against the privatization of housekeeping.[11] She got involved in the BLM protests following the murder of Darrius Stewart in 2015, giving ground support to people while also working on housing organizing.[12] In 2020, BLM provided her with a fellowship, which proved to be transformative. This opportunity for study equipped her with a broader political understanding of the structural nexus of over-policing the poor regardless of any criminal wrongdoing, gentrification, displacement, and the central role of capitalism in the entire enterprise.¹³ This on-the-ground training became real when she went to Louisville to assist in the organizing following the police murder of Breonna Taylor. There, she saw the nexus operating in real time: she learned how police had continually raided Taylor's apartment complex, along with others in the neighborhood, forcing people to move, making clear the connective tissue between poverty, policing, gentrification, and capitalism.¹⁴

Rev. Earle Fisher began his activist journey when he came to Memphis in 1999 to attend LeMoyne-Owen College on a basketball scholarship. When his assistant coach was terminated, he organized and petitioned to get him rehired. Once he answered the call to ministry and attended divinity school, he encountered Black Theology, which focused his liberatory ethic. When he took the pulpit at Abyssinian in 2011, he used the platform to organize his congregation around social and political empowerment for Black liberation. At the same time, he attempted to organize the clergy, starting the Southern Action Coalition (SAC) around 2011 to identify conscious clergy in different neighborhoods who could respond to their neighborhood crises in an organized, collective manner. That attempt was slow at first until the Darrius Stewart murder. The work done by Fisher and a host of others helped bring attention to the tragedy and amplify the voices of the Stewart family. Fisher's role as member of the clergy was crucial. At one of the first public meetings after the incident, his remarks resonated with the family enough that he became one of the central conduits between them and other groups. He subsequently created the Memphis Grassroots Organizations Coalition (MGOC) to unify efforts to find justice for Stewart without any person or group feeling siloed or marginalized. To facilitate this, MGOC sent a petition around the city and convened a mass meeting at Abyssinian to figure out ways to collectively confront inequality in Memphis.¹⁵

Rev. Fisher's petition drew Shahidah Jones to the meeting in Abyssinian, an event which helped set her path. For Jones, the meeting represented a return to an organizing tradition she recognized from childhood. Raised as a Muslim in Memphis, Jones's uncle (after whom she is named) was a Black Panther, a member of the

Nation of Islam, and one of the first members of the Muslim Mosque in Memphis. In college, she became active with the Jena Six protests. Trayvon Martin's murder further piqued her organizing interests, and she began seeking out a grassroots organization that could support her growing curiosity and dedication to social change. Her first stop was the Mid-South Peace and Justice Center, where she began learning the basics of community organizing. After work in different organizations, she found her place during the aftermath of Darrius Stewart's murder, the event she says "made me an activist."[16]

Even in these early stages of their activist journeys, Fisher and Jones note the rise of factions within the protests and stark disagreements over how best to attend to the needs of the Stewart family following his murder. They gained a greater understanding of the impact the exploitation of his death had on his family and how those tensions affected the movement from within. Both Fisher and Jones bemoan the exploitation from all directions. Fisher remembers how skepticism around people's motives plagued early organizing meetings. People tried to exploit the movement itself. As he puts it, too many "were in it for personal platform building and notoriety [rather] than a genuine ultimate advancement of a social political agenda towards equity, justice, love, and truth."[17] Jones says it more bluntly, stating that many of the organizations that "popped up" were too concerned about funding and money. She criticizes them for showing up for Black death but not for Black *life*.[18] Those committed to transformation have to deal with exploitation within movement spaces as they shape the scope and trajectory of their work.

When Jones attended the first meeting to organize a Memphis BLM chapter at the National Civil Rights Museum in 2015, she saw older activists in the room berating and rejecting passionate and committed young people with no organizing skills. Jones's experience speaks directly to the generational friction within the BFS and how that friction damages coalition building. Jones and others yearned for a space where both elders and younger, emerging activists could learn from each other while stressing the importance of historical context, empathy, and grace. Even within the germinating BLM chapter, Jones witnessed again how some people used the brand for self-aggrandizement, and she recognized that pattern from the marketing and communication experience she brought with her. In her initial role with the group, she had used her skills to elevate the BLM social media presence.[19] She received additional organizing training by BLM members anchored in queer and Black feminist theory, a lens that sharpened her own social and political analysis, as it did for so many of the activists showcased in this book. She honed her own practice through trial and error, and within five months she stepped into the BLM leadership ranks in 2016. She found her political home.

The politics of respectability is enmeshed with generational differences. Older leaders frequently remind younger activists about the "correct" or most "appropriate" way to conduct the business of social change. Rev. Fisher and other young activists encountered this firsthand. Fisher labels the older civil rights organizations with historical roots, some predating the mass Civil Rights Movement, as "legacy" organizations. When police murdered Darrius Stewart in 2015, the subsequent organizational scrambling for influence and airtime between legacy and newer organizations reflected what Fisher and others saw as conflict over the control of the microphone rather than a real pursuit of justice for the Stewart family. Collective unfamiliarity, he argues, between organizations trying to advocate for the family widened chasms of misunderstanding and mistrust. Addressing these obstacles required Herculean efforts to unify in order to properly advocate for victims rather than exacerbate their suffering.[20] Jones concurs, adding that if organizations do not reveal their personal goals and motives, then exploitation can occur. Organizers on the ground feel the most impact, and, she adds wryly, "sometimes it feels like fighting with a blindfold."[21]

Yet Fisher, Jones, Sherman, and Adams managed to cultivate relationships that allowed them, through understanding and debate, to work out their "jagged edges" of distrust.[22] This is not endemic to Memphis's movement. Research and testimony show how movement communities that form coalitions struggle from within. Expecting social and political movements to exist in total harmony requires a journey to the idyllic yet to materialize, and when so much is at stake, often the friction creates sparks. In the 1960s, as multiple organizations worked in cities across the country toward the common goal of eradicating Jim Crow, they fought constantly among themselves. Those attempting to thwart their efforts worked to manipulate these cracks to fracture the progress of tentative coalitions. When we spoke about this history, some of which is highlighted in this book, Jones exasperatedly noted an additional element contributing to internal dissension: misrepresentation in the media. She and Fisher recounted numerous instances where the media attributed almost any public actions to BLM, even when other groups had sponsored the action. The attribution of *any* public protest to BLM attracted bad publicity, misunderstanding, and anger.[23]

The Nichols campaign in Memphis highlighted a host of truths to the activists themselves after years of trial and error and hard grind. Amber Sherman maintains that by 2023, organizers were better prepared than in previous protest moments. In 2020, after George Floyd's murder, she recognized a lack of education around policing and policy in the neighborhoods where she organized and the need for more robust strategy in that area. Her own experiences and policy work in Louisville, where she traveled to support activists following Breonna Taylor's murder, prepared her for rapid response with more coordination between organizations. She saw firsthand how activists used data about police stops, arrests, and racial disparities to confront officials with irrefutable facts. This work was also deeply coalitional: multiple people in multiple organizations helped in pooling resources and made pushing out information to more people possible, all while strategizing to both avoid burnout and maintain the pressure with people power.[24]

Sherman's participation in a 2020 BLM fellowship designed by Jones and others focused on political education, strategy, and the basics of organizing. The fellowship helped build her confidence as an organizer and critical thinker. With no application process prohibiting people from benefiting, the fellowship gave opportunities to those who showed interest, highlighting BLM's intentional goal of bringing young people up and through, building the foundations for effective organizers and a base of activists in real time.[25] Sherman recognized that Black women in the organization were "getting shit done," using their connections and political knowledge and resisting the assertions of Black men who wanted to take over the programs (and the money) without producing any results. She credits Black feminist thought for shaping and honing her activism over time, and her organizing work in the wake of Breonna Taylor's murder helped her to recognize the importance of intersectionality, which opened her up to the multiple dynamics in play regarding that case. Even in the midst of the chaos of movement work, the education of movement members remained—and remains—a central objective.

As Joshua Adams notes, some Memphis activists describe their city as "a new Confederacy." They only partially jest. Although Memphis is a majority Black city, and the majority of its elected officials are Black, racial subordination runs deep and shadows every aspect of life. Underfunded public schools, an antediluvian transportation system, substandard wages causing high rates of poverty, and a criminal justice system designed to punish poor (mostly Black) people regardless of actual guilt or innocence lie at the center of the city's dilemmas. However, over the past decade, an emergent, re-energized grassroots coalition of organizations has countered the "new Confederacy," each designed to confront some aspect of the inequity that Memphians encounter. The Justice and Safety Alliance (JSA), encapsulating a muscular multiracial democratic united front, is one of the powerful signs of this growth and development, which sent a clear message across the state about the extent of the people power available to deal with threats to democracy and civil liberties. Adams emphasizes that the existence of JSA, and BLM's role in it, is a testament to how the policy framing of the BFS in recent years has been institutionalized in ways unimaginable a few years ago. As Adams puts it, "Folks came together saying, 'We need a different understanding of what public safety looks like. We need a different understanding of what the city budget looks like.' Within JSA there is an understanding that the police are not producing this idea of safety that we need. There's an understanding that there's not enough democracy in the county locally."[26] The impact of grassroots mobilization and political education bore fruit in the successful effort to unseat Amy Weirich, the county district attorney who had earned the reputation as "one of the most problematic prosecutors in the entire country."[27]

In Memphis, the layers of organizing in recent years produced an activist community primed to act in coordination in the early months of 2023. Decarcerate Memphis formed in 2020 in an effort to confront an expanding federal presence in law enforcement in the city. A central portion of their work was working with "community leaders, activists, attorneys, strategists, clergy, and concerned citizens" to produce data related to pretextual traffic stops and build support for an end to the practice.[28] On December 6, 2022, Decarcerate members presented the results of their research to the City Council, declaring pretextual stops as racist and dangerous. A month later, on January 7, 2023, police officers murdered Tyre Nichols after making a pretextual stop.[29] Activists then convened to plan a process of engagement and coordinate their demands to the city and the police department.

The first step was to reach out to Nichols's family to inquire about their needs and demands. The family's central demands were: to release the video of the violent interaction between Nichols and the SCORPION Unit, the special unit of the MPD designed to combat crime in targeted sections of the city; to name all of the officers on the scene; to charge the officers responsible for the murder; and to end the SCORPION Unit. A consortium of organizations, including #BLM, Decarcerate Memphis, Memphis for All, Youth Justice Action Council, Memphis Interfaith Coalition for Action and Hope (MICAH), Gifts of Life Ministries, and others staged protests demanding each and every one of these demands. For people living outside the city, it was easy to chalk up initial police cooperation regarding the video to the heinous nature of its content. City officials spared few words describing the violent behavior captured on the video.[30] Yet another driving force behind the release was the momentum gained in recent years by grassroots organizations who have become well versed in making public demands of local authorities and who, by 2023, were more than ready to respond if officials did not meet those demands.

After the city released the police recordings of the fatal encounter, activists organized a second peaceful takeover of the Interstate 40 bridge. The bridge takeover was reminiscent of the previous instance on I-40, where upward of a thousand people shut down traffic for over five hours in 2016. This time, however, organizers were more coordinated, more seasoned. As the reporter from MLK50 reported, "The rage of Memphians is deep, but focused. As helicopters and a drone whirled above, organizers passed out water, some displaying yellow armbands and designated as marshals. This wasn't a mob. This was a strategy."[31] When protesters overran the bridge, obstructing trucks and commerce, Mayor Jim Strickland tried to find the leadership source to end the protest. Amber Sherman was the agreed-upon point of contact. When he reached her by phone, her demand was simple: shut down the SCORPION Unit. After he hung up, he inquired who *else* he could talk to in order to negotiate. The answer to that question: Amber Sherman. For decades, as Sherman and Adams observe, the Memphis Police Department had acted like a rogue agency.[32] The demand to immediately disband the SCORPION unit came not only from a bereaved family, but also from a large segment of the city haunted (and harassed) by its existence. The SCORPION Unit had a well-earned reputation for terrorizing residents and escalating the most basic of infractions, like a broken taillight, to brutal attacks.[33]

By this time the activists had ascertained the city's chain of power and knew that the mayor, along with the police chief, had the power to disband the unit. Despite an initial resistance to make the move, the mayor disbanded the unit after local public pressure and substantial coordinated protests. Other specific demands accompanied the order to end the SCORPION Unit. Throughout the early months of 2023, activists continued marches and protests and brought that same energy to Memphis City Council and County Commission meetings in an effort to pass police reforms. Ultimately, they succeeded: the broad coalition convinced a majority of City Council members to pass a series of ordinances that banned the use of unmarked cars in traffic stops; banned police stops for low-level offenses (such as broken taillights); established regular data collection on traffic stops; required regular reporting by the police department to the Civilian Law Enforcement Review Board; and created a new independent review process for excessive-force complaints.[34] The coordinated protests, policy push, political education, and media blasts executed in Memphis powerfully confront the persistent myth of spontaneous direct action and demonstrate the intentional, intelligent planning and strategy that almost always lies at the heart of sustained action.

So, where do we go from here? What is forward progress at this point? We asked these questions to the four Memphis activists. After the long game executed in the shadow of Tyre Nichols's death, Amber Sherman stresses the need to keep the police and elected officials accountable. In Memphis, the next ordinance goal is to disband the Organized Crime Unit. This requires constant pressure, energy, and replenishable labor. BLM has developed training around strategic organizing and education to cultivate a savvy public. This is not the work of a shortsighted organization. Rather, it is the work of a committed band of people who understand the importance of implementing long-term strategies in the pursuit of liberation. The information war is real, as politicians try to limit education while never using the city's history to appraise the current moment, and activists must teach the impact of history and the current implications. In this way, Sherman has recognized increased levels of support from those not on the frontlines, with a broadening of the age range and older people more motivated to organize now that they have information. In the end, she realizes that while her formal college education gave her the tools to study, she does most of the work on her own. To see how they fared, she reads about Black women activists such as Ella Baker, Fannie Lou Hamer, and Pauli Murray.[35]

Part of that on-the-ground education means learning about what one can do as an individual, how to manage stress, and how to pace oneself accordingly to ward off burn out. For Sherman, that means taking time off to rest, being careful and thoughtful in the work, and always analyzing her motives. "You need to *care*," she stresses.[36] BLM is more than just work; these activists engage in relational organizing, socializing, and holding events to find joy and build in rest. Joshua Adams mentions the stipends available to help folks find rest and that skateboarding provides his outlet. That is what freedom feels like, he argues, and it is important to experience it while also fighting for more.[37]

Memphis is a case study of how to get things done in real time, and veteran activists are committed to creating models and templates to assist local campaigns across the county and beyond. Joshua Adams mentioned two more examples of coalition building: he identified a grassroots coalition between BLM, Memphis Artists for Change, and Black Men Build as one that deals with the deep heavy counseling and healing work for those most affected by policing, poverty trauma, and community violence. This mitigates the effects of the long-term struggle alongside the policy-making imperative. Then he told us how JSA met with Alabama Forward (a similar group) regarding voter suppression and the exchange of ideas for increased voter participation. Cross-pollination needs to continue.[38]

All of the activists agree that there is no way around the work, and it is everyone's responsibility to work. Shahidah Jones insists that everyone should, at some point, stand at the literal frontlines of struggle and protest—regardless of positionality, rank, status, or age. Regardless of talent and roles, she stresses that everyone needs training as an organizer, to know their history and to demonstrate their commitment. She repeats, "There is no separation between us and the streets; there is no separation between your job and the streets; there is no separation between the frontlines of the movement and the back of the movement; there is no separation."[39] Rev. Fisher concurs, adding that it is important for everyone to eyewitness the "miraculous, magnificent, and messy activism and organizing."[40] The reliance solely on the virtual space to organize creates obstacles when too many grassroots people cannot navigate it easily and too many poor folk do not have wireless access in their homes, which necessitates combining technology with traditional strategies to reach the people. Yet, in spite of the many obstacles and challenges facing activists in the city, Adams recognizes that their efforts have not been in vain. "People have been fighting and coming together around certain agendas and visions for the last few years. I think that's actually pretty amazing."[41]

Ultimately, we come full circle: history *does* matter. It matters to organizers training activists and executing protests and strategies, as the Memphis case study clearly shows. It matters to those not (yet) on the frontlines: to understand the struggle, its deep roots in the nation's very fabric, and then to act/vote accordingly. It matters enough to prompt white supremacists to try to suppress it. *From Rights to Lives* offers histories that do the work of connecting mass-movement work throughout the Black Freedom Struggle along a series of topics to demonstrate the messy interconnectedness that binds us together as moral citizens and stewards of the world. *From Rights to Lives* leaves frayed ends, and it purposefully prompts more questions, more scenarios and case studies, and hopefully more scholarship and research. As the activists remind us, there is much to do.

NOTES

1. Rather than detail the murder here, see Kaitlyn Radde, "Four Ex-Memphis Police Officers Charged with Tyre Nichols' Murder Have Been Decertified," National Public Radio, March 24, 2023, https://www.npr.org/2023/03/24/1165859546/tyre-nichols-memphis-police-officers-decertified for the details.
2. Jeanne Theoharis and Komozi Woodard, eds., *Groundwork: Local Black Freedom Movements in America* (New York: New York University Press, 2005), 7.
3. It is important for us to emphasize that this is not a comprehensive overview of the events in Memphis in the wake of Tyre Nichols' murder. We have neither the time nor space to provide such an analysis. However, we do believe that this exploration can provide some critical insights into the movement work that took place in Memphis that culminated in the first half of 2023.
4. Abyssinian Missionary Baptist Church, "Meet Our Pastor! Reverend Earle J. Fisher, PhD," accessed May 24, 2023, https://abcministries1.wildapricot.org/Meet-our-Pastor!/; Memphis Grassroots Organizations Coalition, Facebook, accessed May 24, 2023, https://www.facebook.com/Memphis-Grassroots-Organizations-Coalition-838482906269758.
5. On labor struggles in Memphis, see Michael Honey, *Southern Labor and Black Civil Rights: Organizing Memphis Workers* (Chicago: University of Illinois Press, 1993); Aram Goudsouzian and Charles McKinney, eds., *An Unseen Light: Black Struggles for Freedom in Memphis, Tennessee* (Lexington: University Press of Kentucky, 2018).
6. For more details, see any of the many biographies on King, as well as Steve Estes, *I Am a Man!: Race, Manhood, and the Civil Rights Movement* (Chapel Hill: University of North Carolina Press, 2005); and Colette Coleman, "The 1968 Sanitation Workers' Strike That Drew MLK to Memphis," History, July 21, 2020, updated May 18, 2023, https://www.history.com/news/sanitation-

workers-strike-memphis. Memphis has a much longer history of Black freedom struggles, beyond the scope of this book.
7. André Munro, "Shooting of Trayvon Martin," *Britannica*, June 29, 2015, https://www.britannica.com/event/shooting-of-Trayvon-Martin.
8. "This Day in History: August 9, 2014: Michael Brown Is Killed by a Police Officer in Ferguson, Missouri," History, August 6, 2020, https://www.history.com/this-day-in-history/michael-brown-killed-by-police-ferguson-mo; and WMCA Action News 5 Staff, "Family: Officer Killed 19-Year-Old after Mistaking Him for Someone Else," Action News 5, July 18, 2015, www.actionnews5.com/story/29578116/man-dead-after-struggle-with-mpd-officer; Jody Callahan, "Marchers Shut Down I-40 Bridge at Memphis during Black Lives Matter Rally," *Commercial Appeal*, July 10, 2016, https://www.commercialappeal.com/story/news/2016/07/10/marchers-shut-down-i40-bridge-at-memphis-during-black-lives-matter-rally/90569834.
9. Joshua Adams, interview by authors, April 28, 2023, via Zoom.
10. See "Council of Federated Organizations (COFO)," SNCC Digital Gateway, SNCC Legacy Project and Duke University, accessed May 25, 2023, https://snccdigital.org/inside-sncc/alliances-relationships/cofo; and "Who We Are: Partner Organizations," Justice and Safety Alliance, accessed May 25, 2023, https://justiceandsafetyalliance.org/partner-organizations.
11. Amber Sherman, interview by authors, May 9, 2023, via Zoom; for Organizing for Action see "OFA Trainings," Obama Alumni, accessed January 15, 2024, https://www.obamaalumniassociation.org/ofa-trainings.
12. Amber Sherman, interview by authors, May 9, 2023, via Zoom.
13. For more information, see Memphis Coalition of Concerned Citizens, Facebook, accessed May 22, 2023, https://www.facebook.com/CoalitionOfMemphis.
14. Amber Sherman, interview by authors.
15. Rev. Dr. Earle Fisher, interview by authors, May 12, 2023, via Zoom.
16. Shahidah Jones, interview by authors, May 12, 2023, via Zoom. For more information about the Jena Six see "Jena Six (2006)," BlackPast, October 21, 2023, https://www.blackpast.org/african-american-history/jena-six-2006.
17. Fisher, interview by authors.
18. Jones, interview by authors.
19. Jones, interview by authors.
20. Fisher, interview by authors; "Memphis Teen 'Was Running Away' when Shot Dead by Police, Witnesses Say," *Guardian*, Dec. 16, 2015, https://www.theguardian.com/us-news/2015/dec/16/memphis-darrius-stewart-moving-away-from-police-officer-shooting-witnesses.
21. Jones, interview by authors.
22. Fisher, interview by authors.
23. Jones, interview by authors.

24. Sherman, interview by authors. Sherman detailed how she built a support team around her who provided food and dog-sitting when required to enable her to focus on the work. She saw this as part of the long-term organizing and planning.
25. Sherman, interview by authors. Bail support stabilized people's lives, and BLM also worked with people to plan and budget, following through with each case toward what it commonly becomes: a dismissal. Other organizations have fellowship opportunities, but these often have more strings attached and are not as extensive as BLM's. Memphis BLM applied for non-profit grant money to provide a small stipend of about $1000 to each recipient.
26. Adams, interview by authors.
27. "Shelby County Voters Oust Prosecutor Who Sought to Execute Pervis Payne," Death Penalty Information Center, Aug. 9, 2022, https://deathpenaltyinfo.org/news/shelby-county-voters-oust-prosecutor-who-sought-to-execute-pervis-payne; Katherine Burgess, "Shelby County Ousts Amy Weirich, Elects Progressive Prosecutor in Steve Mulroy," *Memphis Commercial Appeal*, Aug. 4, 2022, https://www.commercialappeal.com/story/news/politics/elections/2022/08/04/shelby-county-district-attorney-election-2022-steve-mulroy-amy-weirich/10162106002/; "Study Ranks Shelby County DA as Most Overzealous Prosecutor," Action News 5, July 13, 2017, https://www.actionnews5.com/story/35878519/study-ranks-shelby-county-da-as-most-overzealous-prosecutor.
28. Decarcerate Memphis website, https://decarceratememphis.com, accessed 9 January 2024.
29. Sherman, interview by authors.
30. Emily Cochrane and Rick Rojas, "The Questions That Remain a Year after Tyre Nichols's Death," *New York Times*, January 7, 2024, https://www.nytimes.com/article/tyre-nichols-memphis-police-dead.html.
31. Adrienne Johnson Martin, "Not Only Peaceful, but Thoughtful Protest," MLK50: Justice through Journalism, accessed May 31, 2023, https://mlk50.com/2023/01/27/not-only-peaceful-but-thoughtful-protest.
32. Adams, interview by authors.
33. Steve Eder, Matthew Rosenberg, Joseph Goldstein, Mike Baker, Kassie Bracken, and Mark Walker, "Muscle Cars, Balaclavas, and Fists: How the Scorpions Rolled through Memphis," *New York Times*, Feb. 4, 2023, updated March 1, 2023, https://www.nytimes.com/2023/02/04/us/memphis-police-scorpion.html.
34. Katherine Burgess, "After Tyre Nichols, Memphis Passes Police Reform on Traffic Stops, Data Transparency," *Memphis Commercial Appeal*, March 7, 2023, https://www.commercialappeal.com/story/news/local/2023/03/07/city-of-memphis-passes-police-reform-on-traffic-stops-data-transparency/69955791007.

35. Sherman, interview by authors.
36. Sherman, interview by authors.
37. Adams, interview by authors.
38. Adams, interview by authors.
39. Jones, interview by authors.
40. Fisher, interview by authors.
41. Adams, interview by authors.

Contributors

SCOTT N. BROOKS is the director of the Global Sport Institute and an associate professor of sociology in the School of Social and Family Dynamics at Arizona State University. He has consulted for the NFL, NCAA, USOPC, USA basketball, MLB, and Adidas, as well as college and high school coaches and athletes. He is the author of *Black Men Can't Shoot* (University of Chicago Press, 2009) and teaches sociology of sport, race relations, and the essentials of sports business: basketball.

MICKELL CARTER is a PhD student in the Department of Africana Studies at Brown University. Her research interests include Black internationalism, twentieth-century social movements, and the intersections between culture and politics. Carter has written for the award-winning blog of the African American Intellectual History Society's (AAIHS) *Black Perspectives*, the American Historical Association's *Perspectives* magazine, and the *Washington Post*. She is also a host for the New Books Network's African American Studies podcast.

CHARITY CLAY is an assistant professor at Xavier University of Louisiana. She teaches classes in sociology and African American and diaspora studies and heads the department's concentration in crime and social justice. She began writing about social media activism with a book chapter entitled "#BlacknessBeLike" in *Systemic Racism: Making Liberty, Justice and Democracy Real* (Miller and Ducey, 2017). She is currently working on a manuscript that extends her concept of Systemic Police Terror. Her forthcoming publication, "From Convergence to Absorption," draws comparisons between the interest-convergence of the Civil Rights Movement and the corporate investment in #BlackLivesMatter.

ARAM GOUDSOUZIAN is the Bizot Family Professor of History at the University of Memphis, where he teaches courses on the modern United States, African American history, and the history of American sports. His books include *Down to the Crossroads: Civil Rights, Black Power, and the Meredith March Against Fear* (Farrar, Straus, and Giroux, 2014) and *King of the Court: Bill Russell and the Basketball Revolution* (University of California Press, 2010). He is also the co-editor, with Charles McKinney, of the essay collection *An Unseen Light: Black Struggles for Freedom in Memphis, Tennessee* (University of Kentucky Press, 2018).

FRANÇOISE N. HAMLIN is the Royce Family Associate Professor of Teaching Excellence in Africana Studies and History at Brown University. She is the author of the award-winning *Crossroads at Clarksdale: The Black Freedom Struggle in the Mississippi Delta after World War II* (University of North Carolina Press, 2012), co-editor of the anthology *These Truly Are The Brave: An Anthology of African American Writings on Citizenship and War* (University of Florida Press, 2015), and editor and annotator of the republication of *The Struggle of Struggles* by activist Vera Pigee (University Press of Mississippi, 2023). She teaches courses on Africana studies, US studies and history, and African American studies and history.

ALTHEA LEGAL-MILLER is a senior lecturer in American history and culture at Canterbury Christ Church University in the United Kingdom. Her scholarship on the Black Lives Matter Movement in the United States and United Kingdom has appeared in *Reclaiming the Great World House: The Global Vision of Martin Luther King Jr.* (University of Georgia Press, 2019) and *Developments in American Politics 9* (Palgrave Macmillan, 2022). She has provided expert commentary on radio and television for the BBC and Channel 5 and teaches courses on American studies and history.

DAVID V. MASON is an associate professor at Rhodes College in Memphis, Tennessee. His documentary photographs have appeared in the *Daily Memphian*, the *Tri-State Defender*, and the *Commercial Appeal*, and in the documentary film *Facing Down Storms: Memphis and the Making of Ida B. Wells*. His analysis of Ernest Withers' photograph of Mose Wright testifying in the Emmett Till murder trial appears in the summer 2022 issue of *Storyboard Memphis*. Author of three books, he is also the editor of *Ecumenica*, a peer-reviewed journal that publishes scholarship on the overlap of performance and religion. He teaches classes on the theory and history of live performance.

CHARLES W. MCKINNEY JR. is the Chair of Africana Studies and an associate professor of history at Rhodes College in Memphis, Tennessee. He is the author of *Greater Freedom: The Evolution of the Civil Rights Struggle in Wilson, North Carolina* (University Press of America, 2010) and co-editor, with Aram Goudsouzian, of *An Unseen Light: Black Struggles for Freedom in Memphis, Tennessee* (University Press of Kentucky, 2018). He teaches courses on the Civil Rights/Black Power era, Black activism, the Black intellectual tradition, and Africana studies. His writing has appeared in newspapers and information venues across the country, including the Memphis *Commercial Appeal*, *USA Today*, *Wall Street Journal*, *Black Perspectives*, and *MLK50: Justice through Journalism*.

PETER PIHOS is an associate professor of history at Western Washington University. He is the president of the United Faculty of Western Washington and the vice president for four-year colleges and universities of AFT Washington. His writings have appeared in *Radical History Review* and *The War on Drugs: A History*, edited by David Farber (New York University Press, 2021). He teaches courses on African American history and the modern United States.

CHRISTOPHE D. RINGER is an associate professor of theological ethics and society at Chicago Theological Seminary. He is the author of *Necropolitics: The Religious Crisis of Mass Incarceration in America* (Lexington Books, 2020) and co-editor with Teresa Smallwood and Emilie M. Townes of *Moved by the Spirit: Religion and the Movement for Black Lives* (Lexington Books, 2023). Ringer also served as a delegate to the Movement for Black Lives Black National Convention on behalf of the Workers Center for Racial Justice.

KISHAUNA SOLJOUR is an assistant professor and the associate director for the Center of Public and Oral History at San Diego State University. She received the 2019 ProQuest Distinguished Dissertation Award from the Council of Graduate Schools in Humanities and Fine Arts for her forthcoming book titled *Beyond the Banlieue: French Postcolonial Migration and the Politics of a Sub-Saharan Identity*. She teaches courses on transnational history, activism and social media, and public humanities.

www.ingramcontent.com/pod-product-compliance
Lightning Source LLC
Chambersburg PA
CBHW020327240426
43665CB00044B/870